Guided Reading:
Making It Work

BY MARY BROWNING SCHULMAN
AND CARLEEN daCRUZ PAYNE

SCHOLASTIC
PROFESSIONAL BOOKS

NEW YORK • TORONTO • LONDON • AUCKLAND • SYDNEY
MEXICO CITY • NEW DELHI • HONG KONG

To my mom, who is always there in different ways for the ten of us.

MBS

*To my endearing husband Dick, who supported my writing with his reviews
of this manuscript—and also by nudging and inspiring the writer in me.
You are the wind beneath my wings.*

CDP

CREDITS

Excerpt from *Copycat* by Joy Cowley, illustrated by Murray Grimsdale. Copyright © 1981, 1990 by Thomas C. Wright, Inc./The Wright Group. Reprinted by permission of The Wright Group.

Excerpt from *Mr. McCready's Cleaning Day* by Tracey Shilling, illustrated by Stephen Michael King. Copyright © 1997 by Scholastic Australia Pty. Ltd. Reprinted by permission.

Excerpt from *The Merry Go Round* by Beverley Randell, illustrated by Nelson Price Milburn. Copyright © 1994 by Beverley Randell, illustrations copyright © 1994 by Nelson Price Milburn. Reprinted by permission of Nelson Price Milburn, Ltd.

Excerpt from *Way I Go to School* by Beverly Randell, Jenny Giles, Annette Smith. Copyright © 1996 by Beverley Randell, Jenny Giles, Annette Smith. Photographs copyright © 1996 by Nelson Price Milburn, Ltd. Reprinted by permission of the publisher.

Excerpt from *Sammy at the Farm* by Kathleen Urmston and Karen Evans, illustrated by Gloria Gedeon. Copyright © 1992 by Kathleen Urmston and Karen Evans. Illustrations copyright © 1992 by Gloria Gedeon. Reprinted by permission of Kaeden Corporation.

Excerpt from *All by Myself* by Mercer Mayer. Copyright © 1983 by Mercer Mayer. Reprinted by permission of Golden Books.

Excerpt from *More Spaghetti, I Say!* by Rita Golden Gelman, illustrated by Jack Kent. Copyright © 1977 by Rita Golden Gelman. Illustrations copyright © 1977 by Jack Kent. Reprinted by permission of Scholastic Inc.

Excerpt from *The Three Little Pigs.* Copyright © 1976, 1971 by Scott Foresman and Company. Reprinted by permission.

Excerpt from *The Greedy Goat* by Faye Bolton, illustrated by Paul Borg. Copyright © 1986 by Faye Bolton. Illustrations copyright © by Paul Borg. Reprinted by permission of Mondo Publishing.

Excerpt from *Nate the Great* by Marjorie Weinman Sharmat, illustrated by Marc Simont. Copyright © 1972 by Marjorie Weinman Sharmat. Illustrations copyright © 1972 by Marc Simont. Reprinted by permission of Penguin Putnam Children's Books.

Excerpt from *Five Brave Explorers* by Wade Hudson, illustrated by Ron Garnett. Copyright © 1995 by Wade Hudson. Illustrations copyright © 1995 by Ron Garnett. Reprinted by permission of Scholastic Inc.

Excerpt from *The Little Red Hen* by Joy Cowley. Copyright © 1986 by Joy Cowley. Illustrations copyright © 1986 by Heinemann Publishers (NZ) Ltd. Reprinted by permission of The Wright Group.

Excerpt from *The Lion's Tail.* Copyright © 1976, 1971 by Scott, Foresman and Company. Reprinted by permission of Scott, Foresman.

Excerpt from *Frog and Toad Together* by Arnold Lobel. Copyright © 1971 by Arnold Lobel. Reprinted by permission of HarperCollins Publishers.

Excerpt from *Spiderman* by Peter Patterson. Copyright © 1999 by Shortland Publications, Inc. Reprinted by permission.

Excerpt from *Mouse's Baby Blanket* by Beverly Swedlow Brown, illustrated by Suzanne Aull. Copyright © 1996 by Beverly Swedlow Brown. Illustrations copyright © 1996 by Suzanne Aull. Reprinted by permission of Seedling Publications, Inc.

Front cover design by Kathy Massaro
Cover photograph by Jay M. Schulman
Interior Design by Kathy Massaro
Illustrations on pages 32, 28, and 25 by Rusty Fletcher.
Illustrations on page 241 by James Graham Hale.
Illustrations on page 247 by Bridget Gilroy.
Illustrations on pages 265–272 by Maxi Chambliss and Bridget Gilroy.

ISBN: 0-439-11639-2
Copyright © 2000 Mary Browning Schulman and Carleen daCruz Payne
Printed in USA

Contents

Acknowledgments

I wish to thank the following people for being involved in this book and therefore being involved in my life.

I am indebted to students, parents, and colleagues at William Halley Elementary who inspirit me to reflect on my beliefs about how children learn to read, how best to teach children to read, and how important it is to continue learning within this profession.

I am grateful to Terry Creamer who I admire and learn from every time I step into her first-grade classroom to either work alongside or to strike up a conversation about reading, writing, and children.

Thank you to my family, who make going home for visits alive with memorable moments I hold dear. Special thanks to my sister Bridget Gilroy for sharing her artistic talents and to Charles Browning, brother and family wordsmith, for reading the manuscript with a critical eye and keen pen.

Finally, I must thank Jay, who changed my life the moment he entered it.

—MBS

The journey of writing this book has been supported by my incredible family and many friends. You are each a unique part of the fabric of my life. I acknowledge with appreciation:

Joanne Ibbotson, principal extraordinaire and friend, who leads by example.

Keith Hall and Phyllis Pajardo, assistant principals, and my colleagues and friends at Centre Ridge Elementary who daily encourage me with their dedication and expertise.

The diverse and wonderful students of Centre Ridge who guide my instruction.

Cathy Yerington, a model teacher, and Dolores Varnon, an exceptional principal, for your love of learning and friendship.

My loving family—Edward and Mary, my parents; Ed Jr., my brother; Dick, my husband; Steve and Brenda, my son and his wife; and Lesley, my daughter—for unforgettable moments, much fun and love.

—CDP

We are indebted to the thoughtful, reflective teachers of William Halley and Centre Ridge Elementary Schools and other colleagues who generously shared their classrooms and teaching with us: Katie Abruzzino, Josie Adler, Susan Altemus, Linda Baughman, Ann Boley, Linda Bowlin, Carrie Campbell, Lisa Chambers, Lori Cleveland, Sarah Cobb, Suzanne Comer, Molly Connolly, Terry Creamer, Amy Dux, Margaret Fisher, Geraldine Henryhand, Diane Hurd, Mary Lambert, Kara Luck, Pamela Mahoney, Joe McGuire, Sally Murray, Michelle Nicolai, Janice Poole, Edith Romaine, Sigrid Ryberg, Joe Silva, Margaret Sonley, and Jennifer Stecker.

To Terry Cooper, Wendy Murray, and Joanna Davis-Swing, editors at Scholastic, for the guided reading of our manuscript and helpful suggestions. To teachers Adele Ames, Judy Lynch, and Tonya Singer, for thoughtfully reading and responding to the manuscript.

Lastly, we are both appreciative of the rewarding experience of collaborating on the writing of this book. We have guided each other as partners in reading and writing.

MBS ~ CDP

Introduction

> " All power to those who have the privilege of
> helping children develop their view of reading! "

—Margaret Mooney, *Reading To, With, and By Children*

*Above:
first-grade students
read from their book
baskets during
independent reading
time.*

Reading is a complex activity. The teaching of reading is even more complex! In this book, we explain the technique of guided reading, reading *with* children. Guided reading provides the supportive framework for the systematic yet flexible instruction readers need to develop their skills. Our teaching with guided reading focuses on what students *can* do to build a framework for further literacy learning. The instructional practices we describe here have been refined during our years of actual classroom experience and represent the best practices we currently use with the students and teachers of the schools we are privileged to serve: Centre Ridge and Halley Elementary.

Stepping into kindergarten through grade-three classrooms, we explore what guided reading is and how it fits into a balanced literacy program. We examine the reading process and describe the reading strategies good readers use.

Next, we discuss the reading stages students progress through and ways to select texts for guided reading. We consider the grouping of students and offer detailed descriptions of guided reading lessons with *emergent, transitional, progressing,* and *fluent* readers. We explore the role of phonics and word study.

We describe a variety of assessment tools such as letter identification, concepts about print, running records, benchmark books, and anecdotal records. These tools will help guide students' placement in the appropriate reading material to ensure continued reading growth. Finally, we look at how to effectively gather, organize, store, and use assessment information.

We've also included an appendix of professional resources, publisher information, a list of titles and levels of children's books, and reproducible forms.

We hope this book will not only provide practical and useful ideas to help you implement guided reading for your students, but also that it will also serve to reaffirm and extend your understanding of reading instruction. As teachers of reading, together we share the gift of literacy, contribute significantly to the quality of our students' lives, and make it possible for them to participate in an educated society.

MBS ~ CDP

1

Guided Reading

It's 9:30 in the morning and Carleen has gathered five emergent-level students around a table for a guided reading lesson. The remaining 18 first graders are busy at literacy centers throughout the classroom. Some of those students are reading familiar poems on an overhead projector, some are at a listening center, some are manipulating magnetic letters to form words they know, others are reading electronic books at the computer, and still others are writing messages for the greeting cards they are creating.

With a quick look around to ensure everyone is on task, Carleen begins her guided reading lesson by showing the five first graders the cover of

Copycat, a book they are reading for the first time. She hands each a copy and gives them a brief introduction that summarizes the basic plot—the story is about a little cat who copies what the big cat does until both of them are scared. Carleen begins a discussion on what being a copycat means; one student says that being a copycat is like playing the game "Simon Says." Another talks about when his little sister kept repeating what he said to annoy him.

After making some personal connections to the topic, the group looks at the pictures to get a sense of the story. Carleen uses words from the text, *steps* and *path*, in her conversation, knowing the students may need help with these words. She asks about what letters they might see at the beginning of these words. The first graders locate *steps* and *path* in the text by pointing to them. They continue to talk about the pictures in the book and discover that a dog scares the cats and that the story reverses with the big cat copying the little cat to find safety in a tree.

Carleen then asks the students to read the story softly to themselves while she observes them reading. During each group lesson Carleen observes all the students reading, but she also focuses on one or two students. She jots some anecdotal notes, recording that Delia was using her finger for one-to-one matching and that Adam was using picture clues. When Carleen planned for this guided reading lesson, she reviewed her anecdotal notes and running records on the students. She knew Jessie was experiencing some difficulty using visual sources of information (grapho-phonic cues) when reading, so she decided to use today's lesson to give him some individualized help and instruction.

▲ The emergent-level book <u>Copycat</u>, from the Wright Group.

Carleen sits near him and notices that as Jessie reads softly, he uses the word *went* for *go* in the sentence, *I go up the steps.* He does not realize his error. She prompts him to check what he has read: "Jessie, *went* makes sense, but read that again and check the beginning of this word." Carleen points to the beginning letter of the word *go*. Jessie rereads the sentence, and this time reads it correctly. She praises him for the correction and for checking the first letter of the word to make sure it looked right. On her guided reading record sheet, she makes note of Jessie's self-correction after her prompting.

When the students finish their reading, they discuss and enjoy the humor of the story. Carleen follows the discussion with some word work, focusing on word patterns. She selects some magnetic letters to show how initial letters can be changed. Carleen displays the word *no* on the white board and says, "This is a word you know. Here's another word you know. It was in your reading today." She forms the word *go*. "This says… [children respond *go*]. Do you see how we can change the first letter of a word to make a new word? Let's try it again." With magnetic letters, Carleen makes another known word, *can*, and then places the word *ran* under it to demonstrate again this important principle of how words work.

Carleen collects the books and sends the group back to their seats. She will later place *Copycat* in their baskets of familiar books to reread during independent reading time. Tomorrow she will take Jessie aside before his guided reading group meets to take a running record on his second reading of *Copycat*. The running record is one of the assessment tools that will provide insights on what sources of information and strategies Jessie uses to read this text independently. Analyzing his running record will help guide her teaching for future lessons with Jessie.

▲ *Carleen uses a magnetic white board with magnetic letters to help students learn about how words work.*

Carleen has just completed a 20-minute guided reading lesson with one group of readers in the class. She provided the support necessary for this particular group of readers, jotted anecdotal notes based on her observations of individual readers at work, and made a specific plan for future instruction. Before beginning with another guided reading group, she will take five to 10 minutes to roam the room, checking whether the students at literacy centers are having any problems and ensuring that they stay on task. Each day she usually meets with two or three guided reading groups, working with each child in a small-group setting about three times per week.

Taking Running Records

Each day Carleen selects several students on whom to take a running record. Over the course of two to three weeks, she will have taken at least one running record on all the students in the class. With readers who are experiencing difficulty, she takes running records two to three times a week. She looks for opportunities to take them during the day, perhaps after lunch or before a guided reading group meets. Other days, a running record is taken after a guided reading lesson or the first thing in the morning as students are settling into the classroom. See pages 134–148 for detailed information on taking and scoring running records. For further information, see *An Observation Survey of Early Literacy* by Marie Clay.

What is Guided Reading?

Guided reading is a structured, practical way of matching reading instruction to the diverse individual readers in the classroom. This approach respects the belief that every child is capable of learning to read and recognizes that children learn to read at varying rates of development.

Guided reading provides the opportunity, in a small-group setting, for the teacher to tailor direct instruction to each student's specific reading needs. Through modeling and prompting, the teacher guides or coaches students to think about the reading process and various reading strategies they need to make sense of the text. She also provides additional practice with reading skills by engaging students in word work, extension activities, or other literacy tasks. Her own instruction is guided by careful assessment and observation of each student's reading.

The goal of guided reading is to help students become better, independent readers. Each time a student participates in a guided reading session, the teacher provides support for him to not only use the strategies and skills he knows in order to read a new text, but also to learn something new about the reading process that he will be able to try on his own. In time, the student begins to extend his repertoire of problem-solving strategies to read new books successfully.

In the early primary grades, guided reading supports children as they are learning how to read. As children become proficient readers, the focus expands to include reading for information, or reading to learn. Guided reading promotes both types of instruction. Although the sessions for readers at each end of the spectrum look very different, they both work from the premise that children advance their reading ability when presented with appropriate reading supports and challenges.

In Halley and Centre Ridge primary classrooms in Fairfax County, Virginia, where we teach, teachers gather four to six students around a table or on the floor. Through their assessment, they have identified students who have similar instructional needs and grouped them together. While the grouping is homogeneous, guided reading groups shift and reform as student needs change. The teacher will meet with each group two to three times a week, and more often with low progress students.

Using careful, ongoing assessment of the students, the teacher chooses a book that will provide appropriate support and challenge to the readers in the group. The group members have not read the selected text, which should be short enough to be read in one sitting. Reading an entire text supports their understanding of and ability to apply the reading skills and strategies being practiced. For more fluent readers, who have mastered decoding and are focusing on more advanced reading comprehension strategies, a longer text that may be read independently over several days is appropriate.

Each child has a copy of the selected text. The teacher provides an introduction to give students a sense of the story and/or text features that the lesson will highlight, being sure to point out possible "tricky parts." Students

▲ Terry Creamer leads an emergent group of readers through a guided reading session.

then read the entire text softly while the teacher observes their reading performance, noticing strategies used and problem areas to be addressed. She guides or coaches students as needed, using modeling and prompting to foster student use of reading strategies. She may take anecdotal notes on the group as a whole, or she may focus on one or two students. The teacher may ask groups of more fluent readers to read independently and silently on their own, reconvening the group later to discuss the text.

After reading, the group returns to the text for discussion, some word work, and/or strategy instruction. A follow-up activity may take place. The teacher evaluates students' responses to the reading and determines the next instructional focus for the group. For example, she might decide to explain punctuation marks, share strategies for tackling an unknown word, or work on predicting possible story events.

A sequence for a typical guided reading lesson follows.

Teaching Sequence for Guided Reading

Before

- Teacher selects four to six students for the group and decides on the focus of the lesson based on the assessment of the students. Some students may require more attention and may be taken individually or in a smaller group of two to three students.

- Teacher chooses a text that will support the selected focus and meet the needs of the group. She plans how to introduce the book, how to model the selected reading skill or strategy, and who to observe during the reading.

During

- Teacher introduces the book. Through discussions with the group, she may do one or more of the following:
  - talk about the illustrations,
  - give a sense of the story or basic plot,
  - call attention to text features,
  - have students make predictions,
  - discuss reading strategies,
  - anticipate challenging words or language structures, or
  - review parts in the text, particularly tricky words.

- Students read the text independently and softly to themselves. The teacher observes the group and coaches individual students as needed; she may focus on one or two students. More advanced readers may read silently at their desks or some other reading area.

- Teacher may record her observations as anecdotal notes (see page 149).

After

- Teacher and students return to the text as a group to discuss and clarify understandings, do some phonics or word work, or review reading strategies.

- Students respond to the text in a variety of ways, both within the group and during independent work time. They may reread the book with a buddy, place the text in a book basket for familiar reading, or complete a book project or extension activity.

- Teacher records her observations and evaluates each student's reading of the text to determine what the students need to learn next. (See Chapter 3, Literacy Stages and Book Selections.) Students may be involved in self-evaluation and goal-setting. This step leads directly into the planning stage of the next guided reading session.

Guided reading represents a different approach from that of traditional reading groups; a comparison of the two is shown below.

Guided Reading Groups	Traditional Reading Groups
The focus is on skills and strategies for independent reading of unfamiliar text.	The focus is on skills to read the selections in the basal text.
There are a variety of responses to reading.	Typically, workbook and worksheet exercises form the response to reading.
Various small trade books are used for reading.	Basal text is the primary book for reading.
Flexible reading groups change based on ongoing assessment as skills or strategies are learned.	Fixed reading groups usually remain together during the reading of the entire basal text.
Reading is connected to the other language arts of writing, speaking, and listening.	Reading tends to be treated as a separate subject.
Students are taught to problem-solve unknown vocabulary using strategies they've learned.	Vocabulary is pre-taught to groups.
Instruction is focused on readers' needs through continuous assessment with a variety of assessment tools.	Instruction is focused on a systematic progression of skills in the basal text as measured by an end of the unit, chapter, or section test.
Students read the whole text independently and softly to themselves.	Students read aloud, page by page, often in round-robin fashion.
Selection of a book by the teacher is matched to readers' instructional needs and interests.	Selection of text focuses on reading needs as determined by the basal reader.

Conditions for Learning

Brian Cambourne, an Australian researcher, has studied and identified conditions for how young children learn to talk. Although children receive no formal lessons in talking, they have multiple opportunities every day to use and develop their language skills. They learn to speak in a very supportive and encouraging environment with many experienced and proficient language users. Cambourne believes these conditions are transferable to literacy instruction in the classroom (Cambourne, 1988).

Our own experience has demonstrated that Cambourne's conditions for learning apply to the acquisition of reading and writing skills. A language arts program that includes reading and writing *to, with,* and *by* children provides a rich environment for literacy growth. The following chart summarizes Cambourne's conditions for learning and shows how they may occur in a balanced literacy program.

Cambourne's Conditions for Learning	How They May Appear in a Balanced Literacy Program
IMMERSION	
Students are immersed in multiple opportunities to read and write that are purposeful and authentic throughout the day and across the curriculum areas.	A print-rich environment which includes read-alouds of literature, some related to the content areas, and writing opportunities based on them, expand the possibilities for immersion. Learning centers provide a variety of purposeful and authentic literacy activities.
DEMONSTRATION	
Students have many demonstrations by teachers of the behaviors and strategies to use while reading and writing.	Shared reading, read-alouds, shared writing, and guided reading allow for plenty of teacher modeling of reading and writing strategies.
ENGAGEMENT	
Learners, no matter what level of proficiency, are active participants and are engaged in literacy activities.	Guided reading groups, literacy centers, and extension activities foster active participation of students at all levels.

Cambourne's Conditions for Learning *(Continued)*	How They May Appear in a Balanced Literacy Program *(Continued)*
EXPECTATION	
Teachers create a supportive classroom atmosphere that helps all students believe that they will learn to read and write.	Shared reading, shared writing, guided reading, and independent reading and writing times provide ways for children to be supported in their belief that they are readers and writers.
RESPONSIBILITY	
Students are given opportunities to make choices and be responsible for their learning through meaningful demonstrations and teacher support.	Literacy centers and independent work time allow students to choose their activities and be responsible for their performance and behavior. Individual reading and writing conferences help students evaluate their own learning and set goals.
APPROXIMATION	
Students' best efforts with print in both reading and writing are encouraged and valued.	All teaching begins by acknowledging what students can do. Teachers accept students' levels and focus on developing strategies and skills one step at a time during shared reading, guided reading, shared writing, guided writing, and individual reading and writing conferences.
EMPLOYMENT	
Students are given time, sometimes independently of the teacher, to use the reading and writing strategies they are learning.	Students practice their reading and writing strategies independently at literacy centers, during independent reading and writing times, and in guided reading groups.
RESPONSE	
Teachers provide specific feedback or response while students are engaged in literacy activities, encouraging their continued success.	Prompts during guided reading, teaching points made after taking running records, and reading and writing conferences acknowledge what students do or need to do.

Although we have explained these conditions as separate items, they all work together and are interwoven daily into literacy learning in classrooms.

Guided Reading in a Balanced Literacy Program

At Centre Ridge and Halley, teachers implement a balanced literacy program that encompasses reading *to*, *with*, and *by* children and writing *to*, *with*, and *by* children (Mooney, 1990). The diagrams below represent a view of a balanced program in reading and writing.

Teacher Directed	Gradual Release of Responsibility	Student Directed

Reading to Students
Readaloud

Shared Reading
*Big Books and Small Books
(Fiction/Nonfiction)
Charts, Poems, Songs,
Nursery Rhymes*

Guided Reading
*Teacher-selected Texts
Homogenous Groups
Focus Lessons*

Reading Workshop
*Literature Discussion Groups
Heterogeneous Groups
Focus Lessons*

Independent Reading
*Student Choice
Familiar Books; D.E.A.R.
Literacy Centers*

Reading **TO**	Reading **WITH**	Reading **BY**

Adapted from *Reading TO, WITH and BY Children* (Margaret E. Mooney, 1990)

Teacher Directed	Gradual Release of Responsibility	Student Directed

Writing To/For Students
Schedules
Procedures/Classroom Routines
Notes

Shared Writing: Language Experience/Interactive Writing
Daily News, Morning Message, Class Message
Literature Retellings/Innovations
Informational Writing

Writing Workshop
Student Choice
Variety of Forms and Topics
Focus Lessons
Conferences

Independent Writing
Student Choice
Variety of Forms and Topics
Journal, Response or Learning Logs
Literacy Centers

Writing **TO/FOR**	Writing **WITH**	Writing **BY**

Adapted from *Reading TO, WITH and BY Children* (Margaret E. Mooney, 1990)

A balanced literacy program allows students to participate in a rich literacy environment. Opportunities for the teacher to model the strategies good readers and writers use occur during read-aloud time and during shared reading and shared writing activities (see chart below). Students practice the skills and strategies they are learning during guided reading and writing and independent reading and writing times. The language arts are carefully and purposefully integrated with the content areas. This complete immersion in literacy supports direct reading instruction in guided reading groups. The next two pages highlight scenes from Halley and Centre Ridge classrooms.

Shared Reading

Shared reading is reading *with* children and involves the reading and rereading of enlarged print (book, poem, nursery rhyme, song) with a class or small group. Most times a Big Book is used, although this is not a requirement. Shared reading invites children of varying levels of ability to participate in the reading experience. Repeated readings can focus on:

- understanding the meaning of print
- concepts about print
- story structure
- reading strategies and behaviors
- genre study

Shared Writing

Shared writing is writing *with* children. The teacher and students talk about what to write. The teacher may act as a scribe or share the pen with the students. Shared writing introduces writing to students through writing. It provides the opportunity for a more experienced writer to demonstrate writing. It helps students accomplish an activity they can't yet do on their own. Shared writing can focus on the following:

- different ways writers plan for writing
- the thought processes that occur during writing
- strategies writers use
- concepts about print
- conventions of written language
- spelling strategies

Shared reading and shared writing typically occur during language arts but may also occur during content area learning.

A Balanced Literacy Program

Reading TO ▶

Jennifer Stecker reads aloud to second graders. Teachers in all our classrooms set the example as "expert" readers by reading aloud at least once per day.

▲ Reading WITH

Kara Luck gathers third graders for direct reading instruction in a small, homogeneous guided reading group.

Suzi Comer uses a Big Book in her shared reading lesson to demonstrate for first graders the reading strategies and skills good readers think about using.

◀ Reading BY

Third-grade students in Margaret Sonley's class have 20 minutes daily to practice their reading during independent reading time.

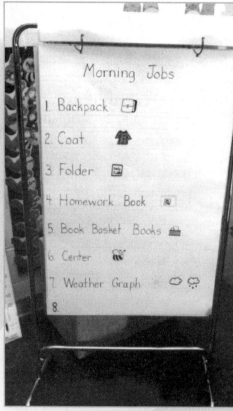

Morning Jobs

1. Backpack
2. Coat
3. Folder
4. Homework Book
5. Book Basket Books
6. Center
7. Weather Graph
8.

Writing TO

Terry Creamer demonstrates that writing has a purpose by finding authentic reasons to write to her first-grade students, such as making a chart of what to do to prepare for the day.

Writing WITH

Michelle Nicolai models writing strategies and skills while composing a morning message with first graders.

Writing BY

Kindergarten students in Sally Murray's class have many opportunities to practice writing independently during Writer's Workshop. Sally gives individual help to her young student writers during this time.

Guided reading is reading *with* children. It is supported by the multiple literacy opportunities teachers provide in their classrooms. The following chapters describe how Centre Ridge and Halley teachers implement guided reading in their classrooms, providing detailed information on establishing and leading groups, practical planning and management ideas, and effective assessment tools.

Understanding the Reading Process

B efore you dive into guided reading, it is helpful to reacquaint yourself with the reading process, for reading is much more than simply decoding words on a page; it is the complex process of making meaning from a variety of symbols and conventions. Experienced readers— such as teachers—read fluently without thinking about or even being aware of their strategies. This section highlights some strategies proficient readers use to navigate texts and provides teacher prompts to encourage beginning readers to use them, too.

Think about what you are doing mentally as you read the following excerpt.

Above: Shared reading of a science Big Book helps Pamela Mahoney's students learn about print and text format.

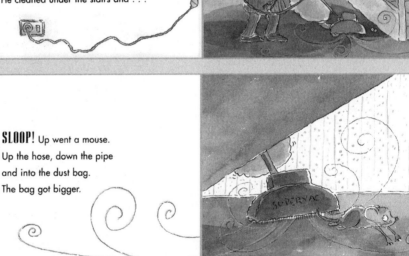

Mr. McCready lost his glasses.
He looked all over the house.

It was cleaning day.
Even though he couldn't see very well,
he got out the vacuum cleaner.
He cleaned under the stairs and . . .

SLOOP! Up went a mouse.
Up the hose, down the pipe
and into the dust bag.
The bag got bigger.

from *Mr. McCready's Cleaning Day*,
Tracey Shilling, Scholastic, 1997,
pp. 1–6

As you read, you probably thought about what it would be like to be without your glasses. You possibly called up a previous experience or had personal knowledge about losing glasses. Perhaps they were on your forehead without your knowing, just like Mr. McCready's glasses were. You may have envisioned your own living room or the inside of your house. You could have reread the word *SLOOP*, or even a few words before it, using meaning cues to confirm that the word makes sense—it represents the sound of the mouse being sucked up by the vacuum cleaner. You might have anticipated or predicted that something will happen to Mr. McCready because there is a mouse in his vacuum cleaner bag. You read left to right on each line and used punctuation to help you understand. Maybe you checked the picture to confirm what you were reading. Your reading was quick and automatic, and you were unaware of the processes you used. You were engaged in making sense of print—READING!

Sources of Information in Text

Readers use three primary sources of information or cues to read a text. They use meaning to tell if what they read is making sense with what is known, fits with previous experiences, and makes sense with the story. Readers use their knowledge of language structure to verify that what is read sounds like the normal patterns of speech and/or book language. They also check visually to see that words look right or have the correct letter/sound association (visual grapho-phonic). As proficient adult readers, we use all of these cues quickly and automatically. When one source of information breaks down, we immediately try another to derive meaning from the print we read.

The diagram below represents how we read and how the sources of information work together.

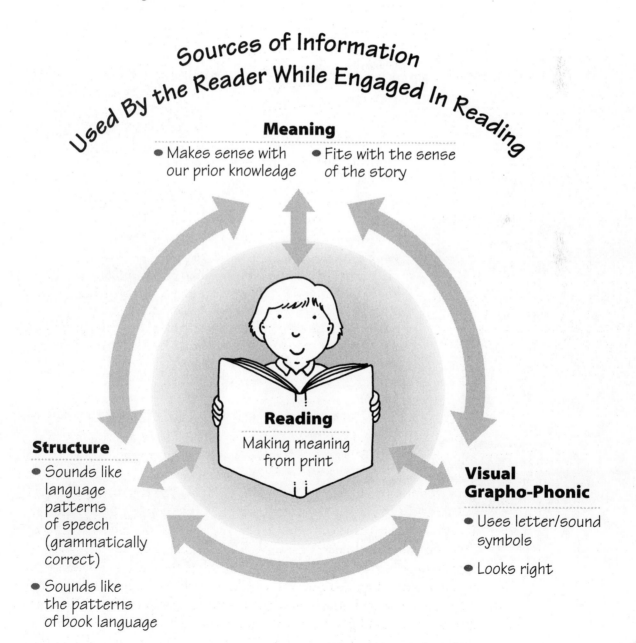

Sources of Information Used By the Reader While Engaged In Reading

Meaning
- Makes sense with our prior knowledge
- Fits with the sense of the story

Reading
Making meaning from print

Structure
- Sounds like language patterns of speech (grammatically correct)
- Sounds like the patterns of book language

Visual Grapho-Phonic
- Uses letter/sound symbols
- Looks right

It is important to help students understand the reading process right from the start. We continually model the use of meaning, language structure, and visual/grapho-phonic cues. Through guided reading, we can teach students how to use various sources of information as they read to get meaning from the text, as well as the strategies or ways to do that. The following chart describes the sources of information readers use and provides some teacher prompts to foster their use.

Description of the Sources of Information: Meaning, Knowledge of Language Structure, Visual/Grapho-Phonic

In running records teachers abbreviate the sources of information as M, S, and V.

Meaning (M)

What we read needs to make sense with our experiences, what we know about the world, and what is happening in the story.

Nick and Kate looked at the cars, too.

Lesley: Nick and Kate liked at the cars, too.

What sources of information is Lesley using and neglecting? She is using structure and visual/grapho-phonic information at the point of error. The word liked looks like looked and is structurally correct, but it does not make sense. Lesley neglects to use meaning as a source of information. Carleen prompts her to think about using meaning when she reads.

Carleen: (Repeats the sentence.) Did that make sense? Read it again, and think about what would make sense.

Prompts to foster the use of meaning as a source of information:

Meaning (M)

- Did that make sense?
- What do you think it could be?
- Let's read it again to make sense.

Knowledge of Language Structure (S)

We use our knowledge of the way we talk to read. Our reading sounds like the language patterns we speak and the language of the books we read.

I go to school in a car.

Steve: I goed to school in a car.

What sources of information is Steve using and neglecting? His oral language patterns may be causing him to use the language structure goed. He attempts to make sense and uses partial visual sources of information. Mary prompts him to think about how it should sound.

Mary: Does that sound right? Can we say it that way?

(Sometimes students reply "yes" because they talk that way. We then have to coach how it sounds in books or in standard English.)

Prompts to foster the use of structure as a source of information:

Knowledge of Language Structure (S)

- Can we say it that way?
- Is that like the way we talk?
- Does that sound right?

Visual/Grapho-phonic (V)

The words we read must match the letters/sounds we see. We look at the first, middle, or last letter of a word, or a familiar part of a word.

Mouse ran under the door.

Brenda: Mouse ran under the table.

What sources of information is Brenda using and neglecting? She is using meaning and structure as sources of information but neglects to use visual information. The word table *makes sense and sounds right but does not look right. Carleen prompts Brenda to check the word to see if it looks right.*

Carleen: That makes sense, but does it look like *table?*

Prompts to foster the use of visual-grapho-phonics as a source of information:

Visual/Grapho-phonic (V)

- Does it look right?
- What letter would you expect to see at the beginning? At the end?
- You saw the little word *be* at the beginning of *beside.*
- Read it again. Get your mouth ready for the first sound.
- Say it slowly.

What are Reading Strategies?

In conjunction with the three sources of information described above, proficient readers use multiple strategies to make meaning from print. They know how to problem-solve new or unknown words, can detect and correct errors while reading, and are able to maintain phrasing in fluent reading. Strategies are mental operations, the in-the-head processes that readers use to read texts. We all use various strategies or actions to get meaning from print—we monitor, search, predict, check, confirm, and self-correct (see the diagram below).

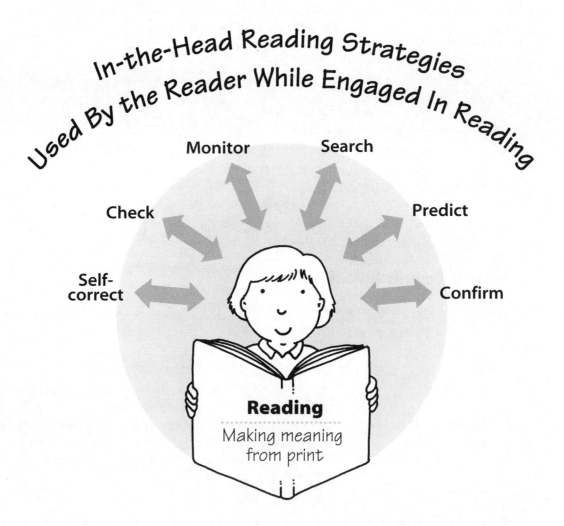

In-the-Head Reading Strategies
Used By the Reader While Engaged In Reading

Monitor   Search

Check   Predict

Self-correct   Confirm

Reading

Making meaning from print

A description of reading strategies and teacher prompts follows. Note that it is just as important to recognize when a student uses a strategy effectively as it is to prompt for the use of a strategy.

Description of Reading Strategy	Teacher Prompts That Encourage Use of Reading Strategies
## MONITOR	
The student notices that something is not right with the reading and may attempt to check and/or correct errors. Good readers monitor their understanding of what they read at all times by integrating all sources of information (meaning, structure of language, and visual/grapho-phonic). This strategy begins early and develops over time as the student becomes a more competent reader.	• Did it match? • What did you notice? • I like the way you noticed something wasn't right. • Something's not right. Why did you stop? • Were you right? How did you know? • How did you know it was _____? • Show me where it wasn't correct.
## SEARCH	

When the reader notices something isn't right in her reading, she searches for more information to correct it. A beginning reader might use only one source of information—meaning, structure of language, or visual/grapho-phonics (**M**, **S**, or **V**)—but with time will learn to try several.	• You said _____.
	  • Does that make sense? (**M**)
	  • Does it sound right? (**S**)
	  • Does it look right? (**V**)
	• If it was ____ , what letter would you expect to see first? Last? Is that what you see?
	• Something's not right on this page. Can you find what's wrong?
	• What do you know that might help?

## PREDICT	
Readers predict words or events in the story as they go along. They use prior knowledge and their knowledge of language, what would make sense, and what would look right (sources of information). Good readers continually predict and revise their predictions during reading.	• Look at the picture. What do you know? • Think about what has happened in the story so far. What would make sense? • What do you think will happen next? • What would you expect to see? (letter[s], word[s])

(Continued on next page)

(Continued from page 29)

Description of Reading Strategy	Teacher Prompts That Encourage Use of Reading Strategies

CHECK

The reader checks that what is read makes sense, looks right, and sounds right. This may occur after an error, or when she comes to an unknown word. The beginning reader may check only one source of information, but as she develops as a reader, she may cross-check one kind of information against another. It's important to note what sources of information the reader is using to check; you can identify them by analyzing a student's running records or through your anecdotal notes (see Chapter 7).

- Check to see if you're right.
- It could be _____, but does it...
  - make sense? **(M)**
  - sound right? **(S)**
  - look right? **(V)**
- What did you notice?
- What did you expect to see?
- Check to see if what you read...
  - makes sense. **(M)**
  - sounds right. **(S)**
  - looks right. **(V)**
- I liked how you tried more than one way to work that out.

CONFIRM

Readers use one or more sources of information (meaning, structure of language, and visual/grapho-phonic) to make certain that what they actually read is what they expected to read. Sometimes readers reread to verify meaning, or to take in the meaning of a sentence as a whole when they've problem-solved a part of it.

- Are you right?
- Did you check to make sure you're right?
- Did you reread to see if you're right?

SELF-CORRECT

Readers often notice on their own that something is not right in the reading. They detect and correct by searching and checking for more information (meaning, structure of language, and visual/grapho-phonic sources of information) to self-correct or make it right.

- I like the way you corrected that all by yourself.
- Were you right? How did you know?
- Something's not right...on that page... in that sentence. Can you find it?

See pages 230–233 in the Appendix for reproducible prompt charts and bookmarks for sources of information and reading strategies.

Reading Behaviors Versus Reading Strategies

Some teachers mistake the observable reading behaviors such as rereading, looking at the picture, pointing, pausing or stopping, or even making the initial sound of a word, as strategies. These observable reading behaviors are not strategies; rather, they provide insights into the sources of information and the "in-the-head" strategy or action that the student may be using while reading. For example, a student may reread in order to search for more visual information. Or she may reread to check and confirm that what she thought she read is actually what is there on the page.

As you work with students, try to sort out the differences between the sources of information available in the text and the "in-the-head" strategies or actions the reader uses to problem-solve while reading. The observable reading behaviors you notice and record, as well as the analysis of running records, will provide insights into both.

Using Prompts to Promote Reading

We use specific prompts to promote the use of the sources of information (meaning, structure of the language, and visual/grapho-phonic) and reading strategies. While we listen to students read aloud, we notice what individual readers do and what needs to be learned next. Verbalizing the process a student used while reading fosters metacognition and provides feedback and encouragement: "I like the way you reread that sentence and thought about what would make sense." Other times, we provide specific prompts to encourage the reader to think and behave a certain way: "That sounds right, but does it look right? Go back and reread it to see if it looks right."

When deciding which prompts to use, we ask ourselves, "What sources of information is the reader using? What sources of information is he neglecting?" We acknowledge what's partially right about the error and then prompt to what's partially wrong or neglected at the point of error.

As you read the previous section, you may have noticed that some of the prompts are distinctly different, while others may seem similar. Prompts can encourage children to utilize different strategies and sources of information in the text while reading. You will develop a sense of which ones are most helpful to students the more you try them, observe students, and record what they do when they read. It's important to use prompts that help students learn to integrate all sources of information. Over-reliance on prompts that focus a student's attention on one source of information, such as visual/grapho-phonic, may lead a student to neglect the other sources of information. As students become more proficient in their reading and learn how to use these strategies on their own, the need for the teacher to use the prompts will lessen because the students take over this task for themselves.

The goal of guided reading is to help students become better, independent readers who are flexible with what they know. Each time they participate in a guided reading session, they learn more about the reading process and practice their reading skills. The diagram below illustrates how the reader integrates the sources of information and reading strategies in the reading process.

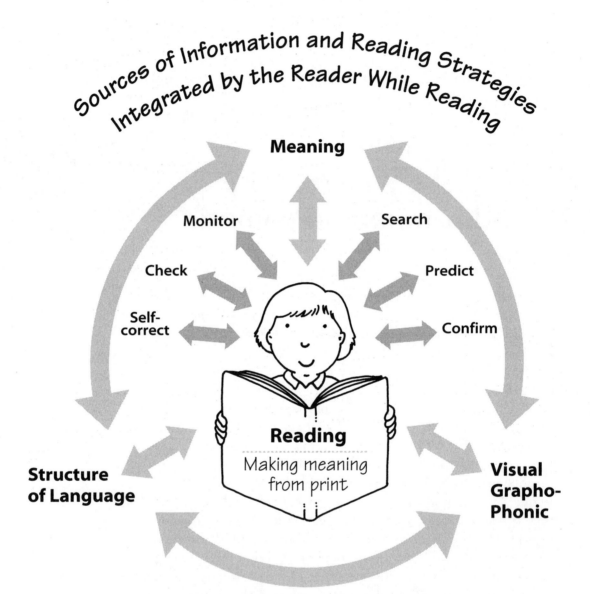

Sources of Information and Reading Strategies Integrated by the Reader While Reading

Meaning

Monitor

Search

Check

Predict

Self-correct

Confirm

Reading

Making meaning from print

Structure of Language

Visual Grapho-Phonic

With careful observation during guided reading, and analysis with assessment tools such as running records, observational checklists, and anecdotal notes, teachers can determine which sources of information and strategies students are using, and which ones they're neglecting, and plan their instruction accordingly. (See Chapter 7 for detailed discussion of these assessment methods.)

Phrasing in Fluent Reading

Students need to understand that the words on the page should sound like spoken language when read. Modeling smooth and expressive reading during shared reading, read-alouds, and guided reading will help students develop this concept. You can also take opportunities during guided reading to demonstrate how to read groups of words together, attend to punctuation, read with appropriate expression and intonation, and adjust the rate of reading.

As students become fluent readers, they are able to put groups of words together in natural, meaningful phrases, the way language should sound; focus on the meaning of a text; and quickly and efficiently use a variety of reading strategies. Students who are word-by-word readers, or who need to stop repeatedly to decode unknown words, may often have difficulty comprehending. They may lack the ability to quickly draw on and use a variety of reading strategies.

Techniques to Try

Try the following techniques to help students with phrasing and fluency.

❧ Model what phrased and fluent reading sounds like, making a connection to the way we talk.

When Carleen visited a kindergarten class, she modeled reading-like-talking using the Big Book *Five Little Monkeys Jumping on the Bed* by Eileen Christelow. During the rereading of the book, Carleen knew that the refrain "No more monkeys jumping on the bed" lent itself to modeling how to read in meaningful phrases and with intonation.

Carleen: "Listen to how I say the words when I read this part. [She reads, "No more monkeys jumping on the bed."] I'm going to ask you to read it the way I do. [Students chant the refrain using the same phrasing and intonation that Carleen modeled.]

❧ Use a tape recorder to improve phrasing and fluency.

With school funds, purchase a cassette tape for each student or visit your local music or variety store and ask for donations of cassette tapes. Tape record students during guided reading or use a parent volunteer to help individual students record their reading of a text. Let students listen to how the reading sounds. Emphasize the parts that are phrased and fluent. These tapes may be sent home quarterly for parents to hear.

❧ Build a core of familiar and easy books students can reread to practice phrasing and fluency.

Use individual baskets or boxes as containers to place familiar books so students can reread to practice phrasing and fluency. Include guided and shared reading books, and student-selected "easy" books. Since these books have been previously read, the need for problem-solving unknown words will be minimal.

> "Why is it important to think about phrasing in fluent reading? The answer is simple. When the reading is phrased like spoken language and the responding is fluent (and some people say fast), then there is a fair chance that the reader can read for meaning and check what he reads against his language knowledge. And his attention can go mainly to the messages."

—Marie Clay, *Reading Recovery: A Guidebook For Teachers in Training*

Choose books that have two to five words on a line.

Books with short, meaningful phrases on a line support the reader during guided reading as they are learning to read groups of words.

Page from an emergent-level book, Merry Go Round by Beverly Randell. ▶

> "Come here, James,"
> said Dad.
> "Come here, Kate.
> Come here, Nick.
> Look at the merry-go-round."

Mrs. Creamer: "Listen to how I slide this group of words together when I read. [She reads the first and second line of text, 'Come here, James,' said Dad.] Did you hear how I read the words together? Now I want you to try it. Make it sound the way I did."

Students reread the phrase. Terry continues to model reading groups of words on the rest of the page and asks students to try it.

Teach students how to read punctuation for emphasis.

When Mary was working with a group of progressing readers, she revisited the book *More Spaghetti, I Say!* by Rita Golden Gelman to demonstrate how to read various punctuation.

> "...I love it.　　I love it so much!"
> I love it.　　　"More than me?"
> I love it.　　　"More than you."
> I do.

Mary: "Let's look at how the reader needs to read this page. There are different kinds of punctuation marks. That helps us know how we need to make our voice sound as we read. What kinds of punctuation marks do you see? [Students respond.] Listen to what I do with my voice when I read the different punctuation marks."

Mary reads the text aloud. She discusses with the students the change in intonation when different punctuation marks are read. They read the refrain together; then they search for various punctuation marks in other places in the book and practice reading them.

Use books that have dialogue so that students develop a sense of how reading sounds like conversation.

Model reading dialogue so students hear how to read with expression and for different characters. Students can then read the familiar dialogue to each other to build fluency.

🐛 Have students do a Reader's Theatre presentation of a text.

For a simplified version of Reader's Theatre, have a group of students perform for their classmates an oral reading of a favorite story, poem, or song with expression and simple gestures. Demonstrate for students how to use voices and gestures for dramatic effect. Give students time to practice their parts; they hold the text during the performance.

🐛 Reproduce copies of favorite songs, rhymes, and poems.

Keep these in a folder, binder, or notebook. Read together as a class, in a small group, or with a partner to practice phrased and fluent reading. Copies may also be sent home for additional practice.

🐛 Prompt students during guided reading to read in a phrased and fluent manner.

Some prompts to try include the following:

- Read so it sounds like you're talking.
- Read it all together.
- Listen to how I read it and make it sound like talk.
- Read groups of words.
- Read the punctuation.

🐛 Set up a reading buddy program.

Start a reading buddy program to provide extra reading practice for primary students. Invite upper-grade students to work with primary students two to four times per week for 10–15 minutes, either first thing in the morning or at the end of the day. Train the upper-grade students to coach their buddies, demonstrating with a primary student if possible.

Have primary students meet their buddies with their book baskets of familiar books from which they will read aloud. After each session, the upper-grade reading buddy records the books read on a "Reading Buddy Record" sheet, which includes titles read, comments, and the date. (See page 242 in the Appendix for a reproducible copy of the reading buddy record sheet.)

🐛 Use masking cards and strips to model phrasing.

Model phrased reading with masking cards or strips. Create the strips from cardstock or use index cards. Choose a familiar or easy book so there is no word solving for the student and read the book aloud, manipulating the masking card or strip to show the student which words you're reading together as a group. Since you are demonstrating phrased and fluent reading, do not stop or talk along the way about why you are reading certain words together; talk about your reading after the demonstration.

After modeling the process for a student, you can ask her to read the book while you move the masking card or strips, helping with the phrasing of the reading, if needed. Accept approximations, letting the student get the

QUICK TIP

Choosing books with a strong story line can help with phrasing and fluency because they support the reader as he predicts events. Some books with strong story lines follow.

Bedtime for Frances
Scholastic, Guided Reading Program

Blind Men and the Elephant
by Karen Backstein

Cloudy with a Chance of Meatballs
by Judi Barrett

Frog and Toad Are Friends
by Arnold Lobel

Mouse Soup
Scholastic, Guided Reading Program

Mr. Putter and Tabby Walk the Dog
by Cynthia Rylant

Noisy Nora
Scholastic, Guided Reading Program

Rumpelstiltskin
Dominie Press, Traditional Tales

Teach Us, Amelia Bedelia
Scholastic, Guided Reading Program

feel and rhythm of what it is to read in a more phrased and fluent manner. You may focus on reading groups of words together, increasing the pace of the reading, or reading in a smooth manner.

Using masking cards

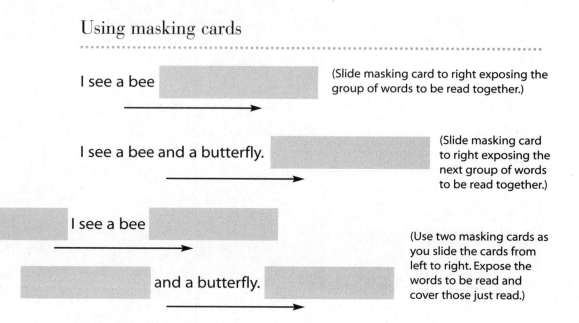

I see a bee ▭ (Slide masking card to right exposing the group of words to be read together.)

I see a bee and a butterfly. ▭ (Slide masking card to right exposing the next group of words to be read together.)

▭ I see a bee ▭

▭ and a butterfly. ▭ (Use two masking cards as you slide the cards from left to right. Expose the words to be read and cover those just read.)

A masking card can be used to either expose or cover up a portion of a longer text for the student.

Once there was a little girl who lived in a cottage in the woods.
Her birthday was very near.
And so she began to plan her party.
Her mother said to her,
"First, you must write the invitations."

(Slide masking card down the text to expose a line at a time.)

To work on the pace of the reading

Slide masking card from left to right covering up the words being read to "push the oral reading along." Slide back to expose the print again if the student has not been able to keep up. Start sliding card slowly covering groups of words. Try on familiar books that the student is rereading for practice.

▭ I see a bee and a butterfly.

Understanding the reading process, knowing the sources of information and strategies employed by smart readers, and providing prompts to support their use contribute to appropriate and effective instruction. In the next chapter, we consider the literacy stages students move through and the book selections we can make to strengthen the reader at each stage of development.

3

Literacy Stages and Book Selections

Mary and I think learning to read is like learning to swim. We don't start out at the deep end of the pool. First, we get used to being in the water. Our students get used to reading by being surrounded with meaningful literacy activities at home or within the classroom. They begin to see reading as a worthwhile activity, and one in which they want to participate.

Above:
Mary considers
possible book titles
she will select for
guided reading.

As novice swimmers, we learn to orchestrate many movements: how to kick our feet, move our arms, and turn our heads in and out of the water to breathe. Students need to learn several reading processes as well: how to use the sources of information (meaning, language structure, and visual/graphophonic cues) to get meaning from print, and when to employ different strategies.

Swim instructors demonstrate each of the appropriate techniques, try various approaches when the students don't "get it," and encourage swimmers to practice their skills until they are able to coordinate the whole process for themselves. Swimmers learn how to swim a little bit at a time. Some learn the process quickly; others take much longer.

Learning to read works much the same way. During guided reading lessons, teachers coach students, demonstrating how to use their knowledge of phonics, language, and meaning to read. We look for "just right" materials to support students' level of reading development and adjust the program based on the assessment of what the readers can do. We recognize that while some will learn to put the process together quickly, others will need more time. The goal is for students to be able to coordinate the process of reading for themselves.

Four Stages of Reading Development

For the purposes of this book, we describe four broad stages of reading development. These stages should help you think about the diverse readers within your classroom, enabling you to match the reading behaviors they display to books that will support their learning. Since students will move through these stages at varying paces, we have not put grade levels with the books. Rather than depend on grade-level designations, we look at each individual reader and instruct within the range of what she can do. This is what makes guided reading so important. The teacher identifies where the individual students are in their developmental stage of reading, and then guides them further toward successful, independent reading.

The first three stages, *emergent, progressing,* and *transitional,* represent the progression from beginning readers to more independent readers. In these stages the focus of instruction is to help students learn to use and integrate the sources of information and reading strategies while reading. Once students have learned to put the reading process together and can read and understand many texts given to them, they have moved to the *fluent* stage of reading. At the fluent stage, guided reading instruction continues, although the focus shifts. Since fluent readers have mastered decoding and are working on more sophisticated reading strategies and skills, after the book introduction they often read the text independently and return to their groups later in the day or week to discuss literary language, author subtleties, and ways to manage challenging and varied texts. Teachers continue to choose text selections that are appropriate to the social and emotional levels of the readers. Students continue to read for pleasure and for information.

The following pages outline the reading characteristics for each stage and provide examples of texts that can be used by children in each stage. We include some of the book features that support the reader in each stage. Within the primary classrooms at Halley and Centre Ridge, teachers have organized their books according to stages. In the Appendix, we list titles of books that can be used for guided reading, and charts of behaviors, book characteristics, and some titles for emergent, progressing, transitional, and fluent readers.

Organizing Your Classroom Library

Classroom libraries and other print materials can be organized in many different ways. Materials might be organized by reading stages or levels by placing colored dots on books for each stage or level. Students use the colored dot system to locate books in their reading range for independent reading time and to return the books to the appropriate place. A section of the classroom library may also be grouped by topics, genres, or authors. The classroom library may be organized by the teacher or with the help of the students.

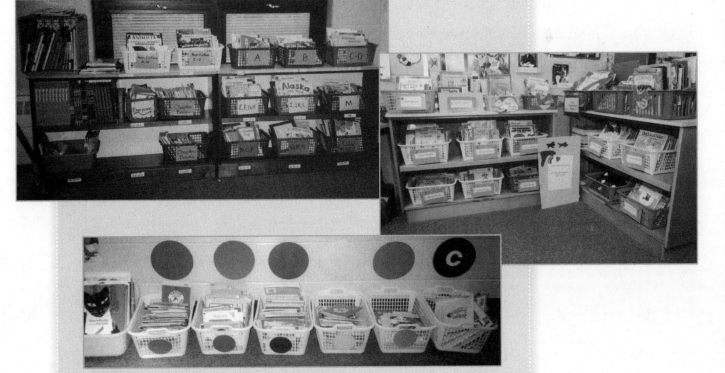

Teachers organize their classroom libraries to suit the needs of their students.

In the *emergent* stage of reading development, the student will display many of the following behaviors.

Emergent Readers:

- understand print carries a message
- display directional movement:
  - —*left* to *right*
  - —*top* to *bottom*
  - —return sweep
- match voice to print with one-to-one word matching by finger pointing
- locate some known words and unknown words
- use picture clues
- recognize difference between a *letter* and a *word*
- may invent text
- begin to use pattern and repetition of text to read
- use oral language/story structure to make a connection to print
- use some letter sounds (beginning/ending)
- begin to use known, high-frequency words to monitor reading

Sample Characteristics of Books
at the **Emergent** Level

I go to school
on a bike.

from <u>Way I Go to School</u> by Beverly Randell, Jenny Giles, and Annette Smith, pp. 6–7

Early in the emergent stage

- consistent placement of print on each page
- illustrations provide high support
- natural language structure
- familiar experiences

- some known high-frequency words
- one/two lines of print (L to R with return sweep)
- predictable, repetitive sentence pattern with one/two word changes

"Woof," barked Sammy.

Sammy saw a horse but the horse didn't see Sammy.

from <u>Sammy at the Farm</u> by Kathleen Urmston and Karen Evans, pp. 8–9

Later in the emergent stage

- some punctuation conventions
- illustrations provide high support
- repeated sentence pattern every few pages
- print in various positions on page

- varied sentence patterns
- multiple lines of print
- familiar objects and experiences
- simple story line

In the *progressing* stage of reading development, the student will display many of the following behaviors.

Progressing Readers:

- have good control of early reading strategies (directionality, one-to-one word matching, locating known and unknown words)

- rely less on pictures and use more information from print

- search the print, check, and self-correct more frequently (both with and without teacher prompting)

- often cross-check one source of information (meaning, language structure, visual/grapho-phonic) with another source

- check and confirm, sometimes using beginning, middle, and ending letters/sounds

- read familiar text with some phrasing and fluency

- start to attend to some punctuation while reading

- begin to build a core of high-frequency words known automatically

- begin to engage in discussions about what is read

Sample Characteristics of Books
at the **Progressing** Level

from <u>All by Myself</u> by Mercer Mayer, pp. 12–13

Early in the progressing stage

- varied placement of print on page
- natural language structures
- variety of simple sentences
- multiple lines of print
- more punctuation conventions
- some repetitive sentence patterns
- illustrations provide moderate to high support

from <u>More Spaghetti, I Say!</u> by Rita Golden Gelman, pp. 22–23

Later in the progressing stage

- variety of sentence patterns and lengths
- variety of punctuation and fonts
- use of direct speech
- longer story (beginning-middle-end)
- illustrations provide moderate support

In the *transitional* stage of reading development, the student will display many of the following behaviors.

Transitional Readers:

- use multiple sources of information (meaning, language structure, visual/grapho-phonic) and a variety of strategies (see page 28) to problem-solve while reading

- make predictions and confirm or revise them while reading

- recognize the importance of monitoring reading for understanding

- use familiar parts of words (beginning, middle, or end) to problem-solve unknown words

- know a large core of high-frequency words automatically

- read many punctuation marks appropriately

- read most texts with phrasing and fluency

- begin to read a greater variety of longer and more complex texts (fiction and informational)

- attend more to story structure and literary language

- engage in discussions about what is read

Sample Characteristics of Books at the **Transitional** Level

from <u>The Three Little Pigs</u>, Scott Foresman, pp. 24–25

The wolf got on top of the house. He called, "Little pig, little pig! I'll come down the chimney and eat you up!"

The third little pig took the cover off the pot of water. The water was very hot. The little pig called, "Come on down!"

Early in the transitional stage

- conventional story
- varied sentence patterns
- more print on page
- some literary language

- variety of literature selections
- illustrations provide some support
- more varied punctuation and fonts

from <u>The Greedy Goat</u> retold by Faye Bolton, pp. 10–11

CLOP-CLOP-CLOP. A donkey came by.
"What's wrong old woman?" asked the donkey.
"A goat's in my house and won't let me in," she said.
"Don't worry," said the donkey. "I'll get the goat out."

KNOCK! KNOCK!
"Who's there?" bleated the goat.
"It's me!" said the donkey.

"Off with you, I'm a fighting goat. My two big horns will rip your coat!"

Later in the transitional stage

- illustrations provide low support
- some challenging vocabulary
- longer selections
- variety of text layout

- more print on page
- developed story line
- font varies in size and type
- literary language

In the *fluent* stage of reading development, the student will display many of the following behaviors.

Fluent Readers:

- use all sources of information (meaning, language structure, visual/grapho-phonic) quickly and flexibly to problem-solve independently

- detect and correct errors, often silently

- use knowledge of how words work (letters/sounds, word parts, and analogies) to efficiently problem-solve unfamiliar words

- read and understand more challenging vocabulary using context and knowledge of how words work

- consistently monitor reading for understanding

- read with phrasing and fluency

- adjust reading pace to accommodate the purposes for reading and difficulty of text

- exhibit an ability to infer author's subtleties in text

- understand and use literary terms and language

- revisit text to support ideas and understandings during literary discussions

- read a variety of genres for information and pleasure

- synthesize and interpret what is read

Sample Characteristics of Books
at the **Fluent** Level

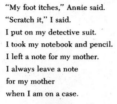

"My foot itches," Annie said.
"Scratch it," I said.
I put on my detective suit.
I took my notebook and pencil.
I left a note for my mother.
I always leave a note
for my mother
when I am on a case.

Dear mother,
I will be back.
I am wearing my
rubbers.
Love,
Nate the Great

I went to Annie's house.
Annie has brown hair
and brown eyes.
And she smiles a lot.
I would like Annie
if I liked girls.

◀ *from* <u>*Nate the Great*</u> *by Marjorie Weinman Sharmat, pp. 12–13*

Early in the fluent stage

- some challenging vocabulary
- literary terms and language
- extended story line
- variety of simple and complex sentences

- longer literature selections (i.e., beginning chapter books)
- fewer illustrations
- more print on a page

companions had traveled three thousand miles.

The people of Mexico City treated the explorers like heroes. Esteban enjoyed the excitement. But there was one question on his mind. During the journey, he and his companions were equals. But what would happen to him now? he wondered. Would he be treated as a free man? Or would he be treated as a slave again? Soon he got his answer.

Esteban had saved Dorantes' life many times. Esteban had great courage and wisdom. He had led the difficult trip across the country. But Dorantes still considered this brave explorer a slave. He sold Esteban to the governor of Mexico City.

Esteban's days as an explorer were not over, though. He was asked to guide an expedition to find the "Seven Cities of Gold." On this trip, he explored land that is now

Arizona and New Mexico.

Sadly, Esteban was killed during the expedition. But he had made his important contributions to history. Esteban was one of the first blacks to explore America. His legend still lives among Native American folklore in the Southwest.

◀ *from* <u>*Five Brave Explorers*</u> *by Wade Hudson, pp. 12–13*

Later in the fluent stage

- more challenging vocabulary
- more complex literary genres
- more complicated text features
- variety of fonts and print layout

- print provides primary source of information
- more complex sentence structures
- more complex story line and concepts
- few to no illustrations

Matching Readers with Books

During each guided reading session, you will spend time introducing the students to the story ideas, linking the text to their personal experiences, and helping them talk and think about the book. The students then read the selection on their own. If there is a good match between the reader and the book, students will be able to read and understand most of the text. They may meet some unknown words, but will be able to problem-solve many of them using a variety of strategies, thereby building confidence and competency as readers.

Clearly, the importance of selecting texts matched to the needs of readers in guided reading groups cannot be overstated. Ongoing assessment—from informal anecdotal notes to more formalized running records—allows teachers to be aware of each student's abilities and needs as a reader. With this knowledge, you can choose books that have appropriate supports and challenges for readers at each stage of their development. Of course, this expertise—being able to match readers with books—takes time to develop. Take advantage of every opportunity you have to acquaint yourself with the books in your classroom library and in the school bookroom. Develop a system for organizing books by levels or stages, so you can easily reach for an appropriate book for a specific reader.

The bookrooms at Centre Ridge and Halley are centrally located and serve as a place to house sets of guided reading books for school-wide use. Books are color-coded and organized by literacy stages.

Always keep in mind the readers, and ask yourself, "What is this book about? What will make it easy? What will make it challenging?" By selecting appropriately, you provide the support for further reading learning to occur. Students will have the opportunity to practice and build on the skills and strategies they know.

Take a look, below, at some specific features to consider in book selection. The importance of these depends on the literacy stage of your students. A reproducible checklist for book selection can be found in the Appendix.

Features to Consider for Book Selection

Concepts in the Book

- Can students relate to concepts or experiences in the text?
- What background knowledge is necessary to understand the text?
- Do events in the story follow a sequential and/or predictable pattern?
- Are students able to understand this type of literary genre?

Illustrations

- Do they provide high, moderate, or low support?
- Where are they located on the page?
- Are they clear or do they need interpretation?

Language/Structure

- Is the text structure repetitive, familiar, or natural to spoken language?
- Are there high-frequency words that can serve as anchors for emergent readers?
- Is there difficult or technical vocabulary that might present a problem?

Text Features/Layout

- How many lines of print on a page?
- Is there clear spacing between words?
- Is the size and placement of the print supportive to the reader?
- Are there unusual print fonts that are distracting or confusing?
- Is the text length appropriate for the reader?
- Are there any unusual text formats—such as diagrams, charts, or maps—that require explanation?

Our next chapter will describe ways to manage guided reading in the classroom, including scheduling, grouping, and using literacy centers.

4

Setting Up and Managing Your Classroom for Guided Reading

*Above:
Students work at literacy activities at centers while Margaret Sonley, the teacher, meets with a guided reading group.*

Once you've decided to implement guided reading in your classroom, you're bound to have lots of questions about how to arrange and manage your room to support this endeavor. Are all my students ready for guided reading? How do I organize my classroom and schedule guided reading into my day? How do I group my students? What are the other students doing while I meet with guided reading groups? These are just a few of the questions you may ask yourself as you plan for guided reading, and this chapter provides some practical answers from experienced teachers we work with.

When Are Children Ready for Guided Reading?

In Halley and Centre Ridge classrooms—as in most classrooms around the country—students enter with a variety of backgrounds and experiences. Some come from homes where reading is a valued activity. As a result, they have an awareness of book-handling concepts, an understanding of story structure and story language, and the ability to share ideas about stories they hear or read. We also have students who have had few literacy experiences, have not attended preschool, or experience English as a second language. How do we handle this disparity in our classrooms?

Our experience has demonstrated that immersing students in a literature-rich environment, modeling reading and writing behaviors, and engaging students in a variety of literacy activities effectively meets the needs of students at all stages of literacy development. Terry Creamer, a first-grade teacher at Halley, faces the challenge of diverse learners each September. She says, "I know that my students' experiences with reading and writing will vary. To meet their needs, I begin by making reading, writing, speaking, and listening a priority. Read-aloud time, shared reading, and shared writing are crucial to my demonstrations of the strategies smart readers and writers use. Through the shared reading of books, poems, and songs, students learn about print and story language. Shared writing activities also support literacy by helping to call attention to both writing and reading concepts. When I provide multiple opportunities for all children to engage in meaningful and purposeful literacy activities, they begin to value and understand that reading and writing are important to their learning." For Terry, establishing reading and writing as important and valuable activities sets the tone for her classroom and introduces students to basic literacy skills.

When students begin to understand and exhibit some of the early literacy concepts described in the following section, guided reading should begin. While you meet with the groups, other students work individually or with partners in literacy centers.

> "What do the children see when they look at the teacher? Do they, in fact, see an adequate model of a literate adult? Do they see a model of an adult who treats literacy as something of personal importance? Do they see someone who reads frequently and for a wide range of purposes? Is there a good match between what teachers say about literacy and what they actually do?"
>
> —Nigel Hall & Anne Robinson, *Looking at Literacy*

A first-grader writes words she knows on a white board. ▶

Literary Concept	How To Assess

A Knowledge of the Alphabet

Students will be able to recognize some of the uppercase and lowercase letters of the alphabet. They may refer to them by letter name, sound, or word association.	Letter Identification; see pages 248–249

A Writing Vocabulary of a Few High-Frequency Words, Including Their Name

If students know how to write a few words, these may serve as anchors in their reading.	Writing Vocabulary; see page 126

An Awareness That Reading Must Make Sense

Students need to know that reading is a meaning-making activity and that the squiggly lines on the page carry a message. Written language sounds similar to the way we talk.	Concepts About Print, page 260

Demonstration of Some Understanding of the Following Early Reading Behaviors

Directional Movement We read a word and lines of print left to right. We read a page of print from top to bottom and the left page before a right page.	Concepts About Print, pages 124–125
One-to-One Word Matching Our eyes are looking at a word at the same time as we are pointing to and reading it.	Concepts About Print, pages 124–125
Locating Known Words We can find known words in the texts we read based on letter/sound relationships and what we know about words.	Word Test, page 124; text reading of benchmark book, page 128
Locating Unknown Words We can find unknown words in the texts we read based on letter/sound relationships and what we know about words.	Observations during shared or guided reading; text reading of benchmark book, page 128

Assessing students at the beginning of the year and monitoring their progress throughout will help you determine who is ready for guided reading. See Chapter 7 for practical assessment tools and this chapter for ideas on engaging the rest of the class while you are meeting with guided reading groups.

Choral Reading

For students who are not yet ready for guided reading, many kindergarten and first-grade teachers use choral reading as a bridge to guided reading. Teachers frequently call together a small group of children who are not yet reading to practice choral reading, a type of shared reading that provides more support from the teacher. Students read aloud a familiar book, poem, song, or nursery rhyme with the teacher. Choral reading with a small group of students allows each student to act like a reader—handling a book on one's own, pointing to approximate one-to-one word matching, practicing left-to-right directional movement, and other concepts about print. This technique strengthens many important early reading behaviors with students before guided reading instruction begins.

> "Children's proficiency in letter naming when they start school is an excellent predictor of their first- and second-grade reading achievement."
>
> —Anderson, Hiebert, Scott, & Wilkinson, *A Nation of Readers*

▲ *After shared reading of a Big Book, a small group of kindergarten students meets with Mary for a choral reading of the text.*

Organizing Your Classroom for Guided Reading

Good management begins with a thoughtful room arrangement and careful selection of materials; the way you organize furniture and supplies will support the learning that takes place within your classroom. For guided reading to be effective, the rest of the class must be engaged in other literacy activities that do not require direct teacher involvement. For most classes, this means literacy centers that accommodate small groups of students. So, a strategically arranged classroom for guided reading would have a class library, inviting spots for individual work, spaces for whole-class gatherings and small-group meetings, and several learning centers.

The classroom floor plan of first-grade teacher Pamela Mahoney shows one design that works well for a wide variety of uses. Pamela says, "I want the learning environment to support whole-group, small-group, and individual activities. I leave a large open area for meeting with the whole class. I keep a chart stand, Big Book easel, and reading/writing supplies close at hand. The word wall is nearby for our use. I also consider where I can work with a small group, yet still have a view of what's happening around the classroom.

"I think about the supplies and materials that will be part of the classroom routine on a recurring basis. Books are all around the room— in the library corner, along a chalkboard tray, and visible in many of the centers. Many of the books are organized in colored baskets by reading stages. Others are sorted by topics, authors, or genres. Students' work is always on display, along with the charts we've generated together about reading, writing, and other topics of study."

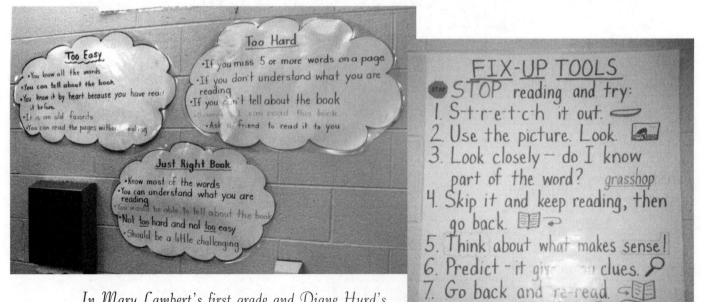

In Mary Lambert's first grade and Diane Hurd's second grade, charts created by the teacher and students together are reminders of literacy learning.

Arranging the room and organizing materials for effective reading and writing workshops takes thought and planning. So before the school year even begins, consider the activities you're planning for your class and the physical layout of your room. With a little ingenuity, you can provide an environment that will support learning all year long.

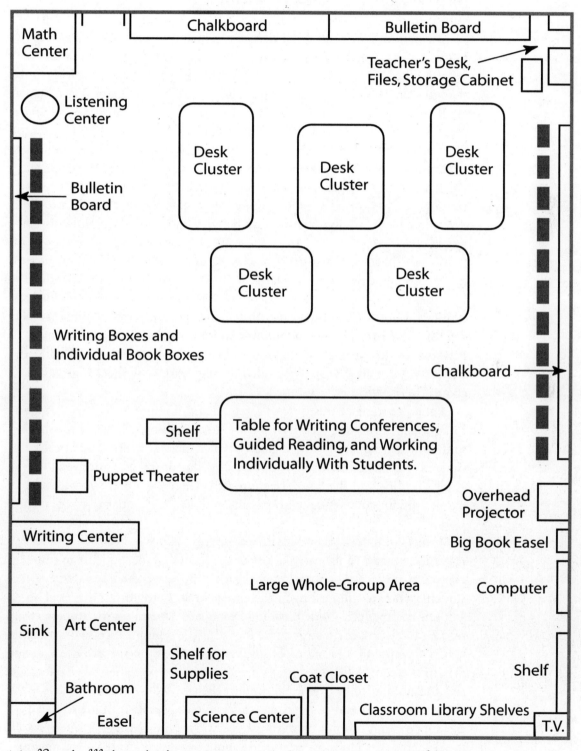

Math Center

Chalkboard

Bulletin Board

Teacher's Desk, Files, Storage Cabinet

Listening Center

Desk Cluster

Desk Cluster

Desk Cluster

Bulletin Board

Desk Cluster

Desk Cluster

Writing Boxes and Individual Book Boxes

Chalkboard

Shelf

Table for Writing Conferences, Guided Reading, and Working Individually With Students.

Puppet Theater

Overhead Projector

Writing Center

Big Book Easel

Large Whole-Group Area

Computer

Sink

Art Center

Shelf for Supplies

Coat Closet

Shelf

Bathroom

Science Center

Classroom Library Shelves

Easel

T.V.

▲ Pamela Mahoney's classroom is organized to support a variety of learning activities.

Scheduling for Guided Reading

In our schools, when primary teachers plan their daily schedules, they set aside a minimum of two hours for language arts and allow time for guided reading each day. Because kindergarten is in session for only a half day in our district, the language arts block is one to one and a half hours, and guided reading occurs only with those children who are already reading.

To determine the time you'll need for guided reading, consider the number of students in your class and the range of reading abilities they possess. Then create your initial groupings; the ideal group size is four to six, though guided reading groups might range from three to eight. Place below-grade or struggling readers in smaller groups. Keep in mind that sessions are short—often 10 to 15 minutes for emergent readers, and 15–30 minutes for more advanced readers. You will want to meet with at-risk groups every day; five meetings over a two-week period for more advanced groups is typical. You'll also want to allow yourself some time for assessment—taking a running record, jotting anecdotal notes, or conducting oral interviews, for example. Finally, allow a few minutes between groups to check in with the rest of class.

Michelle Nicolai, a first-grade teacher, plans an hour of guided reading instruction per day. Michelle relates, "Depending on the number of students I have in my class and the range of readers, I may form five to six guided reading groups. I typically meet with two groups of four to six students each day for approximately twenty minutes. With low-progress readers, I may have two or three students in a group or may take a student individually. In a two-week period, I will have guided reading sessions with each group about five or six times.

"I also use some of this time to assess the reading progress of my students. I might take a running record or record anecdotal notes. I keep a notebook so that my assessment occurs regularly, which enables me to look at each student on a consistent basis. This helps me determine my groups for guided reading and the book selection. My assessment notebook will help me prepare for conferences with parents and determine quarterly report card grades."

Molly Connolly, a second-grade teacher, also allots an hour for guided reading each day. Molly says, "Most of the second-grade students in my classroom are transitional and fluent readers; however, there are always some students who are still reading at the emergent and progressing stages. The amount of time for a guided reading lesson will depend on the students' reading levels and my instructional focus for the group. I meet with students for 15–25 minutes depending on the range of the readers. I also think about the strategies and skills they need, the length and type of book I've selected, and the amount of instructional support they'll need from me.

"The emergent and progressing readers typically read with me so that I can support and prompt them to use specific reading strategies. These are the students that I'm most concerned about because they are still struggling to put the reading process together. I try to meet with them not only during

▲ First graders read together at a poetry center.

guided reading time, but also individually a few times a week during our daily scheduled independent reading time. Sometimes my transitional and fluent readers read with me when they need guidance through a more challenging text. Other times they read on their own after the book introduction and return later in the day, or in the next day or two, to discuss and revisit portions of the text. I want them to be able to support what they've learned or understand by referring to certain portions of the text.

"Frequently, I jot notes about students' reading or do a running record so that I am monitoring each student's reading progress. This helps me determine when to move students from one guided reading group to another and when to provide more instructional support."

Experiment with different time frames and schedules to see what works best for you. Let's take a look at Michelle Nicolai's first-grade and Molly Connolly's second-grade schedules.

Daily Schedule—Michelle Nicolai's First Grade

Language Arts Block: 8:40–11:15

8:30 – 8:40	**Arrival** *Students prepare for the day: early-bird activities, book and literacy center selections, informal conversations.*
8:40 – 9:10	**Morning Meeting** *Calendar, weather, shared writing (morning message/daily news or retelling of a shared experience or innovation on a text), or shared reading (Big Books/small books, poems, charts, songs).*
9:10 – 10:10	**Guided Reading & Literacy Centers** *Michelle meets with two guided reading groups daily for approximately 20 minutes while other students work at literacy centers. She includes time for ongoing assessment of several students each day. Between groups, she briefly checks and assists students at literacy centers as needed.*
10:10 – 10:30	**D.E.A.R. (Drop Everything and Read)** *First graders read independently. Michelle roams to check student book selection, and provides individual reading instruction for students.*
10:30 – 11:15	**Writing** *Focus lessons on writing and shared writing with whole class or small groups. Students write independently on topics of their choosing. Michelle confers with individuals or small groups. Students share their writing.*
11:15 – 12:00	**Lunch & Recess**
12:00 – 12:15	**Read-Aloud** *A variety of genres, authors, and topics from the first-grade curriculum are included as part of the read-aloud.*
12:15 – 1:15	**Math** *Students use manipulatives for problem-solving and computation; occasional read-aloud and shared writing/reading related to math concepts.*
1:15 – 2:05	**Science/Social Studies/Art/Technology** *Hands-on learning in the content areas; some read-aloud and shared writing/shared reading; class observational/learning log related to content areas.*
2:05 – 2:15	**Snack**
2:15 – 2:45	**P.E./Music/Library**
2:45 – 3:00	**Closing/Dismissal**

Daily Schedule—Molly Connolly's Second Grade

Language Arts Block: 9:00–12:00

8:45 – 9:00   **Arrival/Prepare for the Day**

9:00 – 9:20   **D.E.A.R. (Drop Everything and Read)**
Students read independently while Molly reads individually with students at risk; she uses some time for ongoing assessment of students.

9:20 – 9:45   **Class Meeting**
Calendar; schedule of events for the day; shared reading/shared writing.

9:45 – 10:45   **Reading**
Molly meets with two guided reading groups daily for 20–25 minutes while remaining students are at literacy centers. She monitors students' reading progress using various assessment tools.

10:45 – 11:45   **Writing**
Focus lessons on writing/shared writing; students write independently on topics of their own choosing while Molly confers with individuals or small groups. Students share writing in progress or published pieces in Author's Chair.

11:45 – 12:00   **Read-Aloud**
A variety of genres, authors, and topics from the second-grade curriculum are included as part of the read-aloud.

12:00 – 12:45   **Lunch & Recess**

12:45 – 1:45   **Math**
Students use manipulatives for problem-solving and computation; occasional read-aloud and shared writing/reading related to math concepts.

1:45 – 2:15   **P.E./Music**

2:15 – 3:15   **Science/Social Studies/Art/Technology**
Hands-on learning in the content areas; some read-aloud and shared writing/reading; observational/learning logs related to content areas.

3:15 – 3:30   **Closing/Dismissal**

Grouping for Guided Reading

In primary classrooms, students are grouped in a variety of ways throughout the day, enabling them to learn from the teacher and from each other. Sometimes students meet as a whole class for read-aloud or for shared reading or shared writing; other times they meet in small groups. Some of these small groups include direct instruction for guided reading or writing, while other times students work together on researching topics of interest or in cooperative content study groups. The next section addresses some particular concerns about grouping for guided reading.

How do I form guided reading groups?

Joe Silva, a second-grade teacher, says, "Guided reading is one place where homogeneous grouping is important. I think it's critical to students' continued reading progress that guided reading groups remain flexible and change often throughout the year. With twenty-five students in my class, I have to think about an efficient use of my time when planning for direct reading instruction.

"To group students for reading, I rely on my assessment. At the beginning of the school year, I start by having individual students read leveled texts. I take a running record and ask the students to retell what they've read to determine their understanding and reading level. Running records not only provide baseline information but also help me to form guided reading groups.

"For example, two students were reading at the progressing level. I noticed when they came to an unknown word one student waited for me to help. The other student asked me for the word. Since these two students were reading at the same reading level and had similar instructional needs, I placed them together in a guided reading group. I knew I would need to prompt or show them what to do when they come to an unknown word.

"The students I'm most concerned about are the emergent and progressing readers in second grade. To help these students improve in their reading ability, I know I need to meet with them more often. I meet with their groups three to four times a week and take a running record on each of them at least once a week. I also keep weekly anecdotal notes on these students. I select texts that have some reading support, and not too many challenges. I observe transitional readers a little less often, taking a running record every two to three weeks and recording anecdotal notes every couple of weeks. With fluent readers, I take anecdotal notes on their reading every three weeks and a running record once or twice each quarter.

"Observing individual students while they read their guided reading books, as well as the analysis of their running records over time, allows me to make the best decisions about each student's placement in groups."

When do you move a student to a different guided reading group?

Terry Creamer, a first-grade teacher, explains, "If I observe a student reading a book easily with few or no challenges, and the past few running records show an accuracy rate of 95% or higher with a good self-correction rate of 1:4 or lower, the books are too easy. In other words, the child can read nearly all the words in the book, does little or no reading work, and reads in a smooth, fluent manner. I need to think about putting the child in a new guided reading group where there will be only a *few* new challenges.

"Conversely, I may observe a student experiencing a lot of difficulty when reading a book. This might include repeated stopping to problem-solve on words, slow word-by-word reading, appealing for help, taking no reading action, or an inability to retell what was read. I review the book selection, recent anecdotal records, and the past few running records. This helps me determine if the difficulty is limited to that particular book or if it is something that is happening frequently when the student reads. If I notice a pattern of difficulty over the past few book selections, moving the student to another guided reading group where the texts are less challenging may help him once again be able to use strategies to problem-solve while reading."

Like other Halley and Centre Ridge teachers, Joe and Terry consider the needs of the students and the results of assessment to decide on guided reading groups, knowing that the groups will shift when students' needs change.

Here's a view of some of the grouping changes in Terry Creamer's first-grade and Joe Silva's second-grade classes over about a six-week period.

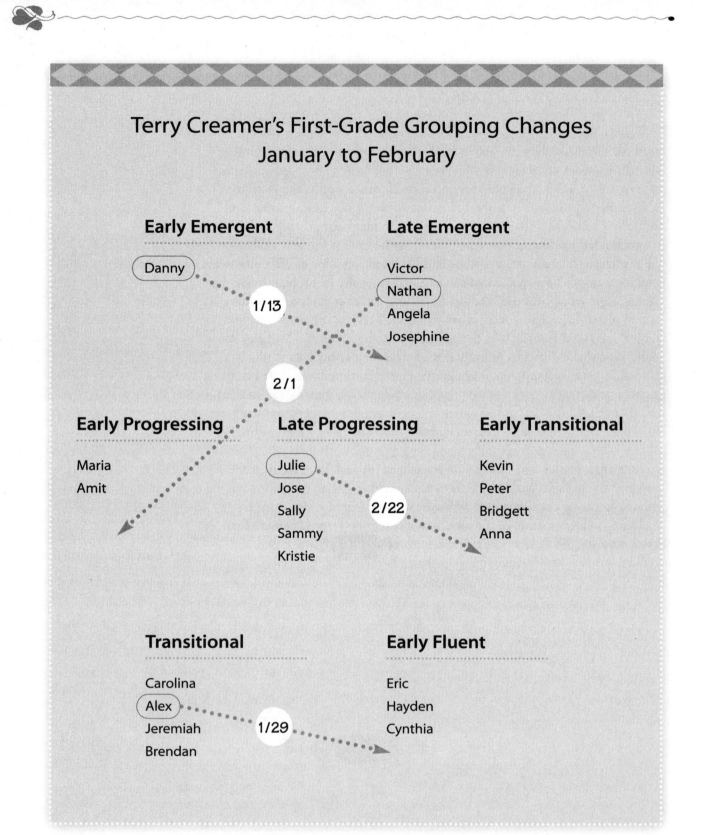

Terry Creamer's First-Grade Grouping Changes
January to February

Early Emergent

(Danny)

1/13

Late Emergent

Victor
(Nathan)
Angela
Josephine

2/1

Early Progressing

Maria
Amit

Late Progressing

(Julie)
Jose
Sally
Sammy
Kristie

2/22

Early Transitional

Kevin
Peter
Bridgett
Anna

Transitional

Carolina
(Alex)
Jeremiah
Brendan

1/29

Early Fluent

Eric
Hayden
Cynthia

Joe Silva's Second-Grade Grouping Changes
Mid-October to December

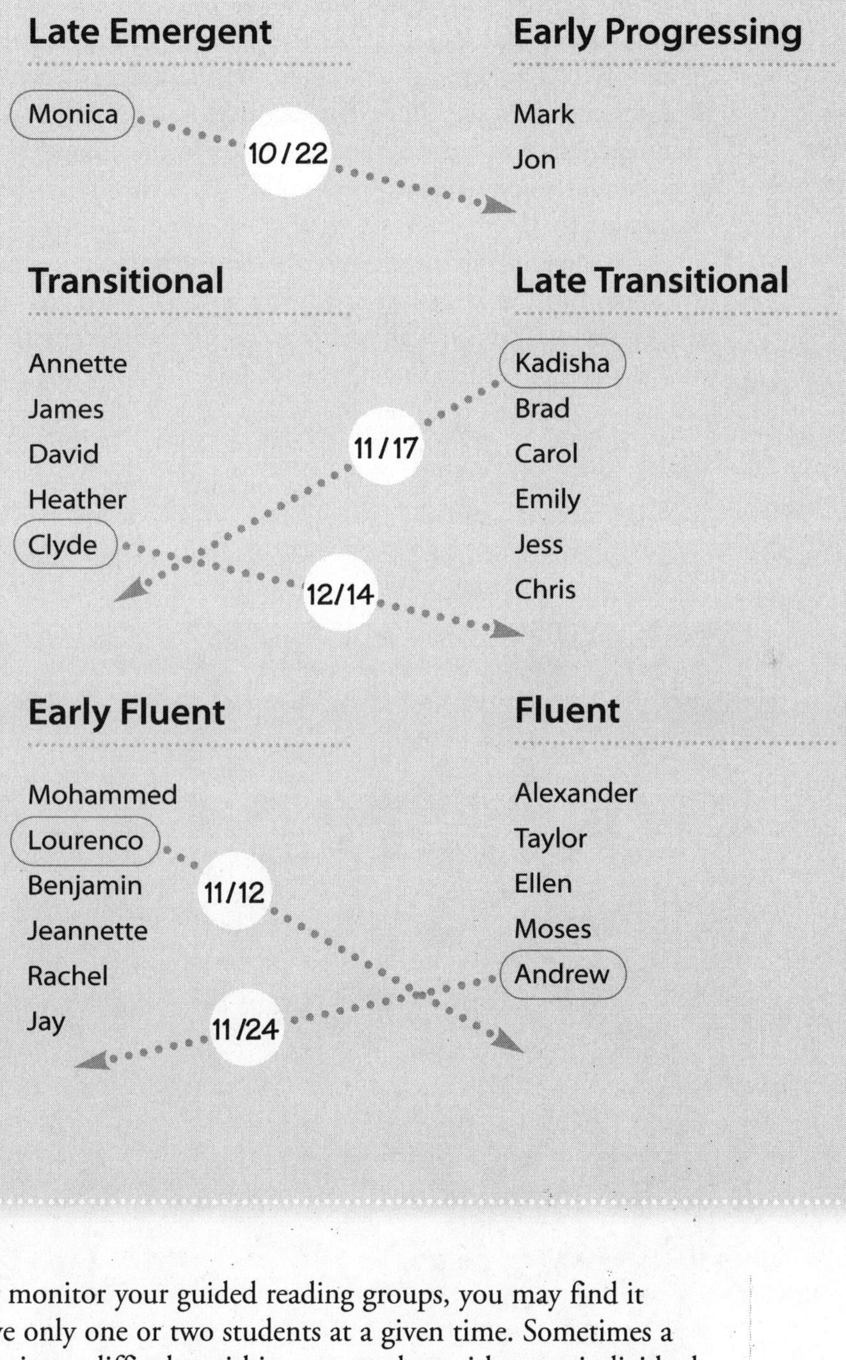

Late Emergent

(Monica)

10/22

Early Progressing

Mark

Jon

Transitional

Annette

James

David

Heather

(Clyde)

11/17

12/14

Late Transitional

(Kadisha)

Brad

Carol

Emily

Jess

Chris

Early Fluent

Mohammed

(Lourenco)

Benjamin

Jeannette

Rachel

Jay

11/12

11/24

Fluent

Alexander

Taylor

Ellen

Moses

(Andrew)

As you closely monitor your guided reading groups, you may find it necessary to move only one or two students at a given time. Sometimes a student may experience difficulty within a group, but with some individual guided reading support (during independent reading), the student may be able to continue reading with the same group.

Setting Up Literacy Centers

As a way of managing the time to meet with small groups of students, teachers often use literacy centers. At literacy centers, students continue to participate in purposeful and authentic literacy activities. These centers provide many opportunities to practice the skills real readers and writers use. They take the place of traditional worksheets and are not meant to be graded.

Literacy centers can be designed to address a wide range of skill levels, learning styles, and interests. Students work in heterogeneous groups that change often. The number of students at each center depends upon the type of center and the space for it. For example, in one first-grade classroom, the listening center has stations for four students, the computer center accommodates one student per computer, and the library center holds up to three students.

When arranging your centers, consider the number of students you want to accommodate at once, the space you have available, and the topics you want to cover. Also think about transitions between centers—will students work at the same center during the whole guided reading period? If so, do they know what to do if they finish early? If not, do they know how to move to another center or activity without disturbing you or other class members? Establishing clear expectations and routines will help centers run smoothly, so you can focus on guided reading groups.

▲ *Kara Luck introduces a social studies center to her third-grade students.*

Kara Luck, a third-grade teacher, shares some advice on managing literacy centers. "In the beginning of the school year, establishing routines is critical. It helps students learn how to work independently. They know what to do, when to do it, and where to go for help. For example, I introduce a few literacy centers at a time, demonstrating how to use the materials and equipment. I have the students sign up and go to the literacy centers to practice. During this time, I make myself available to answer questions and guide students in the appropriate use of each center before I expect them to use the centers independently. This takes a couple of weeks, but I know that when I spend time helping students with the classroom routines, my guided reading instructional time will be effectively used. The students will know what to do if I'm not immediately available."

Things to Consider When Setting Up Literacy Centers

- Establish a manageable number of centers that can be changed easily and routinely.

- Plan time to introduce and demonstrate how each center operates. Some teachers do this during scheduled shared reading-writing time.

- Consider the physical arrangement of the centers to permit movement and a balance of quiet and noisy areas.

- Design centers to meet the range of all learners, addressing a variety of interests and learning styles.

- Have supplies accessible and labeled for independent student use.

- Create signs or charts that communicate functional information and directions, such as "How to Use the Tape Player."

- Develop a plan for the rotation of students through centers and a way to keep track of the centers.

- Provide an opportunity for students to select centers.

- Develop a signal or a problem-solving technique for students to use while they are at centers and you are working with other students.

- Periodically review what's working and not working at centers.

Make your own
language
arts record-
keeping sheet. Use
the reproducible
on page 240 of
the Appendix.
Have students
illustrate or use
computer clip art
for the icons.

Weekly Language Arts Record Sheet

Name: _____

Date: _____

Date: _____

Date: _____

Date: _____

Date: _____

Managing and Organizing Literacy Centers

There are a variety of ways to organize and manage centers. Some teachers have students select literacy centers, while others choose the centers for the students to ensure they regularly rotate through them. No matter which approach you take, it is important to have a record-keeping system in place to monitor student participation in various centers. Shown below are samples of how teachers organize and manage classroom centers.

To monitor students' literacy activities, Suzi Comer's first grade students complete a center record sheet each day.

Carleen created a pocket chart for literacy centers in a first-grade classroom. Students' names were written on two sets of tongue depressors. One set was grouped heterogeneously and placed in the pockets for the various literacy centers. The other set was grouped homogeneously and placed in the pockets for guided reading. Names were moved daily by Carleen to ensure that students worked at each center activity and that she met with scheduled guided reading groups. Each day students recorded how they spent their language arts time on the "Weekly Language Arts Record Sheet." These were sent home in student work folders.

When you arrive...
* Sharpen 2 pencils
* Choose a Center
* Choose 2 Books for D.E.A.R.
* Begin your Morning Work

Centers

POEMS

Second-grade teacher Diane Hurd is beginning to implement guided reading and literacy centers in her classroom. Early in the year she sets a goal of meeting with one guided reading group each day as she works at establishing routines for the literacy centers.

Diane creates a literacy center board with icons. She glues a photo of the student on a clothespin. As students arrive in the morning, they choose the center they will attend. She talks with students about the importance of choosing different centers. Each day one group of students is selected by Diane for guided reading.

To keep track of the centers, Diane Hurd maintains a weekly record sheet where she checks off the centers the second-grade students attend daily. She records book titles selected for guided reading and any follow-up activities, titles of software, and other notations that help her keep track of day-to-day activities.

Mrs. Hurd's Class 10-19/10-22 dates	Guided Reading	Listening Center	Computer	Writing Center	Spelling Activities	Overhead	Buddy Reading	Art
1. Eric	✓ Emily		✓(Money Wks)					✓(w/Brian)
2. Haley	✓ and Attie		✓(Kid Pix)	✓ (puppet)	✓ velcro board			✓(painting)
3. Pietro	✓ xmas	✓				✓ (spelling words)		
4. Sarah	✓ glasses			✓(puppet for Three Pigs)				✓(painting)
5. Andrew	✓		✓(Money Town)	✓(a poetry bk)				✓(painting)
6. Caitlyn	✓ Crunchy Munch		✓(Money Town)	✓(puppets for Three Pigs)				✓(painting)
7. Noopur	✓		✓(Kid Pix)					✓(painting)
8. Taylor	✓ do play		✓(Money Town)	✓(puppet for Three Pig)		✓ (spelling words)		✓(painting)
9. Tommy	✓ mess puppets		✓	✓(Pop-up card)				✓(painting)
10. Kenny	✓		✓		✓ velcro board			
11. Brian	✓			✓(puppets)		✓(writing a story on the plastic paper)	✓(w/Eric)	
12. Louis	✓		✓(Money Town)	✓(puppet for Three Pigs)	✓ white board			
13. Kellie	✓ It Didn't Frighten Me				✓(white board)			✓(painting)
14. Manny	✓ Make a book using the same pattern as the story.	✓		✓ (puppet)	✓(white board)			
15. Danielle	✓	✓						✓(painting)
16. Nick	✓	✓	✓(Money Town)					✓(painting)
17. Samantha	✓	*	✓(Money Town)	✓(popupcard)				
18. Demetrius	✓			✓(popupcard)	✓(magnetic letters)	✓(write on plastic paper)		
19. Vincent	✓ Oh! No! make your own hole picture	✓✓(Twice)	✓(Kid Pix)					
20. Manmeet	✓				✓			✓(painting)
21. Kate	ESL Guided	✓	✓(Check Works)	✓(Journal)				✓(painting)
22. Brenda	ESL Reading	✓		✓ (puppet)	✓(white board)			✓(painting)
23. Yessica	ESL with ESL		✓(Kid Pix)		✓(white board)			✓(painting)
24. Tammy	ESL Teacher Baby Bear's Present		✓(Kid Pix)	✓(puppet)	✓(white board)			✓(painting)
25								

(handwritten note in Listening Center column: A Terrible Day by Patricia Reilly Giff / It was a book on Tape / I did enjoy it.)

Second-grade teacher Carrie Campbell's goals were to meet with guided reading groups more often and to provide students with additional time on the computer each week. She designed the following rotation schedule for reading and writing.

Carrie took her one-and-a-half-hour language arts block and divided it into three 30-minute sessions. On the chalkboard she listed the centers and labeled three columns: one, two, and three. Each 30-minute session had the same five centers. They included guided reading with the teacher, a follow-up reading activity, a writing center, independent reading, and the computer.

Students were assigned a class number based on the alphabetical order of their name. Carrie created three sets of student numbers using different shapes and colors, and placed a magnetic strip on the back of each. This let her move the students among the centers each day. Green circles indicated what the students would do first, red rectangles showed what they would do next, and blue trapezoids what they would do last. Carrie and her students could look down the column to see where they would be for each 30-minute block of time.

In the morning before students arrived, Carrie set up the rotation schedule for the day based on what students had done the previous day.

▼

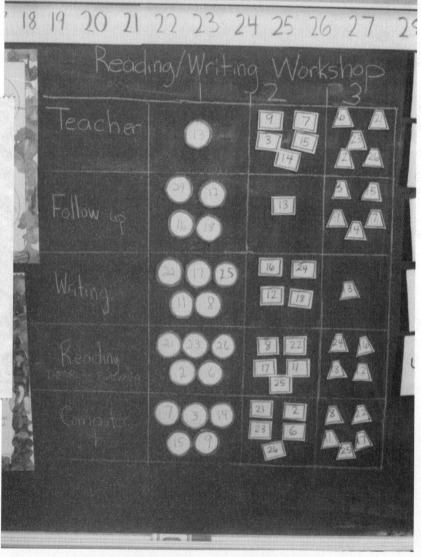

QUICK TIP

To make rotation shapes, use cardstock paper, pre-cut calendar shapes, or small close-up photos of students' heads. Label each with a student name or number. Laminate and attach a magnetic strip or Velcro to each one to make it easy to move as rotations change.

Reading/Writing Workshop Rotation Schedule

Literacy Activity	Session 1 (30 minute session)	Session 2 (30 minute session)	Session 3 (30 minute session)
Guided Reading With the Teacher	⑦ ③ ⑮ ⑭ ⑨	☐ ☐ ☐ ☐ ☐	☐ ☐ ☐ ☐ ☐
Follow-up ◆ Reading with buddy ◆ Reading response journal ◆ Reading activity ◆ Word study activity	○○○○ ○○○	7 3 15 14 9	☐ ☐ ☐
Independent Writing	○○	☐ ☐ ☐ ☐ ☐	7 3 15 14 9
Independent Reading Drop Everything and Read (D.E.A.R.) (rereading familiar books from book basket or guided reading book)	○○○ ○○○	☐ ☐	☐ ☐ ☐ ☐
Computer ◆ Electronic books ◆ Math software ◆ Word processing/ drawing software ◆ Bookmark Internet Sites	○○○ ○○○	☐☐ ☐☐ ☐☐	☐ ☐

The rotation schedule shows the five literacy activities students cycle through on a continuous basis during the 1 1/2-hour reading/language arts workshop. Each activity session is 30 minutes long. Students rotate through three activities each day. For example, the group that has guided reading with the teacher starts with that literacy activity because the previous day they ended the rotation with the fifth activity, computers. For the second 30-minute session, this same group of students will do a follow-up activity. For the last 30-minute session, these students will be working on independent writing. Tomorrow, they will begin with independent reading, move to computers, and finish with guided reading with the teacher. After each 30-minute session, the teacher takes a few minutes to walk around the room and check on students before beginning the next guided reading group. This rotation schedule allows the teacher to meet with three guided reading groups each day. When starting a rotation schedule, keep sessions short and gradually increase them to help students learn to stay on task.

Susan Altemus' third-grade students select the literacy activities they will spend time doing each day while she meets with two or three guided reading groups. These include reading independently or with a partner, working on computers, doing book projects, or visiting the school library. To monitor students' choices and to encourage accountability, Susan spends the first or last five minutes of the reading workshop recording notes on a status-of-the-class record sheet. She asks the students, "What will you be working on today?" and "What did you accomplish today?" and records their responses. Susan refers to this sheet when she meets with students during individual reading conferences and when she helps students set reading goals.

Status of the Class

	Name	Monday 11/15	Tuesday 11/16	Wednesday 11/17	Thursday 11/18	Friday 11/19
1	Alex	IR pp 4-12 GB				
2	Kathy	MA problem solving				
3	Brian	GRT: NF Sharks				
4	Kyla	IR pp 4-12 GB Bk				
5	Jade	GRT: NF Sharks				
6	Carl	WS: Suff +20				
7	Tammy	MA problem solving				
8	Donna	SCI: observ butterflies				
9	Eric	WS: Suff +20				
10	Karen	GRT: NF Sharks				
11	Jeffery	IR pp 4-12 GR BK				
12	Dylan	LIB : research				
13	Erica	BR w/ Shana GR bk				
14	Joe	LIB : Research				
15	Jane	GRT: NF Sharks				
16	Max	LIB : research				
17	Matthew	IR pp 4-12 GR BK				
18	Sarah	BR w/ Emly Buttd				
19	Michelle	SCI - obs. butterflies				
20	Miguel	LIB : research				
21	Emily	BR w/ Sarah Buttd				
22	Ana	GRT: NF Sharks				
23	Scott	GRT: NF Sharks				
24	Shana	BR w/ Erica GR bk				
25	Tyrone	Computers / Living Bk				
26						
27						
28						

Codes:
Independent Reading = IR   Writing Activity = WTG   Social Studies Activity = SS   Science Activity = SCI   Library = LIB
Buddy Reading = BR   Word Study = WS   Math Activity = MA   Guided Reading with Teacher = GRT   Art/Book Project = ABP
Computers = CMP   Poetry Journal = PJ

Possible Literacy Centers for Reading and Writing

The number of possible literacy centers is limited only by your imagination. Below are some sample centers with suggested materials and activities to help get you started.

Retelling Centers

Students use props or role-play to dramatize or retell stories.

Suggested Materials:

- story pieces on a flannel board
- hand and finger puppets (commercial/child-created)
- transparency stories
- wooden, magnetic story characters

Reading Centers

Students read a variety of materials in various ways.

Suggested Materials:

- familiar books from book boxes/baskets
- Big Books from shared reading
- books published by the class and individual students
- books from read-aloud and the classroom library
- electronic computer books
- listening station (assorted books with matching tapes)
- overhead transparencies of poems, songs, and nursery rhymes

Suggested Activities:

- read around the room (charts, poems, student writings, messages, pocket charts with sentence strips)
- buddy reading
- read to a stuffed animal or puppet

Writing Centers

Students compose and publish work in a variety of genres.

Suggested Materials:

- materials for students to publish books (picture stamps with stamp pad, pencils, crayons, markers, variety of sizes and types of paper, blank books, stapler, dictionary or picture dictionary, ABC chart)
- stories on the chalkboard or whiteboard easel
- reading journal/learning log (individual or class)
- greeting cards for students to make and send
- class message board/mailbox
- computer writing software (previously demonstrated by the teacher)

Letter and Word Study Centers

Students work with a variety of materials to reinforce letter and word skills.

Suggested Materials:

- magnetic letters to sort by attributes or to make known words
- clay, sand, Wikki Stix,™ and water pens to form letters or words
- sandpaper and tactile letters to trace or sort
- alphabet stamps with stamp pad to create books
- Magna-Doodle™ to practice letters and known words
- alphabet letter cards to sort
- letter books to read
- alphabet stencils to trace letters and words
- chalkboard or whiteboard

Additional literacy centers can include math, science, social studies, and art.

The next two pages show examples of literacy centers in kindergarten, first-, second-, and third-grade classrooms where students are engaged in meaningful literacy activities while the teacher meets with a guided reading group.

Literacy Centers in Grades K–3

Listening Center

Margaret Sonley's third graders listen to a favorite book at the listening station. Sometimes she provides an activity to do after listening.

Spelling Center

Jennifer Stecker's second-grade students take turns giving practice spelling tests to each other using a whiteboard, chalkboard, or magnetic letters.

Letter and Word Study Center

Diane Hurd's second graders use a variety of materials to explore letters and words.

Overhead Center

Mary Lambert's first-grade students read poetry selections at the overhead center. Sometimes the overhead center has a focus on writing or math.

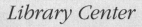

Library Center

Terry Creamer's first graders select books from the library corner to read. Sometimes they reread favorite Big Books from shared reading, "read around the room," or reread guided reading books from their personal book baskets.

◀ Writing Center

Geraldine Henryhand's first graders create greeting cards at the writing center.

▲ Art Center

Diane Hurd's second-grade students use a variety of materials to create original book projects.

◀ Here, her students create personal messages with alphabet letter sponges.

(Continued on next page)

Literacy Centers
in Grades K–3

(Continued from page 73)

Science Center ▶

Terry Creamer's first-grade students illustrate what they see when they observe items at the science center.

◀ Social Studies Center

Kara Luck's third graders have opportunities to explore geography concepts with maps and globes at the social studies center.

Building Center ▶

Edith Romaine's first graders use the Lego™ sets at the building center to create an original design. They write captions and display them on Styrofoam trays to share with the class.

Math Center

Terry Creamer's first graders use the overhead to do math-related activities and use other math manipulatives.

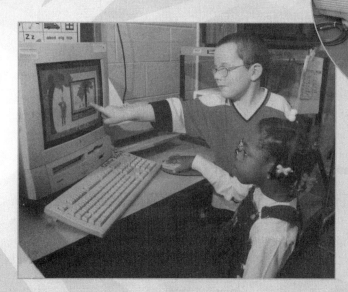

Computer Center

Lori Cleveland's third graders compose a story at the computer center which will be printed and added to their writing folder.

Katie Abruzzino's kindergarten students listen to a living book on the computer.

Drama/Storytelling Center

Linda Bowlin's first-grade students use the flannel board to recreate a familiar story.

When students clearly know what is expected of them, teachers have the time and opportunity to meet with small groups or individual students for guided reading. In our next chapter, we share sample lessons for emergent, progressing, transitional, and fluent readers.

5

Guided Reading Lessons

This chapter describes examples of actual guided reading lessons. In all of these lessons, the teacher first selects and previews the book to be read by the small group, then considers what supports and challenges are in the text (see Chapter 3), and what students will need help with during the book introduction.

The book should have some new challenges the students can problem-solve, both with and without teacher prompts. The goal is for students to read successfully a complete text on their own, using the strategies they know to problem-solve while reading.

Above:
Joe McGuire meets
with a first-grade
group of readers for
guided reading.

> "Good first teaching requires a responsive approach where the teacher is aware of what the child can do, what situations will be appropriate to assist the child to meet the next challenges, and what support will be needed. Responsive teaching ensures each step is secure enough to be a springboard for the next learning and that the learner has the resources and confidence for success. Understanding the learning and reading processes and being familiar with the materials available are as important as knowing the children in one's care. Good teaching can only occur when all three are operating harmoniously."

—Margaret Mooney,
Developing Life-long Readers

At the beginning of each lesson, introduce the book conversationally and engage students in a dialogue about the text. You may choose to focus on the illustrations, story line, words, repetitive or unusual language, text features, or any "tricky" parts. Depending upon the readers in the group, their varied experiences, and the text that will be read, some introductions will be brief and others lengthy.

While you may plan to address a specific reading strategy or skill during the lesson, *always take your cues from the group and address the needs that arise from each particular interaction.*

Possible Focus Points for Book Introductions

We include a list of possible focus points for book introductions below. While it is not a comprehensive list, it may help you plan your guided reading lessons. Choose those points that match the needs of your readers and are supported by your book selection.

For most book introductions:
- set a purpose for reading
- activate prior knowledge about the topic
- connect to previous experience(s)
- discuss story line, plot, setting, title, author
- link to a similar story/reading
- have students predict and anticipate story events
- discuss illustrations and their meaning

Consider the following, depending on your students' levels and needs:
- use some of the language from the book
- prompt students to repeat a phrase to hold in their heads while reading
- call attention to concepts about print
- point out "tricky" parts in the text, i.e., words, language structure, concept, spelling pattern
- draw attention to concepts or pattern changes in language structure or story events
- prompt students to predict letter(s) or the sound/symbol at the beginning, middle, or end of a word
- prompt students to locate one or two words

- ask students to predict, search, check, and confirm in a portion of the text
- confirm and reinforce students' understanding of reading strategies and behaviors previously taught, i.e., rereading, one-to-one word matching by finger pointing, checking the first letter
- point out special text features, i.e., format, layout, diagram, unusual vocabulary
- highlight specific elements of story structure from the beginning, middle, or ending parts of the story; theme; author's writing style
- highlight use of punctuation and its meaning
- prompt students to examine text for information to clarify their thinking and understanding of the text
- support students' understanding of literary genres
- teach something new, i.e., previewing a text, reading a diagram

> The teacher's introduction creates a scaffold within which children can complete a first reading of a whole story.
>
> —Marie Clay, "Introducing a New Storybook to Young Readers"

▲ Carleen's students preview the illustrations in a non-fiction book during her book introduction.

Guided Reading Lesson with an Emergent Reading Group

Sarah Cobb has a group of three emergent readers in her kindergarten class. Sarah acknowledges, "I know that I need to be teaching reading to kindergarten children who show they want to read and who display many of the early reading behaviors. While observing these students in shared reading and writing activities and during independent reading and writing, I noticed that they were understanding some important concepts about print. During independent reading time, they frequently chose to reread the easy, repetitive books I used during shared reading. They pointed to the words as they read and at times even self-corrected errors. When writing, they could hear and record many sounds in words and had a small core of high-frequency words they could write. When I see students attending to print in both reading and writing, then I know they are ready to begin guided reading.

"I often begin by selecting books with predictable, repetitive language, one or two lines of print, highly supportive illustrations, and with some of the words the students know how to read and write. I meet with this group twice a week. After each guided reading session, I choose one or two students that I will do a running record on the following day to note what strategies the students are using or overlooking. This helps me to know what I need to teach and what type of book I will need to select next."

For this guided reading lesson, Sarah selected the emergent book *The Little Red Hen* by Joy Cowley because she knew it had some supports and a few challenges for the students. They were familiar with another version of the story that had been shared as a read-aloud, and this version had several of the words the students could read and write (*me, the, no, cat, dog*). The students would encounter, for the first time, dialogue, speech bubbles, and three lines of print. Part of the exchange between Sarah and her students as they read the emergent book, *The Little Red Hen* by Joy Cowley, follows on page 82. The chart on the next page highlights the reading behaviors of emergent readers, the characteristics of books appropriate for such readers, and some sample titles of emergent-level books.

We include a review of ideas to think about for emergent readers. ▶

Emergent Readers:

- learn print carries a message
- display directional movement:
  - –*left* to *right*
  - –*top* to *bottom*
  - return sweep
- match voice to print with one-to-one word matching
- locate some known words and unknown words
- use picture clues
- recognize difference between a *letter* and a *word*
- may invent text
- begin to use pattern and repetition of text to read
- use oral language/story structure to make a connection to print
- use some letter sounds (beginning/ending)
- begin to use known, high-frequency words to monitor reading

Book Characteristics— Emergent Readers

Early

- consistent placement of print on each page
- illustrations provide high support
- natural language structure
- familiar experiences
- some known, high-frequency words
- one/two lines of print (L to R with return sweep)
- predictable, repetitive sentence pattern with one/two word changes

Later

- some punctuation conventions
- illustrations provide high support
- repeated sentence pattern every few pages
- print in various positions on page
- varied sentence patterns
- multiple lines of print
- familiar objects and experiences
- simple story line

Some Titles of Emergent Level Books

A Bear Lived in a Cave,
  Little Red Readers, Sundance

Cat on the Mat, Brian Wildsmith

The Cat Who Loved Red,
  Lynn Salem and J. Stewart

The Chick and the Duckling, Mira Ginsburg

Dad's Shirt, Joy Readers, Dominie

Father Bear Goes Fishing,
  PM Story Books, Rigby

Freddie the Frog, First Start, Rigby

The Ghost, Story Box, Wright Group

Have You Seen My Duckling?, Nancy Tafuri

I Like, Literacy 2000, Rigby

I Went Walking, Sue Williams

James is Hiding, Windmill, Rigby

Jolly Roger, the Pirate, PM Extensions, Rigby

Lazy Mary, Read-Togethers, Wright Group

Little Pig, Windmill, Wright Group

Little Red Hen, Windmill, Wright Group

Lunch at the Zoo,
  Wendy Blaxland and C. Bimage

Making a Memory, Margaret Ballinger

Not Enough Water,
  Shane Armstrong and S. Hartley

What Has Stripes?, Margaret Ballinger

Sarah: Remember, we first talk about the pictures together before we read the book. That helps us to think about what we will read. Look at the picture on the cover of *The Little Red Hen* book. We read a story about Little Red Hen before. What do you remember about the story?

Charlie: The little red hen wants help but nobody will give her help.

Martina: The cow and the dog and the duck won't help her.

Keith: They won't help her make the bread, and she eats it all by herself.

Sarah: You're right. In the story the little red hen asks her friends over and over again for help.

☙ recalls an action plan for getting ready to read; connects to previous experience and knowledge of the story; prompts students to check the picture

Sarah: Now, let's see what friends she asks for help. Turn to page two.

Keith: A pig.

Sarah: The little red hen said, "Help me," and the pig said…

(Students chime in, "No.")

Sarah: That's right. What letter would you expect to see at the beginning of help?

Keith: H.

Sarah: See if you can put your fingers around the word help.

(Students frame the word *help* with their index fingers.)

Sarah: Let's point and read that page together.

(Students and teacher read page 2 together.)

Sarah: Let's see what happens next.

Charlie: She wants help with the corn and the cat says, "No."

Sarah: That's right; she says, "Help me."
          Look on page six. Who does she say "Help me" to next?

Martina: The dog.

Sarah: Will he help?

(Students say, "No.")

☙ provides and reinforces some of the language of the text; encourages students to use pictures; prompts students to predict a beginning letter and locate a word

Sarah: Look at the next page.

(Students turn to pages 8 & 9.)

Sarah: Look how they wrote the words on this page. They used speech bubbles to show us who is doing the talking. See how this little part in the bubble points down to the character talking. Little Red Hen is saying…

(Students say, "Help me.")

Sarah: That's right. "Help me," but they say…

(Students: "No, No, No.")

Sarah: What will happen next?

(Students turn to page 10 & 11.)

Martina: They're playing cards and they say, "No," and they won't help.

Sarah: That's right. They say, "No." Look on the next page.

(Students turn to pages 12 & 13.)

Keith: She's making bread and they still won't help her.

(Students turn to pages 14 & 15.)

Sarah: Oh, here are those speech bubbles again. Now when she says, "Help me," what do they say?

(Students say, "Yes. Yes. Yes.")

> **points out a special text feature—speech bubbles; prompts students to predict and confirm using the pictures (meaning) and the text**

Sarah: Do you think she'll share?

Keith: No, she'll eat it all herself.

Sarah: Let's look.

(Students turn to page 16 and say, "no.")

Sarah: How do you know? Can you prove it?

Keith: It says no.

Martina: Look at their faces. Their faces are sad.

Sarah: That's right. The word no helps us and the picture helps us too. Now I want you to point with your finger and read the book on your own. While you read, I will be listening to you. You might notice that I'm writing, and that's to help me remember what you do when you read so I can share that with you. Let's read the title together. Then, you can begin to read in a soft voice.

> **prompts students to predict ending; helps students to confirm using information from the pictures and the words in the text]**

Students read the text on their own while Sarah notes on her record sheet what they do while they read. During the reading she prompts individual students to help them problem-solve various words.

Text	Martina's Reading
"Help me,"	✓ ✓ <u>plant</u>
said the little red hen.	✓ ✓ ✓ ✓ ✓

Sarah: Try that page again and point as you read.

(Martina reads again and notices as she points that the word *plant* is not on the page.)

Sarah: This time you made your finger match the words you read in the book.

After the reading, Sarah and the students briefly discuss their favorite pages. She also has them locate one or two words they know. On the following day, Sarah will take a running record on Martina while Keith and Charlie partner-read. Later, the students will take home *The Little Red Hen* to share with their families.

Mrs. Guthrie, a parent volunteer, helps her second-grade son, Chad, select a book for Take Home Reading. ▶

Take Home Reading Program:
Parents and Children Reading Together

The Take Home Reading Program at Centre Ridge involves nightly reading at home by first- and second-grade students with their parents, a significant adult in the home, or an older sibling. It is an opportunity to have extra reading practice and provides a book to those students without reading material in the home.

How does it work?

- Books are leveled using a school-wide literacy scale and placed by levels in baskets. Reading Recovery®, the Pinnell and Fountas *Guided Reading* booklists, or the titles found in the Appendix may also be used for leveling books.

- Teacher reading assessments determine the level of text the student will read. The text level is closely monitored by the teacher with changes occurring during the year as the individual student's reading ability progresses.

- Parent volunteers, trained by the first- and second-grade teachers, come into the school daily to help students select a book from the appropriate leveled basket. They listen to the students read the book or a portion of it.

- The date and title of the book taken home by the student is recorded on a record sheet by the parent volunteer.

- The student takes the book home in a folder and/or envelope and reads the text with a parent, adult, or older sibling in the home. The parent signs the record sheet and, if desired, makes a comment to the teacher. The folder/envelope is returned the following day so students may select another book to take home.

Take Home Reading Bookmarks

Some teachers include a bookmark with the take home reading book. The bookmark will describe if this is a book to be read *to* the child, a book that will be read *by* the child, or a book to be read *with* the child. Suggestions are given to the parents on how to read a book *to*, *with*, or *by* their child. On page 241 in the Appendix you will find these bookmarks as reproducibles.

Take Home Reading Program

Sample Recordkeeping

Week of_____

Take Home Reading Inventory for Mahoney

Name/Folder #	Basket/Level	Mon.	Tues.	Wed.	Thurs.	Fri.
Joshua	1.					
Laura	2.					
Philip	3.					
Samantha	4.					
Felicia	5.					
DJ	6.					
Jamie	7.					
Daniel	8.					
Amanda	9.					
Richmond	10.					
Cavi	11.					
Angela	12.					
Michael	13.					
Andrew	14.					
Caroline	15.					
Tyler	16.					
Elizabeth	17.					
Cynthia	18.					
Jennifer	19.					
Hahram	20.					
Shane	21.					
Rachael	22.					
Anthony	23.					
Ronald	24.					
Sarah	25.					
Peter	26.					

Record : X if the folder/book is returned.
0 if the folder/book is not returned.
AB if the child is absent.

Take Home Reading
Books I Have Read

Title	#	Signature	Comments

▲ *Samples of Pamela Mahoney's teacher and student record-keeping sheets used for the Take Home Reading Program in her first grade.*

Guided Reading Lesson with a Progressing Reading Group

Mary has a group of five first-grade students who are reading at a progressing level. Their running records show that some of them are not consistently using all sources of information (meaning, structure, visual cues) to problem-solve on new text. Mary thought selecting the book *The Lion's Tail* (Scott Foresman) would support the students during the first reading because it has a predictable story line, some repetitive sentence patterns, supportive illustrations, and simple conversational dialogue. While previewing the book, she thought the literary language of the opening phrase "once upon a time" and several of the contractions might present a problem. Her guided reading conversation with this group follows on the next page; characteristics of progressing readers and the books that support them appear on page 91.

from The Lion's Tail. Copyright © 1976, 1971 by Scott, Foresman and Company. Reprinted by permission of Scott, Foresman.

(Continued on next page)

(Continued from page 87)

Mary: *The Lion's Tail* is a story about a lion who is very sad because he can't find his tail. Some animal friends come along and ask him why he's sad. This story begins like make-believe stories. Do you know some of the ways make-believe stories can begin?

Lucas: Once upon a time?

Cole: A long time ago.

Mary: You're both right. Take a look at the first page to see how this story begins. Let's read it together.

(The students and Mary read the first sentence, "Once upon a time a lion couldn't find his tail.")

🍀 **gives the students a sense of the story line; focuses on literary language; asks students to check and confirm using the text**

Mary: There's a word I want you to look at in the sentence "Once upon a time a lion couldn't find his tail." It's on other pages in the book too. It's the word *couldn't.* Can you find it?

(Students locate *couldn't*.)

Mary: It's another way of saying *could not*. We'll talk more about words like *couldn't* after you read. We know the lion's sad because he couldn't find his tail. Look at the picture. Who came along to help him?

prompts students to locate a word in the text; provides some of the language and phrasing from the story (*came along*); asks students to predict, using the pictures for meaning

Cole: A mouse.

Mary: The mouse wants to know why the lion's so sad. Let's turn the page and see what the lion says.

(Students look at pages 4 & 5.)

Mary: He said, "I…"

(Students say "…can't find my tail.")

Mary: So the mouse helped him look for it. But you know what? He couldn't find the lion's tail. Look through the rest of the book to see who else helped and who found his tail.

(Students continue to look through the book on their own and make comments about other animal characters and events.)

Mary: So where was the lion's tail?

Cindy: He was sitting on it.

Mary: How do you know?

Cindy: I looked at the picture.

Mary: The pictures can help, can't they? Let's look at the page and see if we can prove it another way.

encourages students to predict, using the pictures for meaning and language structure; provides the opportunity to preview part of text independently; checks on students' understanding of the story line and plot; prompts students to verify information in more than one way

Mary: Now you're ready to read the story on your own. Remember to think about the story and what's happening as you read.

Students read softly to themselves at the table while Mary observes their reading. She notices that Lucas is reading word by word and decides to show him how to read groups of words to make his reading more phrased and fluent.

Mary: Listen to how I read this. I'm going to read it like the character is talking. "/I can't/…find my tail./" You try it.

(Lucas echoes the phrasing of the sentence.)

Mary: Here's how I would read this part. /I'll/...look for it./ You try.

(Lucas repeats the sentence.)

Mary: Now when you come to the parts where characters talk, make it sound like they're talking by reading groups of words.

(Mary continues to listen to Lucas read and acknowledges once or twice when he reads groups of words in a phrased and fluent manner.)

🐚 models phrasing and fluency, acknowledges some of students' use

Mary follows up the students' reading with a discussion about the humor in the story. Some of the students share their favorite parts. Then, she uses magnetic letters to focus on the contractions *I'll, can't,* and *couldn't*, words from *The Lion's Tail,* as part of their word work. Tomorrow Mary will take a running record on Lucas and Jenna. Later, the students will place this book in their book baskets to read independently.

▲ *After the guided reading of* <u>The Lion's Tail</u>, *Mary does some word work with contractions.*

We include a review of ideas to think about for progressing readers. ▶

Progressing Readers:

- have good control of early reading strategies (directionality, one-to-one word matching, locating known and unknown words)
- rely less on pictures and use more information from print
- search the print, check, and self-correct more frequently (both with and without teacher prompting)
- often cross-check one source of information (meaning, language structure, visual/grapho-phonic) with another source
- check and confirm, sometimes using *beginning*, *middle*, and *ending* letters/sounds
- read familiar text with some phrasing and fluency
- begin to attend to punctuation while reading
- begin to build a core of high-frequency words known automatically
- begin to engage in discussions about what is read

Book Characteristics— Progressing Readers

Early

- varied placement of print on page
- natural language structures
- variety of simple sentences
- multiple lines of print
- more punctuation conventions
- some repetitive sentence patterns
- illustrations provide moderate to high support

Later

- variety of sentence patterns and lengths
- variety of punctuation and fonts
- use of direct speech
- longer story (beginning-middle-end)
- illustrations provide moderate support

Some Titles of Progressing Level Books

The Biggest Cake in the World, Ready to Read, Pacific Learning

Billy Goats Gruff, Read It Yourself, Ladybird

Buzzzzzz Said the Bee, Hello Reader, Scholastic

Carla's Breakfast, Leslie Harper

Catch That Frog, Reading Unlimited, Scott Foresman

Cookie's Week, Cindy Ward

Dressed Up Sammy, K. Urmston and K. Evans

Five Little Monkeys Jumping on the Bed, Eileen Christelow

I Love Camping, Carousel Readers, Dominie Press

The Lion's Tail, Reading Unlimited, Scott Foresman

Messy Mark, First Start, Troll

My Friends, Little Celebrations, Scott Foresman

Notes From Mom, L. Salem and J. Stewart

Notes To Dad, J. Stewart and L. Salem

Papa's Spaghetti, Literacy 2000, Rigby

Rosie's Walk, Pat Hutchins

T-Shirts, Ready to Read, Pacific Learning

Two Little Dogs, Story Box, Wright Group

Who Will Be My Mother?, Read-Togethers, Wright Group

Witch's Haircut, Windmill—Wright Group

Guided Reading Lesson with a Transitional Reading Group

Near the end of the school year, Terry Creamer has a group of strong transitional readers. She plans to have them read a selection from an easy chapter book because they are able to problem-solve on the run, and use multiple reading strategies. Terry has observed that they also need to learn how to look at word parts when they come to longer words. Terry decides to use the text *Frog and Toad Together* by Arnold Lobel; she begins her guided reading lesson by talking about chapter books.

Terry: This is a chapter book called *Frog and Toad Together*. Let's look at the table of contents to see all the different chapters in this book.

(The students open the book to the table of contents and together read the chapter titles.)

From Frog and Toad Together by Arnold Lobel. Copyright © 1971 by Arnold Lobel. Reprinted by permission of HarperCollins Publishers.

We include a review of ideas to think about for transitional readers. ▶

Transitional Readers:

- 🐾 use multiple sources of information (meaning, language structure, visual/grapho-phonic) and a variety of strategies to problem-solve while reading
- 🐾 make predictions and confirm or revise them while reading
- 🐾 recognize the importance of monitoring reading for understanding
- 🐾 use familiar parts of words (beginning, middle, or end) to problem-solve unknown words
- 🐾 know a large core of high-frequency words automatically
- 🐾 read many punctuation marks appropriately
- 🐾 read most texts with phrasing and fluency
- 🐾 begin to read a greater variety of longer and more complex texts (fiction and non-fiction)
- 🐾 attend more to story structure and literary language
- 🐾 engage in discussions about what is read

Book Characteristics— Transitional Readers

Early
- 🐾 conventional story
- 🐾 varied sentence patterns
- 🐾 more print on page
- 🐾 some literary language
- 🐾 variety of literature selections
- 🐾 illustrations provide some support
- 🐾 more varied punctuation and fonts

Later
- 🐾 illustrations provide low support
- 🐾 some challenging vocabulary
- 🐾 longer selections
- 🐾 variety of text layout
- 🐾 more print on page
- 🐾 developed story line
- 🐾 font varies in size and type
- 🐾 literary language

Some Titles of Transitional Level Books

Caterpillars, Bookshop, Mondo

Clifford the Big Red Dog, Norman Bridwell

The Elves and the Shoemaker, New Way, Steck-Vaughn

The Enormous Watermelon, Traditional Tales, Rigby

Father Bear Comes Home, E. H. Minarik

Fox and His Friends, Edward and James Marshall

Frog and Toad Are Friends, Arnold Lobel

Gifts For Dad, K. Urmston and K. Evans

The Greedy Goat, Bookshop, Mondo

How Fire Came to Earth, Literacy 2000, Rigby

How Turtle Raced Beaver, Literacy 2000, Rigby

Insects, Reading Discovery, Scholastic

The Missing Necklace, Reading Unlimited, Scott Foresman

Mom's Haircut, Literacy 2000, Rigby

Old Woman Who Lived in a Vinegar Bottle, Bookshop, Mondo

Rosa at the Zoo, Ready to Read, Pacific Learning

The Snowy Day, Ezra Jack Keats

The Three Little Pigs, Reading Corners, Dominie Press

Very Hungry Caterpillar, Eric Carle

Whose Mouse Are You?, Robert Kraus

Terry:	Each chapter is a story. We're going to read the chapter called "A List." If you want to read any other chapters later on, you can. "A List" is a story about Toad and how he made a list of things he had to do. Let's turn to page 6 and read Toad's list.

(Students read the list together.)

Terry:	Something happens to his list in the story. Let's look through the story and talk together about what we think has happened.
Peter:	He wrote all the things he had to do that day.
Chelsea:	He keeps crossing out the things he does.
Ella:	He goes to Frog's house with his list.
Phyllis:	The wind blew his list away.

🍀 **prepares students for reading a chapter book; reads a relevant portion of the text with the students; previews and encourages them to anticipate story events**

Terry:	Your job is to read the whole story to see what Toad does. We'll meet again the day after tomorrow to talk about what happens. Here are some sticky-notes. Remember to use these if you come to a word you don't know. After you write the word, put the sticky-note on the page where the word is. When we meet, we'll talk about the story and any words you found.

🍀 **sets a purpose for reading; gives responsibility to students to locate unusual or difficult words in the text during reading; provides students with a time frame for completing the text reading**

Terry knows these transitional readers are able to read the text on their own; however, she plans to listen to them read a favorite page during independent reading time. This serves as an informal check on her students. Terry sometimes records this information on her anecdotal record sheet. When the group meets in two days, Terry will give them a few minutes to preview the story to recall story events. Then they will talk about the story and what happened to Toad and his list. She also plans to look at the words the students have recorded on their sticky-notes; she will use part of the guided reading session to teach word-solving strategies in the context of what the students are reading.

◀ *As an extension activity, a first grader, wrote a reading response to the Frog and Toad story, "A Lost Button."*

A Lost Button

Toad lost a button. Frog helped him look for it. I think that Toad will find his button soon because don't they always find the things they're looking for in books.

> 4-21
> A Lost Button
> Toed lost a button
> Fog hlept him look
> for it I thing that
> Toed wbil find his
> Button soon
> because dowt
>
> thay olwas
> find the things
> thaeir tooking
> for in books

Guided Reading Lesson with a Fluent Reading Group

Introducing Nonfiction

Carleen is working with a group of six fluent readers in a third-grade class. Since these students are beginning to read for information, she has decided to introduce them to the genre of nonfiction. Carleen wants students to understand that reading for information is different from reading stories, and that when we read for information, we can be selective about the parts of the book we choose to read. She plans to cover a few of the following features:

Nonfiction Features: Some Teaching Points

- acknowledgments
- afterword
- appendix
- author's notes
- bold/italic print
- captions
- charts
- diagrams
- glossary
- graphs
- index
- introduction
- labels
- maps
- realistic illustrations/ real photographs
- subtitles
- table of contents

Possible Genre Studies

Fluent readers should be encouraged to explore a variety of genres in their reading. Below is a list of possible genre studies you could conduct in your class.

- biography/autobiography
- fables
- fairy tales
- fantasy
- historical fiction
- how-to books
- legends
- mysteries
- myths
- nonfiction
- nursery rhymes
- picture books
- plays
- poetry
- *pourquoi* tales (just-so stories)
- realistic fiction
- tall tales
- trickster tales
- science fiction

On the next page, we include a review of ideas to think about for fluent readers.

Fluent Readers:

- use all sources of information (meaning, language structure, visual/graphophonic) quickly and flexibly to problem-solve independently
- detect and correct errors, often silently
- use knowledge of how words work (letters/sounds, word parts, and analogies) to efficiently problem-solve unfamiliar words
- read and understand more challenging vocabulary using context and knowledge of how words work
- consistently monitor reading for understanding
- read with phrasing and fluency
- adjust reading pace to accommodate the purposes for reading and the difficulty of the text
- exhibit an ability to infer the author's subtleties in the text
- revisit text to support ideas and understandings during literary discussions
- read a variety of genres for information and pleasure
- synthesize and interpret what is read

Book Characteristics— Fluent Readers

Early

- some challenging vocabulary
- literary terms and language
- extended story line
- variety of simple and complex sentences
- longer literature selections (e.g., beginning chapter books)
- fewer illustrations
- more print on a page

Later

- more challenging vocabulary
- more complex literary genres
- more complicated text features
- variety of fonts and print layouts
- print provides primary source of information
- more complex sentence structures
- more complex story line and concepts
- few to no illustrations

Some Titles of Fluent Level Books

Amber Brown is Not a Crayon, Paula Danzinger

Amelia Bedelia and the Surprise Shower, Peggy Parish

Best Clown in Town, Tom Bradley

Box Car Children Mystery of the Missing Cat, Gertrude C. Warner

Bravest Dog Ever: The True Story of Balto Natalie Standiford

Bringing the Rain to Kapiti Plain, Verna Aardema

Cam Jansen and the Mystery of the Monster Movie, David Adler

Canoe Diary, Nic Bishop

Chair For My Mother, Vera B. Williams

Commander Toad in Space, Jane Yolen

Duck in the Gun, Joy Cowley

Exploring the Titanic, Robert D. Ballard

Five True Dog Stories, Margaret Davidson

Gregory, the Terrible Eater, M. Weinman Sharmat

Henry and Mudge in Puddle Trouble, Cynthia Rylant

Nate the Great, M. Weinman Sharmat

Shark Lady, Ann McGovern

Skyfire, Frank Asch

Spiders, Bookshop, Mondo

Story of the White House, Kate Waters

Carleen selects the text *Spider Man*. A table of contents, headings, photographs with captions, and an index are features of this book that she can help the students understand as they begin to explore nonfiction texts. Here's a view of what the group did over several days.

Carleen: We're going to start reading a book today called *Spider Man*. It's a nonfiction book. What do you know about nonfiction? I'll record what you say on our chart.

Peter: It tells true stories.

Ryan: There are interesting facts.

Amanda: It tells you things to learn.

(Carleen puts the students' responses on a chart titled, "What We Know About Nonfiction.")

Carleen: That's a good start to our list of ideas about nonfiction. We'll add to the chart as we discover new things. Let's look at our nonfiction book about spiders. We're going to do a "quick-book-look" to see how the author set up this book to give the reader information about spiders. He uses some special ways that are different from the way storybooks are put together. I'll give you a few minutes to look through the book on your own.

(Carleen lets students browse through the book.)

🐛 **explores students' understanding of nonfiction genre; provides time for students to preview nonfiction texts on their own**

Quick-Book-Look Technique

Use the quick-book-look technique to have students preview a text. Students do not read the text but look quickly through it for special features. This can be done in pairs or small groups with all students looking at the same book title or different book titles. Students record on paper the features they noticed. These are shared later in a class discussion and recorded on a chart, "What We Know About Nonfiction." A good way to introduce this technique is to first model the steps using one of the nonfiction books you read aloud in class. On page 243 in the Appendix you will find a reproducible nonfiction quick-book-look form.

Two third-grade students worked together to do a quick-book-look of a nonfiction book. They were looking for nonfiction features in the text. ▶

Nonfiction Books-- Quick Book Look

Name: Holly and Eric

Things you found:

. Which Habitat?

- flaps so you can find what animal in what habitat.

- Pictures - real life (photo)

- Info on the side

- Glossary in back
(no index)

Carleen: What special things did you notice?

Kristen: There are pictures.

Carleen: Yes, the pictures are real photographs. Frequently, nonfiction books have real photographs. Do you know why?

Peter: It helps you get a real idea of what things look like.

Carleen: You're right. Did you notice anything else?

Ricardo: There's some writing under the pictures.

Carleen: Good checking. Does anyone know what we call that?

(Students shake their heads *no*.)

Carleen: We call that a *caption*. It gives us more information about the photograph. Let's look at pages 4 and 5. Can you find the captions? How many did you find?

Meet My Friends

Now I'm going to introduce you to my friends the spiders. First, though, you need to realize that spiders' faces differ considerably.

Nearly all spiders have eight eyes, which can be arranged in a variety of ways. Spiders which build webs have small eyes and often cannot see very well.

Many web-building spiders have four eyes in the middle of their faces and two on either side, like this brown garden spider.

Some spiders have all their eyes in one cluster on top of their heads, like this tarantula, a funnel-web spider.

Hunting spiders don't make webs for catching their food. Instead, they run after insects, or stalk them. They need at least two really big eyes to help them see clearly.

Many hunting spiders have two big eyes in front and six smaller ones in different positions, like this jumping spider.

Other hunting spiders, like this long-haired forest spider, have four large eyes and two smaller ones.

Try bending over a jumping spider and blinking slowly. Spiders can't blink, and jumping spiders find eyes fascinating. They will often look up and wonder who you are.

4   5

From Spider Man, *Rigby, Literacy 2000, pp. 4–5.*

Ricardo: Four.

Carleen: Yes, Ricardo. What do you notice about the captions?

Ricardo: The words are smaller.

Ryan: Sometimes the caption is underneath the picture or beside it.

Carleen: How would we read these two pages?

Amanda: I think you should look at the photographs and read the captions first.

Peter: I think you can read all the words on page 4 and then all the words on page 5 and save the captions under the photographs for last.

Ryan: You can read all of the words on page 4 and then read the captions under or beside the photographs. Then do the same on page 5.

Carleen: You're all right. What's important is that you read the captions under the photographs because the author is giving you more information about spiders.

(Carleen and the students continue to talk about other features in the book, such as the table of contents, bold headings, and a photo index. They discuss the purpose of these features for the reader. Later these ideas will be added to the chart about nonfiction.)

Carleen: We've talked about how the author has arranged the nonfiction book, *Spider Man*, in our guided reading lesson today. Tomorrow we'll begin by sharing what we already know about spiders. Then we'll read a part of the book.

🐛 **helps students construct an understanding of features of nonfiction; introduces vocabulary specific to nonfiction texts; checks on students' understanding; explores multiple ways of reading one feature of nonfiction**

For several days, Carleen and the students meet. They read and discuss what they are learning about spiders. Because this book has specific vocabulary about spiders, Carleen reminds the students to record any difficult words on their word cards. Students write the word and the page number where the word is located. When the guided reading group meets, part of the time will be spent on word-solving.

Word Cards

Texts that contain challenging vocabulary or technical language require specific instruction in how to analyze and take apart these words. We need to teach students how to problem-solve unknown words in the context of what they read, and we have found word cards are an effective tool for doing so.

Use a 3-inch by 8-inch piece of manila construction paper or similar paper (scraps from a local print shop are perfect). Students put their names at the top of the 3-inch side and write *word* and *page number* beneath their names.

As students read the text, they cite the page number and record any words they cannot pronounce or do not understand. The word cards are brought to the guided reading group for word study. We discuss ways to problem-solve the unknown word and return to the book to read the word in context. We use a white board or chalkboard to look at familiar parts of the word, such as prefixes and suffixes. This technique helps students look at words in a meaningful context rather than in isolation. It also helps identify students who need additional help in word study. See page 244 in Appendix for reproducible word cards.

While they are reading, students record on their personal word card the words they cannot read or do not understand. They bring these to the guided reading group where the group problem-solves these unknown words together.

Name: Sandy	
Word	**Page Number**
intricate	p. 6
spinnerets	p. 7
serenade	p. 9
delicate	p. 16
blotchy	p. 19

Carleen planned an extension activity following the reading of *Spider Man*. During independent work time, the students brainstormed a word map of spider words and met with partners to classify the words. At the next guided reading lesson, they shared their categories with the group. Carleen took the categorized words, typed them, and made copies for students to place in their reading logs. Students were encouraged to continue to add new spider words to the list.

Guided reading changes as readers progress. While students depend heavily on the teacher at first, they gradually assume more responsibility for their own reading as they learn strategies to problem-solve a variety of texts independently. The guided reading session is a time the teacher can teach or reinforce a strategy or skill students need help with, and where students can bring their problems and questions. The next chapter examines how teachers integrate phonics and word study into guided reading so students learn about words in the context of what they read.

6

Phonics and Word Study

Like all teachers, we are always trying to find opportunities to help students understand how words work in our language. Guided reading is one place we can consistently talk about phonics and word study because students continually meet new words in their reading. Sometimes we focus on a few words from the text that may present a problem before students read a selection; other times, we help students with words that are tricky during the reading of a passage. Or we may explore a few words after reading. As with strategy instruction, it often depends on the students, their needs, and the book we have selected.

Above:
Susan Altemus and third-grade students frequently do their phonics and word study during guided reading sessions.

Susan Altemus, a third-grade teacher at Halley, explains: "Today we discussed the letter cluster *ph*. The main character in the story had a photographic memory. I noticed as I listened to individual students read a portion of their guided reading text aloud that the word *photographic* was tricky for a few of them. I chose to make that our word study focus when the students returned to the guided reading group to discuss the part they'd read. We clapped the syllables in *photographic* and searched for what we already knew about the word and its meaning. We talked about the difference between how it looks and how it sounds, and that *ph* can occur at the beginning, middle, or end of words. Next, we brainstormed a quick list of *ph* words, and sorted them based on where the letter cluster occurred in the word. I followed this up by inviting my students to be on the lookout for additional *ph* words in their independent reading. Later, we added these to the list we generated in the guided reading session."

Susan Altemus and her third graders listed all the ph words they knew and found in the books they were reading. ▶

Other Word Study Ideas

- **consonants**

  b...<u>b</u>all   <u>b</u>ath   <u>b</u>ear

- **consonant blends/clusters**

  <u>bl</u>ue   <u>gr</u>ass   <u>st</u>op

- **digraphs**

  <u>ch</u>eese   <u>th</u>is   <u>sh</u>e

- **vowels (long and short)**

  c<u>a</u>t   g<u>o</u>   sh<u>i</u>ne

- **vowel patterns**

  l<u>oo</u>k   b<u>oy</u>   n<u>ew</u>

- **contractions**

  I'll = I will   we've = we have   can't = cannot

- **compound words**

  into   airplane   birthday

- **plurals**

  dog-dogs   cry-cries   foot-feet

- **homophones**

  to   two   too

- **affixes**

  <u>un</u>tie   look<u>ing</u>   return<u>ed</u>

Like other primary teachers at Centre Ridge and Halley, Susan recognizes that students need to understand how the written language system works and how it's related to reading and writing. We all want students to be flexible and quick in solving words they need in reading and writing. What students already know about letters and words will help them learn more new words and will support them to quickly and efficiently problem-solve unknown words.

Planning for Word Study

To help students become word-solvers, we plan for word study instruction in guided reading lessons. In general, it's a good idea to preview the day's text for tricky words; you may want to address these in the book introduction. Also look for words that illustrate a word-study principle that you've planned to cover. And always be alert for words students have problems with while they read—you can talk about these words after the reading or make a note of them for future lessons. Following are some more specific ideas for planning word study for guided reading groups:

- Preview books students read to identify words that might present a problem for students, e.g., the meaning or decoding.
- Use words students know to teach principles about how words work.
- Spend only two to four minutes with a few words to teach a principle.
- Use magnetic letters with emergent and progressing readers so you or students can manipulate the letters.
- Demonstrate on a white board, chalkboard, or paper to show how letters and/or words work.
- Revisit the reading selection after making a teaching point so students see the word in context.
- Explore the meaning of words as part of word study.
- Select words for word study from students' writing and reading.

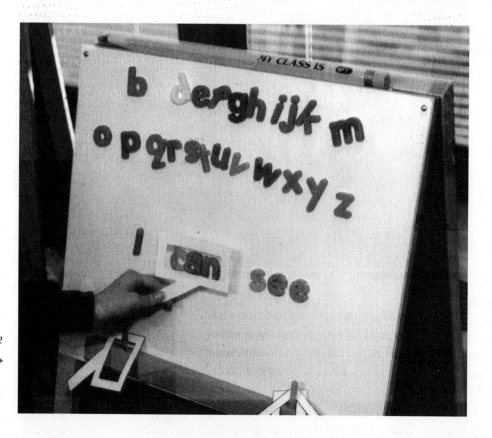

First-grade teacher Pamela Mahoney uses different-size masking cards during word study, shared reading, and shared writing. (See page 239 in the Appendix for reproducible masking cards.) ▶

Some Principles for Letter and Word Study

There are ample opportunities to learn about letters and words in the classroom during shared reading and shared writing and during independent reading and writing. You can also plan for more direct ways to teach how letters and words work in the context of what students are reading before, during, and after guided reading. These opportunities help students learn over time how letters and words work. Depending on the students, the order and focus of the instruction will vary.

The following list shows examples of some principles for letter and word study. The list is not inclusive or in order of instruction. See pages 245–246 in the Appendix for a reproducible copy of this list.

Some Principles for Letter and Word Study

- **a group of letters makes a word**

    Stephen   mom   go

- **letters in words are read left to right**

- **words can vary in length (long or short)**

    I   Alexandra   like

- **letters have an alphabetic sequence**

    a, b, c, …x, y, z

- **letters in words represent sounds**

    /n/ as in *nut*

- **sounds of the letters can be heard in words**

    c-a-t   n-e-s-t   s-t-a-n-d

- **words are the same in writing and reading**

(I use the same letters to write the word *dog* that I see when I read the word *dog*.)

- **initial letters can be uppercase or lowercase**

    it   the
    It   The

(Continued on next page)

(Continued from page 105)

Some Principles for Letter and Word Study

- **initial letters can be changed**

like	day
bike	play

- **final letters can be changed**

is	cat
it	can

- **letters can be added to the ends of words**

play	plays	playing	played	player
see	sees	seeing	seen	

- **words can be abbreviated or shortened**

isn't	VA
is not	Virginia

- **words can be put together to make a new word**

to day	can not
today	cannot

- **letter clusters at the beginning of words can be changed**

play	stop
stay	shop

- **letter clusters at the end of words can be changed**

track	past
trash	path

- **letters can be added to the first part of words or word segments**

it	an
sit	ran

- **letters can be added to the beginning and end of words**

and	stand	standing
mind	remind	reminder

(Continued on next page)

(Continued from page 106)

Some Principles for Letter and Word Study

 **middle letters can be changed**

cat   big
cut   bug

 **words can be learned through analogy**

no   went   stop
go   sent   day
                        stay

 **letter clusters in the middle of words can be changed**

farm   green
form   grain

 **some words sound the same but are spelled differently and have different meanings**

see   blue   to
sea   blew   too
                        two

 **some words are spelled the same but sound differently and may have different meanings**

read   bow
read   bow

 **some words look differently than they sound**

eight   buy   eyes

 **some words have silent letters**

knit   right   lamb

 **some words can be broken into parts or syllables**

dinosaur   understand   wonderful

Through letter and word work, we're teaching students to become aware of how to work with what they know to figure out new words. We help them construct words and take words apart, which they will need to do when they write and read. Assessment will help you determine where your students are, which principles they understand, and which they need to learn.

Snapshots of Letter and Word Study During Guided Reading

We can look at how letters and words work before, during, or after the students read a selection in a guided reading lesson. The following snapshots show how word study can be integrated into guided reading lessons.

Principle: Some words have silent letters.

When Mary previewed *Mouse's Baby Blanket* by Beverly Swerdlow Brown for a group of emergent readers, she identified the word *knit* as one that would probably be tricky for students. During the book introduction, she used magnetic letters to show that *k* was a silent letter in the word *knit*. Mary's conversation went something like this.

Mary: Let's look at this word. It's in our story many times. There's something tricky about it.

(Mary makes the word *knit* with magnetic letters and points to the letter *k*.)

Mary: See the *k* at the beginning. It's silent. When we say this word, we begin with the sound of this letter.

(Mary points to the letter *n*.)

Mary: Now look here. There's another part of this word that you know.

(Mary points to the word part *it*.)

Pierre: I know, *it*.

Mary: That's right. Let's look at the whole word and try it together. It says...

Students: Knit.

Mary: Now, let's find *knit* on the first page of the book.

(Students frame the word *knit* with their index fingers. Then they read the sentence together.)

Mouse began to knit.
Mouse began to knit
a baby blanket.
But it became too big.

from *Mouse's Baby Blanket*,
by *Beverly Swerdlow Brown*.

Principles: Letters can be added to words; Some words look different than they sound.

When the transitional-level guided reading group completed reading *The Three Little Pigs* (Scott Foresman) with reading teacher Josie Adler, they talked about the story. Some of the children revisited the book to read aloud their favorite parts. Following previous lessons, Josie planned to discuss the different sounds of the suffix *ed* within the context of the story.

Josie: Turn to page 11. Read the page to yourself. As you read, I want you to look at the words *huffed* and *puffed* and think about what you hear at the end.

(Students read the text.)

Josie: What did you hear at the end of the words *huffed* and *puffed*?

Danielle: Sounds like /t/, a t.

Josie: Yes, but take a look. It sounds like a t, but what letters do you see at the end?

Mike: E-d.

Josie: That's right. Remember we've discussed how *e-d* can sometimes have the sound of t. Now, I want you to look at page 10. Check to see if you can find another word that ends with *e-d*.

Dee: *Called*.

Josie: How does the *e-d* sound in this word?

Stacey: Like a d.

Josie: Right. We found out that *ed* can have two different sounds. Let's say the words and listen to how they sound at the end.

(Children say the words *called* and *huffed*.)

Josie: When you're reading and you see *e-d* at the end of a word, notice how it sounds. You might discover that *e-d* can have still another sound. Now, let's read these two pages together.

After the reading, you can have students find *-ed* words in the book and sort them by the sound *-ed* makes, reinforcing the principle taught.

"Then I'll huff and I'll puff and I'll blow your house in!" called the wolf.

So he huffed and he puffed and he blew the house in.

from <u>The Three Little Pigs</u>, *Scott Foresman.*

Principle: *Some words can be broken into parts or syllables.*

Another opportunity to engage in word study occurred when Carleen met with a fluent guided reading group to discuss the book *Bats*. The students came to the table with a copy of the book and individual word cards (see page 99). On the word cards, students recorded any words they were unable to read or understand and the page on which the word was found. Carleen and the students began by discussing the details in the book. Their discussion led naturally to some of the words that presented difficulty for the students. Here's a portion of their conversation.

Abby: I had a word on page 12 that I didn't know. I don't know how to say it. It's spelled *c-a-r-n-i-v-o-r-o-u-s.*

(Carleen writes the word on a white board.)

Carleen: Was this word tricky for anyone else?

(A few children say *yes.*)

Carleen: Let's look at it. What do you know about this word?

Abby: I see *car* in it.

Carleen: Good. You've got the first part. Let's look at the next part. (Carleen uses a large masking strip and shows *niv.*) This much says…

Abby: *Carniv.*

Carleen: Can you add the last part? (Carleen slides the masking strip to *orous.*) Say it fast. *Carniv…*

Students: *Carnivorous.*

Carleen: Good, *carnivorous.* See how taking the word apart helped us figure out the whole word? Now remember, it's not only important to be able to pronounce the word. We need to know what the word means too. Who knows what *carnivorous* means?

Lee: I think I know what it means, but I'm not sure. I think it has to do with what they eat.

Carleen: Well, let's check and see if there is more information in the book or whether we have to go to another source. Who can find where we need to look in the book?

(Students returned to the text and reread page 12, discovering that the meaning of *carnivorous* was stated in one of the sentences. Then the students checked to see if the word was listed in the glossary.)

Building Resources for Letter and Word Work within the Classroom

Guided reading is one opportunity for direct instruction in phonics and word work, but you can build a climate for letter and word learning throughout the day. Here are some of the ways you can promote learning about letters and words in your classroom.

Alphabet Charts and Alphabet Books

Alphabet charts and alphabet books help acquaint students with the names of letters, letter sounds, word associations, and letter formation. Students come to learn that there is more than one symbol for each letter, that fonts can vary, that sounds can vary for some letters, and that the letters of the alphabet have a sequence. Themed alphabet books can extend students' vocabulary, concepts, and background knowledge.

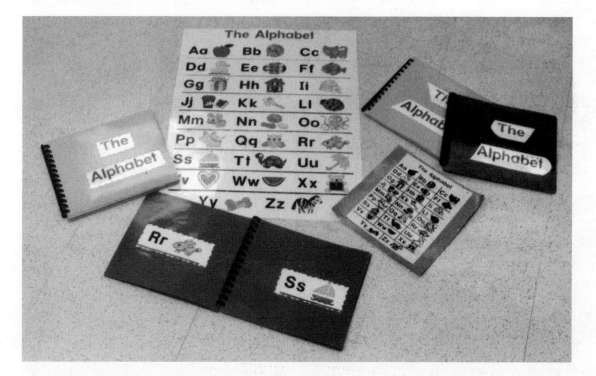

▲ *Primary teachers use the same alphabet chart to provide students with a consistent letter/sound symbol association throughout the grades. The chart is posted near reading and writing areas for easy reference. See page 247 in the Appendix for a reproducible, desk-size alphabet chart.*

Amy Dux's first graders created their own alphabet chart and books.

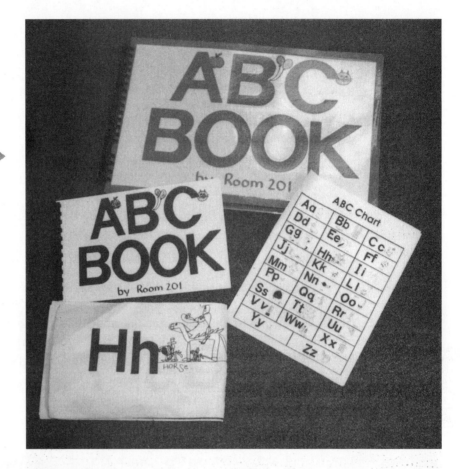

▲ First graders from Mrs. Creamer's room read a variety of alphabet books.

Tips for Using Alphabet Charts and Books

- Purchase many different types of alphabet books for the classroom library. Place them together for easy access. Encourage students to select an alphabet book that they can read independently to keep in their personal book basket.

- Read a variety of commercial and class-created alphabet books during read aloud time and/or shared reading.

- Create a class alphabet Big Book and make individual smaller versions. Include students' names.

- Chant the alphabet chart (a...a...apple, b...b...balloon) to build a familiarity with letter/sound association.

- Cut up the alphabet chart to make individual, lap-size alphabet books. Place in the classroom library.

- Reduce the size of the alphabet chart to 8-1/2 by 11 inches or smaller for students to use when writing independently at their desks or at the writing center.

- Cut up the alphabet chart so students can sequence the letters at a pocket-chart center.

- Cut up two alphabet charts, mount each set on different-colored tag board. Have students match the letters from the two sets. Store each set by color in a resealable plastic bag.

- Make content-specific alphabet books to include such topics as animals, plants, and space.

- Create an alphabet word mural with students. Divide paper into sections for each letter of the alphabet. Use newspapers and magazines to find letters with varying fonts and pictures for each letter. Include students' names and drawings on the mural. Post at eye level for independent reading.

Letter and Word Explorations

Exploring and working with letters and words in different ways helps students learn distinctive features about print. They notice the similarities and differences in how letters look, and they use this knowledge in the context of reading and writing.

◀ *Kindergarten students use a variety of mediums to write letters and words.*

Second-grade students use magnetic letters to practice individual spelling words. ▶

◀ *A second-grade student explores words by adding affixes to root words.*

Letter and Word Explorations

- During shared reading and shared writing, help students notice features about print and the meanings of words. When looking at letters and words, use a variety of tools such as highlighter tape, Wikki Stix,™ masking frames (see reproducible on page 239 in the Appendix), sticky-notes, plastic framing wands, and masking strips.

- Demonstrate how to clap and listen for parts of words (syllables) to help students write longer words and to look for familiar parts when reading.

- Teach students how to say words slowly to listen for the letter sounds they hear. Ask questions such as: *What letter sounds can you hear in…? What did you hear first? What did you hear next?* Model this in shared writing.

- Demonstrate how to check and confirm words in reading by saying the word slowly and pointing to the letters across the word at the same time.

- Purchase plastic and wooden letter and word tiles or magnetic letters for students to sort letters, make known words, and practice spelling words.

- Sort magnetic, plastic, or wooden letters by various attributes, i.e., letters with curves, circles, long and short sticks, color, lowercase and uppercase.

- Use clay to form letters, names, and words. Roll 10–15 pieces of clay into eight-inch lengths to manipulate into various letters and words. Store in a resealable bag for reuse and accessibility.

- Practice letter formation with water pens, fat chalk, markers, colored glitter glue, sand, salt, shaving cream in a tray, or finger paint in a resealable plastic bag. Use white boards, chalkboards, Magna-Doodles,™ or magic slates for a writing surface.

- Use alphabet stencils, stamps, sponges, and cookie cutters for students to make letters and words they know.

- Use magnetic letters or a white board to explore and practice how words work, i.e., change the first, middle, or final letter; add a prefix or a suffix; break into parts and remake. (See Principles for Letter and Word Study in this chapter for more ideas.)

- Create puzzles for students to match letters, letter/sound symbols, and high-frequency words.

- Make Big Book and small book versions for letters, blends, or digraphs. Use commercial stickers, computer clip art, or student drawings for illustrations. Add these to the classroom library.

- Create alliterations for consonants, blends, or digraphs, i.e. "Happy Harry had a huge hamburger." Have students illustrate and compile into a class book.

- Use commercial software to type letters and words on the computer, using a variety of fonts.

Word Walls

Word walls help students develop a common bank of words for writing, provide an opportunity to view words in another setting, and promote an awareness that words have a correct spelling. Select a place in the classroom to display high-frequency words students meet repeatedly in their reading and writing. Place the word wall at a comfortable height for students and arrange the words in alphabetical order. Demonstrate how to use the word wall during shared writing activities.

◀ Terry Creamer, a first-grade teacher, sets up a word wall to build an interest in words and to help develop a common core of words that students will meet frequently in reading and writing. She begins with students' names. Frequently, she uses words from the wall to teach new words.

During independent reading time, first-grader Victoria sometimes chooses to read her personal word bank, which consists of words that she knows how to write and read. ▶

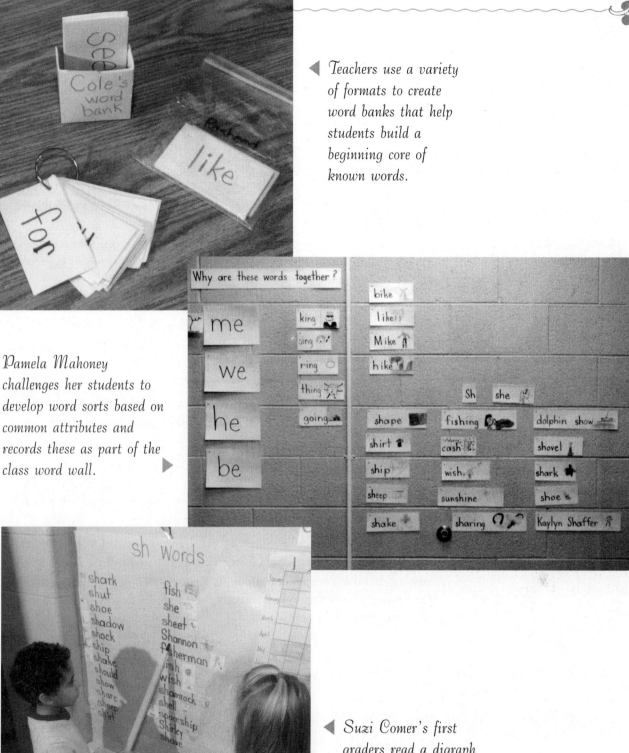

◀ Teachers use a variety of formats to create word banks that help students build a beginning core of known words.

Pamela Mahoney challenges her students to develop word sorts based on common attributes and records these as part of the class word wall. ▶

◀ Suzi Comer's first graders read a digraph chart the class brainstormed together.

For more information on developing and using word banks and word walls, see

Phonics That Work!
   by Janiel Wagstaff

Phonics They Use
   by Patricia
   Cunningham

Teaching Reading and Writing with Word Walls
   by Janiel Wagstaff

Words Their Way
   by Donald Bear et al.

Word Walls: Tips for Success

- Begin word walls with student names, the words students are already able to write (refer to students' writing vocabulary assessments), or words that are used repeatedly in the morning message or daily news.

- Use the words on the word wall to demonstrate strategies that show how words work and how they are used in reading and writing. For example, if I know the word *like*, it can help me get to the word *bike*. If I know the beginning letters of *stop* and the last part of *day*, I can make the new word *stay* (analogies).

- Plan extension activities using the word wall. Sort words by letter(s), sound(s), syllables, affixes, patterns, and topics.

- Play "I Spy a Word" with words on the word wall to help children notice concepts and features about print. For example, the teacher or student says, "I spy a word that begins and ends with the same letter," (*mom*) or "I spy a word that has a double letter in the middle and is the name of someone in the classroom" (*Tammy*). Students locate the word on the word wall.

- Use the word wall to help students learn about alphabetical order. Discuss how this helps to find words faster. Make a link to the use of the dictionary.

- Create word walls of content-specific vocabulary during a unit of study. Following the unit of study, cut the words apart and reorganize them to make a dictionary. Or, put the words on sentence strips, punch a hole for a metal ring, and place in the classroom library.

- Make class word banks by putting words from the word wall on four-by-six-inch blank index cards. Place in a file box or punch a hole in the top, left-hand corner and secure with a metal ring. Students can refer to these when they write independently and can practice reading the words during independent reading.

Word Study Resources

To help students learn why and how to use resources, build a collection of reference materials to include picture and junior dictionaries, thesauruses, atlases, rhyming dictionaries, children's encyclopedias, computer software, commercially prepared word lists, topic word books, and writer's reference books. Demonstrate when and how to use these resources during reading and writing instruction.

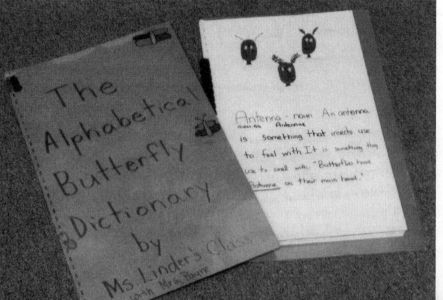

Third graders in Aimee Linder's class created a class reference dictionary during their science unit of study on butterflies.

Students use commercially produced dictionaries for personal words needed in writing.

Word Study Resources

- Purchase a variety of paperback versions of up-to-date reference materials to enable regular and less costly replacement. Organize these resource materials in a box or basket separate from the classroom library so students can easily find and use them.

- Create class Big Book dictionaries from topics of study in the content areas. Use commercial stickers, computer clip art, or student drawings for illustrations. Add these to the classroom resource library.

- Plan a reference scavenger hunt after students have been introduced to and used a variety of reference materials. Prepare a series of questions that ask students to identify the type of reference materials they would use to find the answer. For example, *What resource could you use to find a synonym for* said? (thesaurus, dictionary) *What resource could you use to find the rules for capitalization?* (writer's reference book, dictionary)

- Help students learn how to use computer writing tools such as the dictionary and thesaurus.

Exploring phonics and words during guided reading instruction provides opportunities for students to become word-solvers. In the next chapter, we discuss a variety of assessment tools teachers can use to help determine what their students already know and what they need to learn, which helps teachers plan for guided reading We also discuss ways to gather, organize, store, and use assessment information.

Assessment and Evaluation in Guided Reading

Assessment in reading can be thought of as taking a snapshot of a reader at work; it allows us to capture information about a reader's progress, which we in turn use to guide our instruction. Assessment is a continuous process that relies heavily on observations of students engaged in the task we are assessing—namely, reading. We observe and interact with students, often recording responses, reading behaviors, and strategies students use while they read. In *The Whole Language Evaluation Book*

(1989), Yetta Goodman refers to this as "kid-watching." We are constant kid-watchers during guided reading lessons, shared reading and shared writing, independent reading and writing, literacy center time, classroom discussions, or, more formally, in one-to-one conferences with students about their reading or writing.

By carefully observing individual students in the course of ongoing classroom activities, we evaluate, reflect, and revise our instructional plans on the basis of what students do. We let students know when they are successful in a learning task, and provide the support they need to complete tasks they are yet unable to do on their own. Equally important, kid-watching is a way for us to evaluate ourselves and our teaching.

Assessment Tools

As teachers we must decide *when*, *what*, and *how often* to assess. Many teachers use consistent types of assessment tools throughout the year to form a picture of each student as a learner during that time. However, in our schools, running records, writing samples, and anecdotal notes are used across the primary grades. Choose only the tools and forms that work for your classroom and students, keeping in mind your purposes for assessment; you can adapt, create, or add other tools as you need them. Since literacy is difficult to assess, use a variety of tools to get a complete picture of students' strengths and needs. It is important to assess at intervals periodically during the year to chronicle student progress and to plan instruction. The information you gather through assessment can be used to decide when students are ready to join guided reading groups, how students should be grouped, and what skills or strategies they need to work on. We describe here a number of assessment tools that you may find helpful when considering the types of information to gather about your students' reading and writing.

Letter Identification

Kindergarten and first-grade teachers assess students' knowledge of the alphabet, letter names, and sounds (Clay, 1993). Some teachers use this assessment with second graders who have made low progress in reading. This tool identifies students who need additional help in learning the alphabet.

How to Use the Alphabet Recognition Sheet

1. Sit beside the student.

2. Give the student the "Student Alphabet Chart" (see page 249 in the Appendix).

3. Begin by asking the student: "What are these?"

4. Point to each letter across the line and ask: "What is this one?"

5. If the student does not answer, use one of the following questions:

   "Do you know its name?"
   "What sound does it make?"
   "Do you know a word that begins like that?"

6. Use the "Alphabet Recognition Record Sheet" to record student responses (see page 248 in the Appendix).

7. Count as correct if the letter name, letter sound, or a word beginning with the letter was given.

8. Total the correct uppercase letters and lowercase letters identified and record in the comments section any observations during the completion of the task.

Victoria's completed "Alphabet Recognition Sheet." ▶

Word Test

It is often helpful to know what words a student recognizes by sight, particularly when the student is just beginning to learn to read. Some of the teachers we work with use the United States version of the word test lists in *An Observation Survey of Early Literacy Achievement* (Clay, 1993) to determine what words a student has accumulated as part of a reading vocabulary. The U.S. version, called the "Ohio Word Test," consists of a list of many high-frequency words from the "Dolch Word List." You might also want to develop your own word list by identifying high-frequency words used in shared reading and shared writing.

Some teachers in grades two and three use the word lists included in the *Qualitative Reading Inventory-II* (QRI-II) (HarperCollins College Publishers, 1995). With the QRI assessment, the student reads a list of words in isolation while the teacher records correct responses, as well as any attempts. The teacher may also note the accuracy of the student's decoding attempts.

Concepts About Print

The Concepts About Print (CAP) assessment helps teachers of emergent readers determine what a student knows about book handling and print concepts. This assessment shows you what students know about reading before they may be actually reading, and helps you decide when students know enough to be a part of a guided reading group. It also determines what teaching techniques will help the students learn more about how print works in our written language.

The teachers we work with use checklists for concepts about print. Some use the checklist in *An Observation Survey of Early Literacy Achievement* (Clay, 1993); others use a modified version our district has adapted from Clay's checklist. Or you may consider using Marie Clay's *Concepts About Print: What Have Children Learned About the Way We Print Language?* (2000), a guide that provides information on administering the CAP assessment. Also, in *The Story Box Level 1 Teacher Guide*, the Wright Group Publishing Company includes CAP checklists for individual students and one to use as a class profile.

QUICK TIP

Teachers can model and discuss concepts about print during shared reading of Big Books, charts, nursery rhymes, and songs. Shared writing, such as morning messages and written retellings of familiar stories, provides another opportunity for teaching these important concepts.

Some of the important concepts include the following:

- book handling (front, back, title, where to begin reading)
- print (not the picture) carries the message
- directional movement (left to right, top to bottom, return sweep, first, last)
- word-by-word matching with finger pointing under each word read orally
- concept of a *letter* and a *word*
- letter, word, and sentence order matters
- letters can be capital or lowercase
- spaces serve a purpose in reading
- punctuation marks have meanings and signal the reader

Benjamin's completed "Concepts About Print Score Sheet." ▶

3 CONCEPTS ABOUT PRINT SCORE SHEET

Date: 1/25   Stones: _____   Sand: ✓   SCORE: 2/124   STANINE GROUP: 8

Name: Benjamin   School: Halley

Recorder: Achulman   Classroom Teacher: Smith

Use the script when administering this test.

Scoring: ✓ (Checkmark) correct response.   • (Dot) incorrect response.

PAGE	SCORE	ITEM	COMMENT
Cover	✓	1. Front of book	
2/3	✓	2. Print contains message	
4/5	✓✓✓✓	3. Where to start 4. Which way to go 5. Return sweep to left 6. Word by word matching	
6	✓	7. First and last concept	
7	✓	8. Bottom of picture	
8/9	✓	9. Begin 'The' (Sand) or 'I' (Stones) bottom line, top OR turn book	
10/11	✓	10. Line order altered	put the and after "hole" & this 1st
12/13	✓✓✓	11. Left page before right 12. One change in word order my with 13. One change in letter order "e" should go there pts to end	
14/15	✓•	14. One change in letter order make a should be of etha; ni → i 15. Meaning of ? when a something in front of	should go here - pts to beg.
16/17	✓••✓	16. Meaning of period/full stop wrong "k." 17. Meaning of comma — end of sentence 18. Meaning of quotation marks 19. Locate M m H h (Sand) OR Tt Bb (Stones)	
18/19	✓	20. Reversible words was, no	
20	✓✓✓✓	21. One letter: two letters splashed; splashed 22. One word: two words in; in the 23. First and last letter of word The; The 24. Capital letter The; The	

© Clay, 1993. Adapted with permission by The Ohio State University/Rev./94

FCPS #1 8/9F

Writing Vocabulary Inventory

At the beginning of the school year and periodically throughout the year, kindergarten through grade-three teachers at Halley and Centre Ridge collect a "Writing Vocabulary Inventory" (WVI) (Clay, 1991). It provides an inventory of known words that each student can write in ten minutes. The WVI helps you determine students' awareness of words and parts of words. In grades two and three, it sometimes provides insights into what students know about the conventions of spelling and how words work. Keep in mind that the WVI is not a spelling test. Some third-grade teachers use the WVI only at the beginning, to obtain baseline information. It may also be used at regular intervals during the year with low-progress students.

Administering the Writing Vocabulary Inventory

The WVI can be done in large groups or small groups depending on the grade level. Find a place with limited print, so that students generate the words themselves rather than copy words from in and around the room.

1. Give the students blank pieces of paper and pencils and say:
"I want to see how many words you can write. Can you write your name?"

(Start the 10-minute timing here.)

After the students finish writing their names, say: *"Think of all of the words you know how to write and write down as many as you can on your paper."*

2. Prompt the students by suggesting categories if they are unable to think of words to write. For example: *"Do you know how to write any...animal words? color words? number words? little words? things you can eat? places you can go? names of people in your family?"*

3. Prompt students with some high-frequency words if they are unable to generate many words suggested by the categories above, such as: *I, go, to, and, my, like, love, cat, play* (see *An Observation Survey of Early Literacy Achievement* [Clay, 1993] for additional examples).

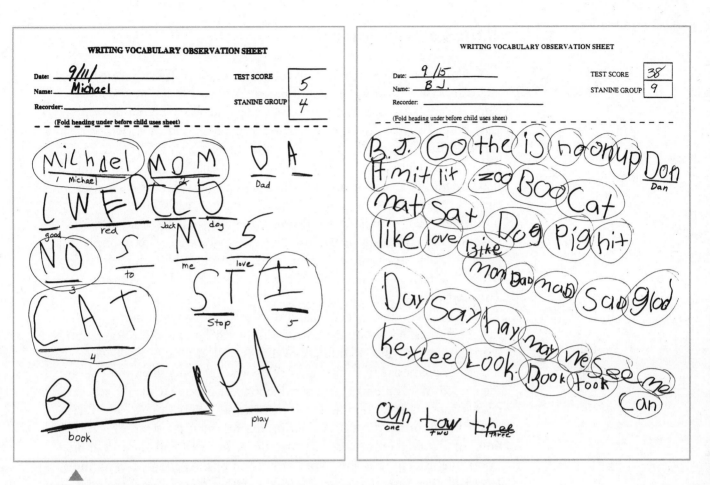

Two first-grade students' completed 10-minute Writing Vocabulary inventories.

Spelling Inventory

To help obtain a general view of students' knowledge of the word system we use in writing, you can administer a spelling inventory as part of their assessment. Many current professional books that focus on spelling are good sources for spelling inventories. To find out more about developmental spelling inventory lists, directions on how to administer them, guidance in analyzing students' spelling responses, and ideas for instruction, you may want to refer to the following professional resources.

- *My Kid Can't Spell* by J. Richard Gentry
- *Spelling in Use* by Lester Laminack and Katie Wood
- *Spelling K–8 Planning and Teaching* by Diane Snowball and Faye Bolton
- *Words Their Way: Word Study for Phonics, Vocabulary, and Spelling Instruction* by Donald R. Bear, Maria Invernizzi, Shane Templeton, and Francine Johnston

Benchmark Books

Walk into any classroom in our schools and you will find a range of readers. Because of this, we identified books we could use to assess the different levels of readers at the various stages of development in *each* classroom. Teachers first met as a grade-level team, and then later as a vertical primary team (K–3), to discuss and select a range of "benchmark books." The teams chose a few titles for each benchmark reading level; the benchmark books had specific features or characteristics for readers at various stages of reading development. A range of texts with a progression of difficulty from kindergarten through grade three is essential to the selection of benchmark books for text-based assessment. For example, first-grade teachers expect most students to be able to read benchmark books within the mid to higher range of the transitional level, i.e., *Pot of Gold* to *Frog and Toad*.

Kindergarten, first-, second-, and third-grade teachers in our schools use the benchmark books for assessment purposes only. A book introduction is written for each benchmark book so that there is uniformity in how teachers introduce the books to students. After the teacher reads the introduction, the student does an oral reading of the book or passage while the teacher takes a running record. However, if the student is very phrased and fluent, and it is too difficult to take a running record, the teacher takes anecdotal notes of observed errors and self-corrections. In either case, after reading aloud, the student retells the story or portion of the passage. If a running record is taken, it is then scored, and the teacher determines if the book is at the frustrational, instructional, or easy level for the student. Teachers use this information to form and plan for guided reading groups at students' instructional levels.

Listed below are some benchmark book titles teachers selected to assess readers at various stages of development in kindergarten through grade-three classrooms. We've included book introductions written by primary classroom teachers for each selection. There is a progression of difficulty through the stages.

Benchmark Book List

Always read the title and the introduction to each benchmark book. A retelling is not included in the early text readings, but begins at the progressing stage.

EMERGENT

Title/Word Count	Author/Publisher	Teacher's Book Introduction
Me (24 words)	Rigby PM Starters	Read the title and say: *This book is about a little girl who tells about all the things she can do. Look at the pictures and tell about what you see she is doing.* Have student preview pictures. Read the title again and say: *Now, point as you read about what the little girl can do.*
I Love My Family (31 words)	Wright Group Sunshine	Read title and say: *This book is about a boy who loves his family. Look at the pictures to find out who the people he loves are before you read.* Read the title again and say: *Now, point as you read about the little boy's family.*
Look for Me (65 words)	Wright Group Story Box	Read title and say: *David is playing a game of hide-and-seek with his mom. Mom looks everywhere for David. First look at the pictures to see where Mom looked.* Read the title again and say: *Now, read to see where Mom finds David.*
The Cat Who Loved Red (63 words)	Seedling Publications	Read title and say: *Once there was a cat that loved the color red so much that everything she had was red. Look at the pictures before you read to find out the things she loved.* Read the title again and say: *Now, read to find out about the cat who loved red.*

Benchmark Book List

PROGRESSING

Title/Word Count	Author/Publisher	Teacher's Book Introduction
The Red Rose (126 words)	Wright Group Story Box	Read title and say: *Mr. Singh had a red rose in his garden. Let's see what he does when a caterpillar, a bird, a cat, and a dog come into his garden. Look at the pictures to see what happens.* Read the title again and say: *Now, read to find out what happened in the garden.*
Bruno's Birthday (32 words)	Rigby Literacy 2000	Read title and say: *Bruno gets some special things for his birthday. Look at the pictures to see what happens on his birthday.* Read the title again and say: *Now, read to find out what he gets.*
Tricking Tracy (125 words)	Rigby Literacy 2000	Read title and say: *Tracy likes to play tricks on her friends. Look at the pictures to find out what happens to her one day when she needs help.* Read the title again and say: *Now, read to find out about the tricks she plays. After you have finished reading, I want you to tell in your own words what happened in this story.*
Susie Goes Shopping (194 words)	Troll Associates First Start°	Read title and say: *Susie's mother did not feel well, so she asked Susie to go shopping for her. Look at the pictures to see what happened when she gave Susie a dollar to buy a loaf of bread at the bakery.* Read the title again and say: *Now, read to find out what happened at the bakery. After you have finished reading, I want you to tell in your own words what happened in this story.*
Three Billy Goats Gruff (387 words)	Scholastic	Read title and say: *There were three billy goats by the name of Gruff who wanted to go to the hillside to make themselves fat. On the way they had to cross a bridge where a great ugly troll lived. Look at the pictures to see what happened when each of the billy goats went to cross the bridge.* Read the title again and say: *Now, read to find what happened when they came to the bridge. After you have finished reading, I want you to tell in your own words what happened in this story.*

Benchmark Book List
TRANSITIONAL

Title/Word Count	Author/Publisher	Teacher's Book Introduction
Mom's Haircut (99 words)	Rigby Literacy 2000	Read title and say: *Mom wanted a haircut. Look at the pictures to see what happened when she tried to get one.* Read the title again and say: *Now, read to find what happened with Mom's haircut.* After you have finished reading, I want you to tell in your own words what happened in this story.
You'll Soon Grow Into Them, Titch (191 words)	Pat Hutchins	Read title and say: *Titch is the youngest child in the family. When he outgrows his clothes, he gets hand-me-down clothes that are too big. Everybody keeps telling Titch, "You'll soon grow into them." Look at the pictures to see what happens.* Read the title again and say: *Now, read to find what happened to Titch.* After you have finished reading, I want you to tell in your own words what happened in this story.
The Pot of Gold (266 words)	Scott Foresman and Company Reading Unlimited	Read title and say: *A mean man named Grumble catches an elf. He knew an elf always has gold, so he told the elf to take him to the gold. Look at the pictures to find out how the elf tricks Grumble.* Read the title again and say: *Now, read to find what happened to Grumble and the elf.* After you have finished reading, I want you to tell in your own words what happened in this story.
The Little Red Hen (pp. 5–33; 277 words)	Scholastic	Read title and say: *The little red hen was hoeing the garden and found some grains of wheat. She knew it would make a delicious cake. Look at the pictures to find out what happened.* Read the title again and say: *Now, read to find what happened when she asked her friends to help.* After you have finished reading, I want you to tell in your own words what happened in this story.
Father Bear Comes Home (pp. 9–15; 199 words)	Else Holmelund Minarik	Read title and say: *I want you to read a chapter in this book called "Little Bear and Owl." Look at the pictures to find out what happens when Little Bear goes down to the river to catch a fish for Mother Bear.* Read the title again and say: *Now, read to find what happens when Little Bear meets Owl down at the river.* After you have finished reading, I want you to tell in your own words what happened in this chapter. Take a running record on pages 9–15; 199 words.
Frog and Toad Are Friends: "The Lost Button" (pp. 28–33; 206 words)	Arnold Lobel	Read title and say: *In this chapter, Toad loses a button and Frog tries to help him find it. Look at the pictures to find out what happened.* Read the title again and say: *Now, read to find out how Frog helps Toad.* After you have finished reading, I want you to tell me in your own words what happened in this chapter. Take a running record on pages 28–33; 206 words.

Benchmark Book List
FLUENT

Title/Word Count	Author/Publisher	Teacher's Book Introduction
Nate the Great and the Sticky Case (pp. 7–12; 194 words [take a running record on this section])	Majorie Weinman Sharmat	Read title and say: *I want you to read a part of this story about Nate the Great, a boy detective. Nate and his dog Sludge are asked to solve the case of a missing dinosaur stamp. Look at the pictures to see where the missing dinosaur stamp was found. Read the title again and say: Now, read to find out about the missing stamp. After you have finished reading, I want you to tell in your own words what happened in this part of the story.*
Hooray for the Golly Sisters (pp. 54–64; 235 words [take a running record on this section])	Betsy Byars	Read title and say: *I want you to read a part of this story about the Golly Sisters. The Golly Sisters want someone to yell, "Hooray for the Golly Sisters," after their show. Read to find out if their wish comes true. After you have finished reading, I want you to tell me in your own words what this part of the story was about.*
Marvin Redpost: Why Pick on Me? (page 1 to top of page 4; 298 words [take a running record on this section])	Louis Sachar	Read title and say: *I want you to read a part of this story about a boy named Marvin Redpost. Marvin and his classmates have to think of a survey question to put in a class time capsule. Read to find out what questions they consider. After you have finished reading, I want you to tell me in your own words what this part of the story was about.*
Cam Jansen and the Mystery of the Dinosaur Bones (pages 1–3; 259 words [take a running record on this section])	David Adler	Read title and say: *I want you to read a part of this story about a girl named Cam Jansen. Cam is a girl detective who has a photographic memory. She can take one look at something and remember everything about it. Read to find out about what happens when Cam goes on a field trip with her class. After you have finished reading, I want you to tell in your own words what this part of the story was about.*
Ramona Quimby, Age 8 (pages 11–14; 438 words [take a running record on this section])	Beverly Cleary	Read title and say: *This book is about a girl named Ramona Quimby. I want you to read the beginning part of the chapter to find out what happens when Ramona gets ready for the first day of school. After you have finished reading, I want you to tell in your own words what this part of the story was about. Now turn to page 11 and begin to read.*
The Chocolate Touch (page 1 to second paragraph on page 4; 313 words [take a running record on this section])	Patrick Skene Catling	Read title and say: *I want you to read a part of this story to find out what a boy by the name of John Midas liked better than anything else. After you have finished reading, I want you to tell you in your own words what happened in this part of the story.*

▲ Some benchmark books that teachers at Halley use as part of their reading assessment with students in grades K–3.

QUICK TIP

Consider purchasing a commercial set of benchmark books such as the *Developmental Reading Assessment* (DRA)(Beavers, 1997). These benchmark books are designed for use in kindergarten through third grade.

Janice Poole, a third-grade teacher, uses the Developmental Reading Assessment to assess and document Kathia's development as a reader. ▶

Running Records

A running record (Clay, 1993 *infra*) of students' oral reading behavior is an essential tool for recording what a student does *while* in the process of reading. The teacher graphically records in a shorthand method everything the student says or does when reading a passage or book, to gain insight on the strategies the student uses effectively and those with which the student needs help.

Running records may be taken on unfamiliar and familiar texts (read once). Often, teachers take running records on books students have read during guided reading. For guided reading purposes, running records are usually taken on the second reading of the text. Teachers may select a few students each day on whom to take a running record.

Analyzing and interpreting the results of a running record can then provide information about what is happening as the student is reading.

How to Take a Running Record

1. Sit next to the student so you can see the text as the student reads aloud. If you're right-handed, sit on the student's right-hand side.

2. Mark the student's every response on the recording sheet (see page 253 in the Appendix) or a blank sheet of paper. Each word read *correctly* is represented by one check mark (✓); you do not record the text.

3. Arrange check marks exactly the way the words are arranged on the page, starting a new line for each line of text and recording page numbers, so that you will be able to tell which check represents each word.

4. Record what the child says above the line; record what the text says below the line when there is a discrepancy between what the reader reads and the text.

5. Record page numbers and mark page breaks with a vertical line.

Here is an example of how an accurately read text would be recorded.

Text: *All Fall Down*	Running Record:
I see a bee.	2. ✓ ✓ ✓ ✓
I see a bee and a butterfly.	4. ✓ ✓ ✓ ✓ ✓ ✓
I see a bee and a butterfly and a bird.	6. ✓ ✓ ✓ ✓ ✓ ✓ ✓ ✓ ✓

Following, you'll find how to record various behaviors students may exhibit during reading.

Substitution

....

When a student reads a word that is different from the text, write the word in the text with the substituted word above it. *Counts as an error if not self-corrected.*

Text:	**Running Record:**
I go up the stairs.	CHILD ✓ ✓ ✓ ✓ steps
	TEXT stairs

If a student tries several times to read a word, record all the trials. *No matter how many attempts are tried, it counts as **only one** error.*

Text:	**Running Record:**
I like my home,	CHILD ✓ ✓ ✓ here/h…/ house
	TEXT home
said the bird.	✓ ✓ ✓

Omission

....

When the student omits a word, record it with a dash. *This counts as an error if not self-corrected.*

Text:	**Running Record:**
I see a bee and a butterfly	✓ ✓ ✓ ✓ ✓ ✓
and a bird and a rabbit.	CHILD ✓ ✓ ✓ ✓ — ✓
	TEXT a

Insertion

....

When the student inserts any additional word(s), record it (them) over an underscore. *Each word inserted counts as an error if not self-corrected.*

Text:	**Running Record:**
Our dog Sam likes	✓ ✓ ✓
to ride in the car.	CHILD ✓ go for a ✓ ✓ ✓
	TEXT —

Repetition

When the student repeats a word or group of words, draw an arrow with an *R* to show where the repeat begins and ends. If the student repeats more than once, record it as R $_2$ or R $_3$, etc., indicating the number of repetitions. *Repetition **is not** counted as an error.*

Text:	**Running Record:**

Have you seen my cat?

(Child reads: Have you, Have you seen my cat? Have you seen my cat?)

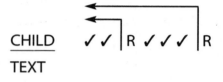

CHILD   ✓ ✓ | R ✓ ✓ ✓ | R

TEXT

Self-correction

When a student succeeds in correcting an error, the error response is recorded, then the letters SC (self-correction) are written after it. *No error is counted.*

Text:	**Running Record:**

It's a baby snake.

CHILD   ✓ ✓ little | SC ✓

TEXT   baby

That's what's inside.   ✓ ✓ ✓

Intervention

When taking a running record, try to intervene as little as possible. This is not a teaching moment. Remember, you want to find out how the student problem-solves when reading text independently. There are, however, a few times to intervene, as described below.

Sometimes a student is unable to proceed because an error is made and he is aware of it, but cannot correct it. Allow a wait time of five to ten seconds for the child to problem-solve. If the child does not make any attempts during that time, simply tell the student the word. Record this as *T* on the same line you record text. *This counts as an error.*

Text:	**Running Record:**

We won't run after him.

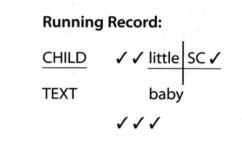

CHILD   ✓ was/went/ wot | ✓ ✓ ✓

TEXT   won't | T

Use your best judgement when and when not to give a Told. For example, names, places or unusual words may be difficult for the child. You would be more likely to just tell the child the word, so the meaning of what she is reading is not lost.

🐛 Record an appeal for help from the student as *A* before using *T* for *told*. *This counts as one error.*

Text: **Running Record:**

Miss Pool's car broke down.   ✓ ✓ ✓ ✓ ✓

CHILD	The/h/ho/have	A		✓ ✓ ✓ ✓ ✓
TEXT	How		T	

"How will I go to school?"

said Miss Pool.   ✓ ✓ ✓

🐛 Sometimes the student may get into a state of confusion or is just unwilling to continue reading. Then you need to intervene in order to start the child reading again by saying, "Try that again." Record this as *TTA* with brackets [ ] around the portion of the text that required assistance. This should not involve any teaching, but you may indicate to the student where to begin again.

Text: **Running Record:**

But I don't love

CHILD	✓ ✓	do	like	to	
TEXT		don't	love	-	
CHILD	✓	on		the	
TEXT		grandpa's		whiskers	TTA

my grandpa's whiskers.

The above confusion counts as one error. Only the second attempt is scored (see below). The student would have a total of three errors with the error of TTA and the two in the sample below.

But I don't love

CHILD	✓ ✓ ✓ like
TEXT	love

my grandpa's whiskers.

CHILD	✓ ✓ beard
TEXT	whiskers

🐛 At times, the teacher may think a child can attempt something in the reading, but she makes no attempt. The teacher may say, "You try it." *This is recorded as YTI and does not count as an error.*

Initial Sound

When the student says the beginning of a word, then quickly says the word in the text, record this behavior by writing the initial sound and a check mark (✓) above the word. *This is not counted as an error or a self-correction,* but indicates the student is using multiple sources of information to problem-solve on text.

Text:	Running Record:		
I can jump,	CHILD	✓ ✓	j ✓
	TEXT		jump
said the grasshopper.		✓ ✓ ✓	

Names

When the student substitutes a name or mispronounces it throughout the passage, *it is counted as an error the first time only.*

Text:	Running Record:	
Maria went outside to play.	CHILD	Mara ✓ ✓ ✓
	TEXT	Maria
Just then her mother called,		✓ ✓ ✓ ✓ ✓
"Maria, come in for dinner."	CHILD	Mara ✓ ✓ ✓
	TEXT	Maria

REMEMBER: Student's responses are placed above the line, while text or any teacher intervention is placed below the line.

The best way to learn how to take running records is through practice. When you begin, explain to students what you are doing and that the running record will help you to be able to share with them what they do when they read. If a student reads too fast for you to keep up, it's okay to ask him to stop for a moment until you catch up. After finishing the record, do some immediate teaching. Begin by highlighting the problem-solving strategies the student used, praising what he did well specifically. For example, *"You ran out of words on this page, so you knew you had to go back and reread to check closer."* Or, *"When you said _____, you knew it didn't make sense, so you checked closer and thought about what else it could be."* When making a teaching point based on what you observed, limit it to one or two points after the child has finished reading.

Summary of Running Record Conventions

Accurate reading

CHILD ✓
TEXT

Substitution (**One error**)

CHILD looks
TEXT   looked

Omission (**One error**)

CHILD ——
TEXT   and

Insertion (**One error**)

CHILD big
TEXT   ——

Repetition or reread
Repeated rereads (**No error**)

↓————————— R
↓————————— R 2, 3, 4, etc.

Self-correction (**No error**)

CHILD looks | SC
TEXT   looked |

Intervention (**One error**)

[ ] teacher assistance
TTA "Try that again."
A Appeal
T Told

Intervention (**no error**)

YTI "You try it."

Student uses initial sound
to problem-solve (**No error**)

CHILD w ✓
TEXT   will

Scoring a Running Record

To calculate the **error rate**, **accuracy rate**, and **self-correction rate**, you will need the following information:

RW = the number of running words in a selection

E = the number of errors a child made while reading (does not include self-corrections)

SC = the number of self-corrections a child made while reading

The **error rate** is most meaningfully expressed as a ratio. It tells you that for every one error, the child read so many words correctly. To compute the ratio, divide the number of running words by the number of errors. For example, if a child read a text containing 104 words (104 running words) and made 8 errors, you would find the ratio of errors to correct words by computing

$$\frac{RW}{E} = \frac{104}{8} = 13$$

So the ratio would be 1:13; for every 1 error, the child read 13 words correctly. If the above calculation does not come out to a whole number, simply round to the nearest number.

You can convert the error rate to an **accuracy rate** by using the conversion table or by using the calculations below. The accuracy rate of the above example is computed this way:

$$\frac{(RW - E)}{E} \times 100 = \frac{(104 - 8)}{104} \times 100 = 92\%$$

This rate will help you determine if a text is easy, instructional, or hard for the student.

EASY 95–100%   **INSTRUCTIONAL** 90–94%   **HARD** 89% or below

The **self-correction rate** tells you that a child corrected one out of so many errors. This rate is also expressed as a ratio. If a child made 8 errors and self-corrected 4 others, the self-correction rate is

$$\frac{(E + SC)}{SC} = \frac{(8 + 4)}{4} = \frac{12}{4} = 3$$

So the self-correction ratio is 1:3; the child is correcting 1 out of every 3 errors.

A self-correction rate of 1:4 or less indicates that a child is self-monitoring.

Conversion Table for Error/Accuracy Rates
for a Running Record

Error Rate	Accuracy Rate (%)	Reading Level
1:200	99.5	
1:100	99	
1:50	98	Easy/Independent Reading Level
1:35	97	
1:25	96	(95–100%)
1:20	95	
1:17	94	
1:14	93	Instructional Reading Level
1:12.5	92	
1:11.75	91	(90–94%)
1:10	90	
1:9	89	
1:8	87.5	Hard/Difficult Reading Level
1:7	85.5	
1:6	83	(89% or below)
1:5	80	
1:4	75	
1:3	66	
1:2	50	

Analyzing the Running Record

Taking and scoring the running record is the first step. Careful analysis of the errors and the self-corrections made by the student while reading is the next important step. When you analyze a running record, examine each attempt and self-correction, deciding what sources of information the reader was using or neglecting *at the point of the error or self-correction*. Mark the type of cues used for each error and self-correction. If you use the sheet on page 253, there is a column for recording this information. Write only the first letter of the cue in the interest of space (Meaning, Structure of language, Visual/grapho-phonic). If you use a blank sheet, just write in the cues at the end of each line.

Thoughtful analysis creates a profile of what sources of information and strategies a student is using, neglecting, or over-relying on when reading. It also provides you with insights on how to help the student become a more strategic reader. As you analyze running records, consider these questions:

- Is the text familiar or unfamiliar?
- Does the student have control of early reading strategies (directionality, word-by-word matching, locating known words, locating unknown words)?
- What types of errors did the student make (did they make sense, sound right, look right)?
- Did the student detect errors and make attempts to problem-solve?
- How does the student problem-solve (picture, rereading, letters/sounds, letter clusters, syllables)?
- Did the student correct the errors? If so, what additional source of information was used (meaning, structure, or visual grapho-phonic)?
- Does the student ask for help? How often? On what type of words?
- How well does the student make use of the strategies that have been taught?
- Is there a pattern of reading behaviors within the running record or across several running records (e.g., no self-correction; uses meaning and structural information, but neglects visual cues; looks at the first letter in unknown words, but doesn't attend to the letters in the rest of the word)?
- How does the reading sound (word-by-word, repeated pausing, some short phrases, longer phrases)?
- Does the student read the punctuation?
- Does the student read with intonation and expression?
- How well does the student understand what is read?
- Do the child's instructional needs match the text selected?
- What is the accuracy rate and self-correction rate? Is the text easy, instructional, or hard?
- What has to be learned next?

Running records are an excellent tool for chronicling reading development over time and monitoring the reading strategies a student uses. The following examples show the process of analyzing and interpreting running records for a series of running records from a reader's emergent through transitional stages.

QUICK TIP

For more detailed information on taking and making sense of running records see An Observation Survey of Early Literacy Achievement (Clay, 1993), Constructive Evaluation of Literate Activity (Johnston, 1992), and Running Records for Classroom Teachers (Clay, 2000).

Running Record

Child's Name: Robb
(Midway through emergent stage)

Date: 10/18

Totals: 3 | 7

Adapted from An Observation Survey by Marie Clay

Left margin annotations:

Robb: "It [butterfly] sounds like an i at the end, but it's a y." (beginning to notice discrepancy between letter and letter sounds)

cross-checks using known words

predicts based on pattern of text and structure of language; may be noticing discrepancy in size of word or may be using a known word

uses meaning and structure cues; neglects visual information (3X)

cross-checks using known words

rereads to confirm and pull meaning together

before reading this page, Robb turns to cover of book and rereads title

Page	Title — All Fall Down		E	SC	Cues Used E	SC
2	✓ ✓ ✓ ✓ I see a bee.					
4	✓ ✓ ✓ ✓ ✓ ✓ ✓ I see a bee and a butterfly.					
6	The|sc ✓ ✓ ✓ ✓ ✓ ✓ I| see a bee and a butterfly ✓ ✓ ✓ and a bird.			1	MⓈV	MSⓥ
8	✓ ✓ ✓ ✓ ✓ ✓ ↓I|sc see|sc I see a bee and a| butterfly ✓ ✓ ✓ ✓ ✓ bunny and a bird and a rabbit.		1	1 1	MⓈV MⓈV MⓈV	MSⓥ MSⓥ
10	✓ ✓ ✓ ✓ ✓ ↓I|sc see|sc ✓ I see a bee and a| butterfly and ✓ ✓ ✓ ✓ bunny ✓ ✓ ✓ a bird and a rabbit and a seal.		1	1 1	MⓈV MⓈV MⓈV	MSⓥ MSⓥ
12	and|sc ✓ ✓ ✓ ✓ I|sc ✓ R I| see a bee and a| butterfly and ✓ ✓ ✓ ✓ bunny ✓ ✓ ✓ a bird and a rabbit and a seal ✓ ✓ ✓ and a ball.		1	1 1	MⓈV MⓈV MⓈV	MSⓥ MSⓥ
14	✓ ✓ ✓ All fall down.		3	7	10100	007

SCORES:
Running words / Errors = 72 / 3

Error Rate 1: 24	Accuracy 95 %	SC Rate 1: 3

☑ **EASY** 95–100%   ☐ **INSTRUCTIONAL** 90–94%   ☐ **HARD** 89% or below

Observations/Analysis of Cues Strategies:

High level of monitoring with this book; cross-checking using visual information; often self-corrects using known words; some evidence of fluency on pages with less print.

▲ *Robb's running record of the emergent-level book All Fall Down. Note: The sample has the text printed for your convenience; a real running record would only have text under the markings when the student made an error.*

Robb's initial reading assessment showed that he was reading at the emergent level. His participation in shared reading and shared writing showed that he had an understanding of many concepts about print and a good control of oral language. Robb knew 45 uppercase and lowercase letters of the alphabet. He was able to write eight words, four of which were names. Since he joined a guided reading group, he has become more secure in early behaviors such as directionality, one-to-one word matching by pointing, and locating known and unknown words.

Robb's current running record on *All Fall Down* shows that he is using meaning and structure as sources of information when reading. He is beginning to monitor and self-correct with known words. He is able to use the pattern of the text to make meaningful predictions about what would make sense next in reading (repeated self-correction of errors: *I/a* and *see/butterfly*).

After the running record, the teacher praised Robb for his self-corrections and the rereading he did to pull the meaning together on page 12. Because Robb is neglecting visual sources of information—not checking to see if words look right—the teacher prompted him to reread page eight and to check the first letter of the last word in the sentence (teacher points to the word *rabbit*). In the next guided reading lesson, the teacher will focus on helping Robb use the visual sources of information to read, along with meaning and structure cues.

QUICK TIP

Record a child's statements and reading behaviors during the running record. They inform your instruction. You make your best guess as to what the child is doing and using because these are "in-the-head" strategies.

Robb's current running record of *Catch That Frog* (see page 144), an early progressing-level text, indicates that at times he uses all sources of information when reading. He is beginning to cross-check meaning and structure with visual information (*helped/put; the/it; had/was; her/happy*). Robb is becoming more phrased and fluent in his reading. He rereads to check and confirm. He is beginning to make more than one attempt on his own to problem-solve, although he is not always successful (*out of/out* for the word *away*).

After the running record, the teacher complimented Robb for rereading to check that what he read made sense, sounded right, and looked right on the last sentence of page 23. The teacher chose to focus on helping Robb to use parts of words and what he knows about other similar words to figure out an unknown word. She prompted Robb to reread page 11 and asked him what he knew about the word *away*. Next, she took the word *away* and showed him with magnetic letters how the two parts worked. Then, she reminded him to look for familiar parts that he knows in words when he reads.

Next lessons will focus on continuing to help Robb learn to integrate meaning, structure, and visual sources of information when reading. Word work will focus on helping Robb see familiar parts or chunks in unknown words when reading.

Running Record

Child's Name: Robb _(early progressing stage)_   **Date:** 12/13

Totals | 4 | 8

Adapted from *An Observation Survey* by Marie Clay

Left margin annotations (pointing to rows):

Predicts using meaning and structural cues; cross-checks for more visual information; self-corrects at the point of error.

Uses all sources of information (meaning, structure, and partial visual)

Uses meaning, structural, and visual (first letter) cues

Monitors; searches and checks for more visual information; self-corrects some errors

Predicts using meaning and structural information; made an attempt to problem-solve when one-to-one was off; made a second attempt but knew it was still wrong; teacher TOLD when student was unable to go on.

Page	Title — Catch That Frog	E	SC	Cues Used E	SC
2	Carol ✓ and ✓ her ✓ mother went ✓ to ✓ the ✓ store. ✓				
3	Her ✓ mother ✓ got ✓ a ✓ cart. ✓				
4	Carol ✓ put helped|sc milk ✓ into|in ✓ the cart. ✓	1	1	(MSV) (MSV)	MSV
5	She ✓ put ✓ bananas ✓ in ✓ the ✓ cart. ✓				
6	A ✓ frog ✓ jumped ✓ out ✓ of ✓ Carol's ✓ pocket. ✓ The ✓ frog ✓ was ✓ Carol's pet. ✓				
7	The ✓ frog ✓ jumped ✓ around|across the ✓ store. ✓ Carol ✓ ran around|after the|sc store)R|sc it. ✓ —	1 1	1	(MSV) (MSV) (MSV) MSV (MSV) MSV	
8	The ✓ frog ✓ jumped ✓ over ✓ the oranges. ✓				
9	It ✓ jumped ✓ under ✓ the ✓ oranges. ✓				
10	Carol ✓ caught ✓ the ✓ frog. ✓				
11	It ✓ got ✓ out of|out away| again. ✓	1		(MSV)	
12	The ✓ frog ✓ jumped ✓ behind ✓ the ✓ R bread. ✓	4 3		7 7 3	0 0 3

SCORES: Running words / Errors = 131 / 4

Error Rate 1: 32   **Accuracy** 96 %   **SC Rate** 1: 2

☑ EASY 95–100%   ☐ INSTRUCTIONAL 90–94%   ☐ HARD 89% or below

Observations/Analysis of Cues Strategies:

Robb is beginning to read in a more phrased and fluent manner; generally used meaning and structural sources of information; predictions often based on meaning and structural information; cross-checking more with visual information (7x), i.e. *helped/put; and/it*; when meaning is lost, Robb consistently goes back to make sense; continue to help Robb search for more visual information

Adapted from *An Observation Survey* by Marie Clay

Page	Title	Catch That Frog	E	SC	Cues Used E	SC

Uses all sources of information to problem-solve at the phrase level

13 It jumped in/ front of the bread. — sc — | | 1 | (MS)V | M S(V)

14 The frog jumped on a boy.

15 and/sc — It/ jumped off the boy. | | 1 | (MS)V | M S(V)

16 The frog jumped around the store. R

18 Carol ran around the store after the frog.

20 The boy ran around the store after the frog.

22 The frog jumped into the cart.

Uses all sources of information: searches for additional visual information, resulting in self-correction

23 Carol came/sc caught/ the frog. | | 1 | (MS)V | M S(V)

Cross-checks one source of information with another source; rereads to confirm and pull meaning together.

She was/ had/sc happy/ her/sc she had her frog back. R | | 1 / 1 | (M)SV / (MS)V | M S(V) / M S(V)

Totals: | | 5 | 553 | 005

▲ *Robb's running record of the progressing-level book* <u>Catch That Frog</u>.

Running Record

Child's Name: Robb
(early transitional stage)

Date: 2/8

				Totals	**E** 6	**SC** 2		

Page	Title		Rosa at the Zoo		E	SC	Cues Used E	SC
2	Dad took us to the zoo. "Let's go and see the monkey," R said Dad. "Me too!" said Rosa.							
3	We lifted R Rosa up. "I like/can sc monkeys," said Rosa. "Let's go and see the lions," I said. "Me, too!" Rosa said/said Rosa.				1 1	1	M S V / M S V M S V M S V	
4	We lifted Rosa up. She looked at the lion. It walked up and down, up and down, laying/looking R sc at us.					1	M S V / M S V	
5	Then the lion roared. Rosa cried.				2	2	341	102

Annotations (left margin):
- rereads to check
- uses meaning and structural cues; cross-checks with visual information at the point of error to self-correct
- predicts using meaning and structural cues
- monitors; rereads because it didn't make sense; searches for more visual information to self-correct

Adapted from An Observation Survey by Marie Clay

SCORES: Running words **135** / Errors **6**

Error Rate 1: **22** **Accuracy** **95**% **SC Rate** 1: **4**

☑ **EASY** 95–100%   ☐ **INSTRUCTIONAL** 90–94%   ☐ **HARD** 89% or below

Observations/Analysis of Cues Strategies:

Robb uses all sources of information and is showing evidence of integrating them (*won't/want/went; lifts/lifted; got/get*). Rereads to check, confirm, and self-correct; reads fluently with phrasing; good pace and intonation; expressive at times; longer sections of text read accurately allows him to attend to message/meaning; select text with a little more challenge so he has some opportunities to learn new things

Page	Title Rosa at the Zoo	E	SC	Cues Used E	SC
	"I don't like lions," she said.				
6	We went to see the elephant. *won't/want* It was having a bath. Rosa likes baths. She looked at the elephant and said, "Me, too! Me, too!"	1		Ⓜ Ⓢ Ⓥ	
7	"No, Rosa," said Dad. R "That bath is for the elephant."				
8	The elephant looked at Rosa. It lifted up its trunk. R *lifts* Woooosh! R Rosa was wet all over. R "There you are," said Dad. "No bath. But you did get a shower." *— got*	1 1 1		Ⓜ Ⓢ Ⓥ USV Ⓜ Ⓢ Ⓥ	
		4	0	333	—

Adapted from An Observation Survey by Marie Clay

predicts using all sources of information

rereads to possibly check or confirm

uses meaning and structural cues; neglects some visual cues here (does not change meaning)

▲ Robb's running record of the transitional book Rosa at the Zoo.

At the transitional stage, Robb consistently integrates meaning, structure, and visual sources of information. He problem-solves quickly, searching for additional information to self-correct. He rereads to check, confirm, and to pull the meaning together. Robb is phrased and fluent with large portions of the text, and he adjusts his pace to problem-solve.

After the running record, the teacher praised Robb for rereading and self-correcting the last line on page four. He checked to make sure what he read made sense, sounded right, and looked right (*laying/looking*). The teacher prompted, "How did you know it was *looking*?" so Robb would think about what sources of information led him to self-correct the error. The teacher made a teaching point of the last sentence on page eight, where there were two errors. She prompted Robb to read that part again to check to see if he could find something that was not right. Robb reread the sentence and self-corrected both errors. The teacher acknowledged that this time Robb made it not only make sense and sound right, but his reading matched what the words looked like.

The teacher plans to select books that will require Robb to do a little more reading work. She will continue to help Robb learn how to integrate meaning, structure, and visual sources of information, and will also focus some teaching on checking the middles and ends of words while reading.

How Often Should I Take a Running Record?

- Take a running record of each **emergent** reader every two to four weeks. Take one more often with students who are not making expected gains.

- Take a running record of each **progressing** and **transitional** reader every four to six weeks and more often with children who are not making expected gains.

- Take a running record of each **fluent** reader quarterly and more often with any student who begins to experience difficulty reading.

Oral Retelling

An oral retelling usually follows either an oral or silent reading. Teachers often ask students to retell a story after finishing a running record on a benchmark book to determine what the student understands about the text read at the progressing, transitional, or fluent level.

The teacher asks the student to close the book and then says: "Tell me everything you can remember about the story in your own words." While the student retells the story, the teacher takes abbreviated notes. If the retelling is vague or incomplete, the teacher prompts with some of what the student has already told. Prompts such as "Tell me more about…" or "What else can you tell about…" may help the student add information omitted from the retelling. A retelling might include some of the following.

- Main idea or topic
- Beginning, middle, end
- Characters, setting, events, problem, resolution
- Important details
- Specific vocabulary or literary language

Anecdotal Notes

Anecdotal notes are used to record observations of students during reading and writing. Develop a schedule that lists who will be observed each day. Use a clipboard, notebook, or folder to record notes. Focus on one or two children *while* they read, and jot brief comments on observable reading behaviors during the reading of the text. Because many of the guided reading groups range from four to six students, teachers at Halley and Centre Ridge are able to record anecdotal notes on each student every two to four weeks. Over time, these notes provide an informative profile of the student-reader. Remember, anecdotal notes serve not only as a record of what the student is doing while reading, but also help direct the next instructional steps.

◀ Terry Creamer's flip chart of anecdotal notes.

QUICK TIP

Use sticky-notes or computer address labels to record anecdotal notes. You will find these notes useful to refer to for report card comments and conversations during parent conferences. (See pages 256–257 in the Appendix for reproducible guided reading group anecdotal record sheets.)

A student page from the anecdotal flip chart booklet ▶

<u>Spider</u> 11-18 • Look at letters! • not using 1st letter - just guessing	12-8 invents text <u>Dan the Flying Man</u> ④ + -am not monitoring; checking		mom dad love to is	
<u>My L. Dog</u> 11-20 • needs finger or leaves out words • good memory for story	~~Ice Cream~~ <u>Little Pig</u> • invents text • not using 1st letter		the cat ~~will~~ and you	
11-24 <u>Where's Your Tooth?</u> Better independence 1-1 off on "it is"	<u>Octopus</u> Dan guesses instead of making 1st sound	1/7 Reviewed known books Farm Concert difficult Who Lives Here	a we me can my	✓ Dan 10 ✓ 11 ✓ 12 ✓ 14
11-25 <u>I Can Write</u> 12-2 Flying + Floating • easy • SC 1-1	1-4 <u>Who Will Help?</u> ④	<u>Father Bear goes fishing</u> ⑤ * Starting to monitor; checked 3X's	1-27 <u>Look for me</u> ⑤ using visual inconsis.	✓ 15 ✓ 16 ✓ 17 ✓ 18
12-3 <u>Family Fun</u> off on 2-3 syllable tries memory only focus on early strategies 1-1; known + unknown words	1-5 <u>What Can You See?</u> • What else ~~needed~~ help	<u>Hide + Seek</u> + - shouted • making progress • working on making 1st sound; using known words to monitor	<u>Dan</u> 2-2 <u>Monkey's Friends</u> small ~~short~~	✓ 19 ✓ 20 ✓ 21 ✓ 22 ✓ 23

Molly Connolly's second grade guided reading status-of-the-class anecdotal notes. ▼

Status of the Class

Date 10/20 - 10/24

Alison	Amal	Billy	Monique	Sol	Tyler
<u>The Big Kick</u> T-looked fluent	<u>The Big Kick</u> good prblm solving + ✓ing	<u>The Big Kick</u> monitors fluency good	<u>The Big Kick</u> sc; ✓ing	<u>The Big Kick</u> good expression ✓ing; monitors; rereads to sc	<u>The Big Kick</u> little diff. appeals 2X's do running rec. tomorrow
Anthony	**Briana**	**Chris**	**Heather**	**Jay**	**Paul**
<u>Cat Who Loved Red</u> rereads to sc. fairly fluent	diff. getting started — picked up pace as she read	no diff. maybe more challenging bk?	good phrasing + expression; able to prblm solve at word level	appealed 1X; prblm solves after prompt to think abt story + ✓ beg of word	good bk selection; able to prblm solve throughout using all sources of info
Denise	**Dylan**	**Kristin**	**Zack**		
<u>I Love My Family</u> good 1-1; prblm solves last pg - rereads	1-1 accurate diff w/ last pg. needed help - Ⓟ meaning	1-1 off — goes back ea. time to match — last pg needed 2 TOLDS	1-1 not firm watching Dylan — diff focusing on text		
Carly	**Greg**	**Lisa**	**Nana**	**Ryan**	
<u>My Little Dog</u> Some diff. w/ pattern; Ⓟ for meaning	points; 1-1 good + firm; solves on own; rereads; ✓s picture	reads w/out. pting; ✓s pic; rereads; ✓ing; using M, S, V + ✓s 2X's	diff. getting started. Once past 4 pg. + sense of pattern able to read; monitors	weak; needed repeated prompts to focus on meaning of story; too hard? ✓ w/ running record	
Bo	**Derrick**	**Joni**	**Melodie**		
<u>Franklin Rides a Bike</u> good predictions Ⓟ to read 1st + pp to self + "prove" which prediction w/ sticky notes	predictions good — gave a couple possible ideas	able to locate prediction w/ sticky note quickly	read other Franklin bks — knew characters		

Oral Interview

Many kinds of information can be gathered from an interview, or literacy conference, as some teachers call it. An interview is an opportunity for a student to talk with you about her experiences as a reader and writer both in and outside of school.

Keep interviews informal so the student feels at ease to talk. You might ask the student to bring a self-selected book and a writing sample as a way to invite her to begin talking about herself as a reader and writer. Here are some of the topics or questions that could be discussed.

1. What are you reading now? How did you choose the book?

2. Do you like to read? Why or why not?

3. What do you like to read (books, genres, authors)?

4. Is reading easy or hard? Why?

5. What do you do when you come to a word you don't know? (Does it match what you observe the child do when she reads?)

It is helpful to record anecdotal notes during the interview.

Book Graph

Some teachers use a book graph to record the books read by a student. It provides a visual representation of the increase in reading difficulty in text levels. Book graphs can be designed to show a student's reading growth through the course of one school year or across the primary years. Here's a sample of the "Developmental Reading Assessment" (DRA) book graph (Beavers, 1997) used with a student. A similar book graph could be designed using benchmark books to show students' reading growth.

To monitor students' reading progress over time, some teachers use the Developmental Reading Assessment Student Book Graph. To indicate the increase in level of text read successfully, teachers record fall and spring text reading levels through the students' primary years. The book graph becomes part of each student's assessment profile.

▼

DRA STUDENT BOOK GRAPH								
Name _____								
44 Danger in the Deep								
40 Old Ben Bailey Meets His Match								
38 Trouble at the Beaver Pond								
34 Be Nice to Josephine								
30 Touchdown!								
28 You Don't Look Beautiful to Me								
24 The Wonderful Day								
20 Green Freddie								
18 A Giant in the Forest								
16 The Pot of Gold								
14 The Wagon								
12 Robert's New Friend								
10 Shoe Boxes								
8 Duke								
6 Why Are We Stopping?								
4 Where Is My Hat?								
3 The "I Like" Game								
2 I Can See								
1 Things That Go								
A Can You Sing?								
	FALL	SPRING	FALL	SPRING	FALL	SPRING	FALL	SPRING
DRA STAGE:								
Grade level School year	Kindergarten		First Grade		Second Grade		Third Grade	

©Upper Arlington City Schools 1996, 1997

DRA STUDENT BOOK GRAPH								
Name _Cole_____								
44 Danger in the Deep								
40 Old Ben Bailey Meets His Match								
38 Trouble at the Beaver Pond								
34 Be Nice to Josephine								
30 Touchdown!								
28 You Don't Look Beautiful to Me								
24 The Wonderful Day								
20 Green Freddie								
18 A Giant in the Forest								
16 The Pot of Gold								
14 The Wagon								
12 Robert's New Friend								
10 Shoe Boxes								
8 Duke								
6 Why Are We Stopping?								
4 Where Is My Hat?								
3 The "I Like" Game								
2 I Can See								
1 Things That Go								
A Can You Sing?								
	FALL	SPRING	FALL	SPRING	FALL	SPRING	FALL	SPRING
DRA STAGE:	Emergent	Early	Early	Transitional				
Grade level School year	Kindergarten 1997-1998		First Grade 1998-1999		Second Grade		Third Grade	

©Upper Arlington City Schools 1996, 1997

Reading Log Record

A reading log record is a list of the books each student has read. They are a way for students to record their reading accomplishments. They also reflect the range of the books students read during the school year. Some teachers have students record whether the book was too easy, just right, or a "someday" (challenging) book. Some record sheets have places for students to record page numbers or make comments about what was read.

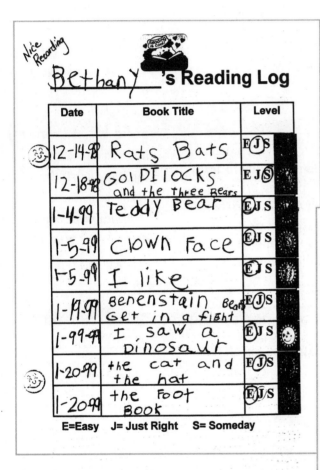

Nice Recording

Bethany's Reading Log

Date	Book Title	Level
12-14-98	Rats Bats	E (J) S
12-18-98	GoI DI 1ocks and the three Bears	E J (S)
1-4-99	Teddy Bear	(E) J S
1-5-99	Clown Face	(E) J S
1-5-99	I like	(E) J S
1-19-99	Benenstain Bears Get in a fight	E (J) S
1-99-99	I saw a Dinosaur	(E) J S
1-20-99	the cat and the hat	E (J) S
1-20-99	the Foot Book	(E) J S

E=Easy   J= Just Right   S= Someday

Students in Suzi Comer's first grade and Mary Lambert's second grade keep reading log records of the books read.

Martin   DEAR Record Sheet

Date	Title
2-6	Matha-Magic
2-17	Magic and Magicians
2-17	ARBor day magic
2-27	ABRACA Dozzle
2-28	I love cats
3-1	a House is a House for...
3-2	Literary imaginations
3-3	Mystery Monsters
3-6	Big road race
3-8	A Terribele fright
3-9	colors
3-10	How speed y is a cheetah
3-11	I love colors
3-12	is it red is it yellow is it blue
3-15	a snake mistake
3-16	the perfect ride
3-17	pig pig rides
3-18	Riddle book

Writing Sample/Writing Sample Assessment Record/Writer's Checklist

Writers create meaning using the same conventions of print that readers encounter when reading actual texts. Likewise, observing students' writing can provide insights into their reading as well as their writing. The writing sample provides information on what the student understands about phonics, language structure, story structure, text features, conventions of print, and the meaning of letters, words, and sentences.

During the first few weeks of school, you can ask students to create a writing sample by drawing a picture and writing about a topic of their choice. Encourage them to write about something or someone they know and care about. Students usually create the sample in one sitting without the help of the teacher. You can use assessment tools such as the "Writing Sample Assessment Record for Early Writing" (see page 260 in Appendix) in kindergarten through grade two and/or the "Writer's Checklist" in grades two and three. Highlight or check the learning behaviors as you observe and analyze the student sample. Some teachers build a picture of the student over time by recording on the checklist with a different colored marker or highlighter pen each time they review a new sample. Writing samples should be collected and reviewed periodically.

MY AND Mi BRITEr
AREPLEG-hooky

KARAN deep 2iNGh

▲ *An emergent reader's writing sample:* <u>Me and my brother are playing hockey</u>.

Writing Sample Assessment Record For Early Writing

Name: _Karan_   Date(s): _9/19_

To build a profile of the writer use a different colored highlighter pen to mark the learning behaviors observed each time a writing sample is reviewed. In the comments section make a note or two about future areas of focus.

Concepts/Conventions of Print

Knows where to begin writing
Knows writing moves left-to-right and top-to-bottom
Leaves spaces between words *Just beginning to show evidence of this*
Correct letter formation *Some difficulty with "M" (bottom to top)*
Concept of letter
Concept of word
Uppercase and lowercase letters used conventionally *Mixes uppercase + lowercase letters*
Approximate spelling *MY MI ME MY*
Conventional spelling of frequently used words *AND ; ARE*
Uses punctuation: periods; question marks; exclamation marks; quotations; commas; apostrophes
Other:_____

Understands That Writing Conveys a Message

Drawing/pictures
Scribble
Print-like symbols
Strings of letters
Writes own name: first name; last name
Letter/sound relationships: beginning; beginning/ending; beginning/medial/ending
Labels for pictures
Words
Phrases (groups of words)
Sentence
Several sentences
Beginning, middle, and end
Details or vocabulary specific to topic
Central idea organized and elaborated
Other: *Drew picture first; observed K. saying words slowly to try to hear sounds in words; reread writing to figure out what the next word should be*
Comments:

Designed by Mary Browning Schulman and Carleen DaCruz Payne

Guided Reading: Making It Work   Scholastic Professional Books

Quick-Reference Assessment Chart

Here is a list of assessment tools to consider when collecting systematic information on students' reading and writing. The type of assessment, description, suggested periodic use, grade-level use, and what to observe, analyze, and reflect on are included.

Assessment Tool	Suggestion for Use	Grade
Letter Identification Knowledge of the alphabet letter names, sounds, or word associations.	Baseline; Quarterly	⟨ K 1 ⟩ 2 3
Word Test List of high-frequency words occurring in reading materials or texts being used.	Baseline; Quarterly	K ⟨ 1 2 3 ⟩
Concepts About Print Check on student's knowledge of book handling and print concepts.	Baseline; mid-year; end-of-year	⟨ K 1 ⟩ 2 3
Writing Vocabulary List of words a student can write independently in 10 minutes (Clay, 1991).	Baseline; Quarterly	⟨ K 1 2 3 ⟩

Observe/Analyze/Reflect

- What does the child call the letters? (ABC's, alphabet, words, numbers, etc.)
- How does the child identify the letter—alphabet name, sound, or word?
- Which letter(s) does the child reverse or confuse?
- Which letters are known/unknown?

- How many and what types of words are in the child's reading vocabulary?
- Which words did the child know quickly? Which words were decoded?
- What types of decoding attempts does the child make on words (letters/sounds, letter clusters, word parts)?
- Are there any word confusions (in/on; was/saw)?

- What does the child know about book handling (front of book, print carries the message, left page before right)?
- Does the child have control over directional movement (where to start, which way to go, return sweep, first and last)?
- Is the child able to demonstrate word-by-word matching?
- What does the child know about letters and words (uppercase and lowercase letters; concept of a letter and word; first letter, last letter)?
- Can the child locate any known words in the text?
- Does the child know the meaning of punctuation (question mark, period, comma, quotation marks)?

- How many and what types of words can the child write correctly?
- What does the child know about letters and letter formation?
- How does the child use uppercase and lowercase letters?
- How does the child attend to space on the paper (left to right; top to bottom; between letters, words, and lines)?
- Are there confusions about letters, words, or letter sounds?
- What does the child know about how words work? Does she link words (day, play, away)? Use analogies/associations (up/down; in/to/into; yellow/sun)? Recognize affixes (jump, jumping, jumped, jumpy; unhappy, rewrite, preview)?

Assessment Tool	Suggestion for Use	Grade
Spelling Inventory List of words to determine how students spell and the corresponding developmental stages of spelling.	Baseline; mid–year; end of year	K 1 (2 3)
Benchmark Books Selected books used to take a running record and/or a retelling to determine the appropriate level of reading text for a student.	Baseline; Quarterly	(K 1 2 3)
Running Records Technique for recording reading behaviors and sources of information used by the student while reading.	Baseline; Ongoing	(K 1 2 3)
Oral Retelling Recalling information or events learned through reading to determine student's comprehension.	Baseline; Quarterly	(K 1 2 3)
Anecdotal Notes Brief, informal notes that record precise observations of reading and writing behaviors.	Ongoing	(K 1 2 3)

Observe/Analyze/Reflect

- What does the child know about writing, letters, words?
- Does the child know beginning letter/sound associations? Beginning of words? Middle of words? End of words?
- Does the child know that most words have a consistent spelling?
- What is the child's developmental stage?
- What does the child use but confuse?
- Does the child know that knowing something about one word can help spell another word?

- Is the child able to read the benchmark book?
- Is the child able to predict what will happen in the story/passage before reading?
- What strategies and sources of information does the running record indicate the child is using?
- Is the child phrased and fluent during the reading?
- Can the child retell the story?
- What level or stage benchmark book was the child able to read with 90% accuracy or better? What was the self-correction rate?

- Is the text familiar/unfamiliar?
- Does the child have control of early reading strategies (directionality, word-by-word matching, locates known word, locates unknown word)?
- What types of errors did the child make (did they make sense, sound right, look right)?
- Did the child detect errors and make attempts to problem-solve?
- How did the reading sound (word-by-word, repeated pausing, some short phrases, phrased and fluent)?
- What is the accuracy rate and self-correction rate? Is the text level easy, instructional, or hard?

- Is the child able to tell what happened in his/her own words?
- Did the child include characters, setting, important details or events?
- Are the events in or out of sequence?
- Did the child use vocabulary or phrases from the story or passage?
- Does the retelling reflect minimal understanding, adequate understanding, or a very strong detailed understanding?

- What reading behaviors are observable?
- What sources of information and strategies does the child use or neglect? (see page 25)
- Does the child detect and correct errors?
- Is the reading phrased and fluent?

Assessment Tool	Suggestion for Use	Grade
Oral Interview Questioning students to gain insights and information on their attitudes, strategies, and goals in reading and writing.	Baseline; Quarterly	K 1 2 3
Book Graph Record of books read by a student, representing the increase in text levels/difficulty.	Beginning of year; end of year	K 1 2 3
Reading Log Record List of books students read, frequently maintained by the students.	Ongoing	K 1 2 3
Writing Sample Picture and/or writing completed by a student independently about a topic of choice.	Baseline; Ongoing	K 1 2 3
Writing Sample Assessment Record/ Writing Checklist List of student writing behaviors observed and analyzed when student writing sample is reviewed.	Baseline; Ongoing	K 1 2 3

Observe/Analyze/Reflect

- What is the child's overall attitude about reading?
- What types of books does the child enjoy reading?
- What does the child say she does when she doesn't know a word? Does it match what you observe the child doing when she reads?

- What level(s) of text difficulty is the student able to read and understand?
- How has the student's reading performance changed over time?
- Is the student at the school's or district's established proficiency level?

- Does the list reflect continued growth as a reader?
- Is the child choosing books that are just right, too easy, or too challenging?
- Is the child reading a variety of genres (fiction, information, poetry)?
- What types of comments or responses does the child tend to record about what is read?

- What beginning concepts about written language does the child use?
- What does the child understand about written conventions of print such as punctuation, capitalization, and spelling?
- Does the child focus on a central idea and elaborate?
- Are ideas organized?
- Is there interesting vocabulary and descriptive details?
- Is there a particular style, tone, voice, audience awareness?

- Is the child able to choose own writing topics?
- What does the child know about the conventions of print?
- How does the child convey meaning (picture, string of letters, beginning and ending letter sounds, sentences)?
- What does the content of the writing show?
- What does revision show?
- Is the child able to talk about his own writing?

Gathering, Organizing, Storing, and Using Assessment Information

Establishing a manageable and useful data-gathering system with opportunities to review and reflect on each student's ongoing learning is critical for making good decisions about what to teach next. Teachers gather, organize, and store assessment information for quick reference in a variety of ways. Some teachers keep current student records in a three-ring binder and quarterly remove all but the last reading and writing assessment, placing these in a student file folder. This method keeps the binder system manageable and provides an opportunity for the teacher to check and think about each student when she files the quarterly assessments in the folder. Other teachers put each student's writing samples and assessment forms in a separate manila folder and alphabetize them in a box or a hanging file crate. Still other teachers record anecdotal notes by dividing a spiral notebook or steno pad into a section for each student.

It's important to begin the school year by gathering baseline information on all students. Often teachers focus on only one or two students a day during the first four to six weeks of school, and they use a variety of assessment tools. From the baseline assessment, teachers can draw some generalizations to determine students' levels of reading and writing and how to form their initial guided reading groups.

Let's view some of the different ways several teachers gather, organize, store, and use student assessment information to plan daily instruction.

Boxes for Each Guided Reading Group

Terry Creamer, a first-grade teacher, collects baseline language arts data at the beginning of the year on all the first graders in her classroom. The baseline information includes a letter identification test, ten-minute writing vocabulary, student writing sample, and running record on a text reading of a benchmark book. She forms guided reading groups based on her analysis of all the assessment information.

Terry says, "Because the students in my class range from emergent readers to fluent readers, it is not unusual to have six or seven guided reading groups when I begin the school year. Analyzing the running records of the leveled benchmark books used in our school, and looking at what students can do in writing, helps me decide how to group students. Once I've formed the guided reading groups, I file each student's baseline data by alphabetical order in a manila folder and store it in a cardboard box. I revisit the baseline assessment information at the first parent conference meeting, comparing where the child was at the beginning of the year with more current assessments, such as running records, anecdotal notes, and writing samples I collect on a regular basis.

"You have to be organized to do guided reading. You have to know who's in the group, their reading level, what the students in the group know, and what they need to learn next. I am always tinkering with my system—always trying to do it better. Teachers have to do what works for them as well as for the students. For example, when I began guided reading this year, I used a flip chart booklet to record anecdotal records during reading and writing. I discovered that because I jot notes quickly in the midst of the students' reading during a guided reading group, I had a hard time flipping back and forth from one student's page to another in that type of booklet. That's when I decided to change what I was doing.

"The system I use now helps with both planning and record keeping. I keep a box for each guided reading group. In the box, I have a group folder, a folder for each student in the group, and multiple copies of the book I selected for the students to read. Inside the group folder, I keep a guided

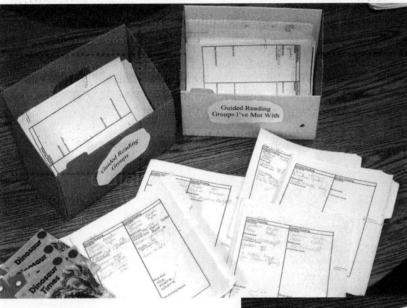

Terry Creamer uses folders and boxes to organize and store materials for guided reading.

reading form that is a combination of a planning sheet and an anecdotal record sheet. I have sections for the following: students in the group; title of the guided reading book; focus of book introduction; word work for that day; list of students to give a running record; and space for anecdotal notes. Each form has space to plan for two guided reading sessions in a row. I refer to the form before the students read, make notations on it while they read, and use it again afterwards to jot additional observations. The anecdotal notes I write, which often include the prompts I use with some students, and the running records I take on students, help me decide what my instruction will focus on next. I like the convenience of being able to look back over lessons as I plan for the next lesson.

"As children progress, the groups change, so I need an easy way to move student assessment information from one group to the next. Having individual folders for each student makes it easy to move a child's folder from one guided reading group's box to another. Keeping track of what students have read, are reading, and thinking ahead to what they will read next, is easy to do with this system."

◀ Terry Creamer's guided reading lesson plan record. (See page 264 in Appendix for reproducible.)

A Notebook and Box System

Molly Connolly has 25 students in her second-grade classroom. She too begins her year by gathering baseline information on her students. Molly explains, "It usually takes about three to four weeks to complete the baseline information I collect on all of my students. I try to meet with two or three students each day and aim for a minimum of eight to ten students each week. My initial reading and writing assessment for each student includes a running record, oral retelling, student writing sample, spelling inventory, and an oral interview. Some of these can be administered as a group while others require individual time with a student.

"I usually start by collecting a writing sample and a spelling inventory because I can gather that from the whole class at once. I review the writing samples and the spelling inventories, looking for students who demonstrate difficulty with written expression. I've found that looking at students' writing is a useful way to determine which students I want to assess first with a running record, retelling, and oral interview.

"However, I am aware that a student who has difficulty with written language can turn out to be a competent reader. That's why it's important to look at reading *and* writing to determine a student's strengths and areas of need. Once I have this baseline information, I decide how to group the students, the number of guided reading groups, and even some of the books I initially select.

"Right now I have five guided reading groups with two to six students in each. A notebook and box system makes it easy to keep track of what I am doing with each group. I use a different colored box and a one-and-one-half inch notebook for each guided reading group. In the front of each notebook, I keep a three-hole-punched clear plastic sleeve with a list of the students in the guided reading group. When students move to another group, I make a new list of the students in the group, and slip it in the plastic sleeve on top of the previous list. This way, I can see how the groups change over time.

"Next, I have a double-sided plastic pocket folder where I keep a copy of the daily guided reading lesson plan and any materials I will use. I have additional pocket folders alphabetized for each student in the group, so I can quickly file or find a student's running records and anecdotal notes. In the last pocket folder, I store all the previous guided reading lesson forms.

"I've been using this system for a while now, and it helps the students keep organized. When they've finished reading, they place the book in their guided reading box, so they'll be ready for the next time we meet."

> " It's important to look at reading and writing to determine a student's strengths and areas of need. "
>
> —Molly Connolly, second-grade teacher

Molly Connolly keeps a guided reading notebook with plastic pocket folders for each group.

A Notebook as the Centerpiece

Carrie Campbell, another second-grade teacher, shares how she gathers, organizes, and stores student assessment information. Carrie says, "I use a large three-inch binder, a clipboard, and file folders to organize and store students' assessment information. The notebook is a place to organize and keep a good portion of the language arts assessment data I collect. Information in the notebook consists of a baseline writing sample, ongoing running records, retellings, quarterly update of a chart with literacy stages our district developed, weekly spelling words along with the pre-tests and post-tests, quarterly spelling inventories, and anecdotal notes from guided reading, independent reading, and writing conferences. Each quarter, I review and remove assessment data into a separate hanging file folder labeled with each student's name.

"I really put a lot of thought into how I set up the notebook. I've tried a number of different ways to organize the assessments, but I find the notebook helps keep everything orderly and in one place. I refer to it when planning for instruction, conferring with parents and resource teachers, and as a reference when I am completing parent reports at the end of each quarter.

"The notebook has pockets in the front and back. In the front pocket, I keep various blank copies of planning and assessment forms such as running records, status of the class grid sheets, and writing checklists. In the back pocket, I keep an extra copy of a reading strategies prompt sheet, a running record conversion table, and various notes and handouts from language arts/reading presentations that I have found helpful.

"I tab the sections with numbers. I start with number one and assign each student in alphabetical order an ascending number. Lilliam D. was number five throughout the year, so whenever I collected any of her assessment data, I would date it and place it in the section following the divider with tab '5'.

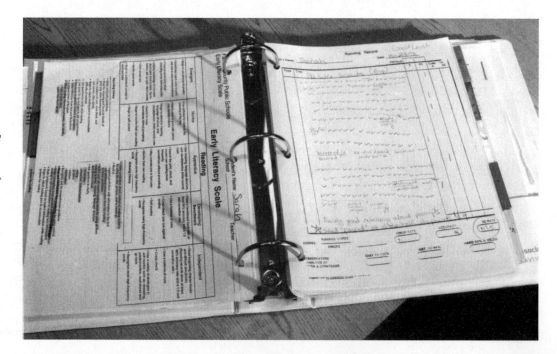

Carrie Campbell uses a large notebook to organize and store guided reading information. ▶

Week of Oct. 25

✓ The Carrot Seed
10/25   Samantha → needs higher level
        Lindsey

✓ Mr. Potter and Tabby
10/26   Walk the Dog
- read   Sandra → still pointing
by   Nelson   to words
yourself
then   Joshua
buddy   Kelly
read   Tila

✓ Frog and Toad are Friends
10/25   Alex — sounding out is
        Sylvana   only strategy observed
        David
        Cody

✓ Arthur's Pet Business
10/25   Sarah
- write   Josh B.
about   Erin
your own Molly
business
idea

✓ The Stories Julian Tells
10/26   Matt
- finish Matthew
book +   NiduK - good
discuss   predictions
favorite
story

✓ Ramona Quimby, Age 8
10/26   Danielle
- read
first
chapter

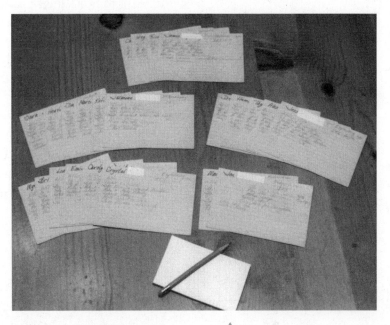

Guided reading groups and book titles Carrie Campbell recorded on one weekly planning sheet.

Susan Altemus, third-grade teacher, keeps track of the books each student reads in guided reading on a 4" x 6" index card. She records the reading stage and the title of the book. Cards are sorted and stacked according to guided reading groups. As students change groups, the index card is moved with the student.

At the very front of the notebook, I store a weekly guided reading group planning sheet. The planning sheet lists the students in the group for that week, the titles of books used with each group, book introduction notes, and the focus for each lesson.

"I put computer labels on a clipboard. I can quickly record the student number at the top of the computer label and begin taking anecdotal notes when I'm sitting in a guided reading group, having a writing conference, or walking around the room during independent reading time. I transfer the label to a blank sheet of paper I keep in each student's section of the binder. This system works for me now, but I am always on the lookout for ways to improve on it."

Questions

Ask myself each day:

1. Did students spend a large amount of time reading?

2. Did students spend a large amount of time writing to an audience?

3. Did I analyze the strategies and errors of some of my students as they read and wrote?

4. Did my students gain confidence/expertise/ experience success in language arts class?

5. Did I create enthusiasm by making lessons interesting—exciting—fun?

In thinking about her students, Susan Altemus asks herself these questions. She keeps them on the front of the file folder she uses for her guided reading planning sheets.

Many of the teachers with whom we work are continually looking for better ways to hone their present systems. Think about your students and what you need to know about their reading and writing. Find time to ask colleagues how they organize their records. Experiment by using the assessment tools you think will help you learn more about what your students know and need to learn next. Good reading and writing assessments are critical to making informed decisions about instruction. When teachers know what students *can do* as readers and writers, the planning and decision-making about how to group and what to teach during guided reading is based on sound instructional information.

See the Appendix for suggested book titles and levels, helpful reproducible forms, publisher information, and professional resources.

Closing Remarks

This book tells the stories of how we work with teachers to provide guided reading instruction for children. We believe throughout the primary grades children should have many opportunities for reading and writing in authentic and meaningful ways. In our schools, we work alongside teachers who strive every day to create a balanced literacy program for the children in their classrooms.

Guided reading, reading with children, is a piece of a balanced literacy program. It provides the supportive framework for the systematic yet flexible instruction needed to develop independent readers. Instruction is guided by careful, ongoing assessment and observation of children. The focus is on the child and what she can do. Instruction is provided in small, homogeneous groups with attention to individual children's needs. To support the reader, books are carefully selected. Each time a child attends a guided reading session, the goal is to help her learn something new about the reading process that she will be able to try the next time she reads.

Making guided reading a part of your daily literacy program will help all children learn to read and become better, independent readers. We hope you will find some of the guided reading ideas within these pages helpful to your teaching.

Appendix

We've collected a variety of materials in the Appendix to help you get started with Guided Reading. You will find a bibliography of professional books, a compilation of educational resource providers, and lists of leveled books appropriate for guided reading lessons, one arranged alphabetically and one by reading level. In addition, we've provided lots of reproducible forms to help you organize and manage your guided reading program, including prompts, record sheets, checklists, learning center icons, and more.

*Above:
Edith Romaine
takes a running
record on a first-
grade student.*

Bibliography

Anderson, Richard C., Elfrieda H. Hiebert, Judith A. Scott, and Wilkinson. *Becoming a Nation of Readers: The Report of the Commission on Reading.* Washington, DC: U.S. Dept. of Education, 1985.

Baltas, Joyce and Susan Shafer, eds. *Scholastic Guide to Balanced Reading K–2.* New York: Scholastic, 1996.

————. *Scholastic Guide to Balanced Reading 3–6.* New York: Scholastic, 1996.

Barron, Marlene. *I Learn to Read and Write the Way I Learn to Talk.* Katonah, NY: Richard C. Owen, 1989.

Bear, Donald. R., Marcia Invernizzi, Shane Templeton, and Francine Johnston. *Words Their Way: Word Study for Phonics, Vocabulary, and Spelling Instruction.* Englewood Cliffs, NJ: Prentice-Hall, 1996.

Braun, Win and Jan Turbill. *Readers Theatre: Scripted Rhymes and Rhythms, Grade 1–6.* Peguis Publishers, 1987.

Butler, Andrea and Jan Turbill. *Towards a Reading-Writing Classroom.* Portsmouth, NH: Heinemann, 1987.

Cambourne, Brian. *The Whole Story: Natural Learning and the Acquisition of Literacy.* Scholastic: New York, 1988.

Clay, Marie. *Becoming Literate.* Portsmouth, NH: Heinemann, 1991.

————. *Running Records for Classroom Teachers.* Portsmouth, NH: Heinemann, 2000.

————. *Concepts About Print: What Have Children Learned About the Way We Print Language?* Portsmouth, NH: Heinemann, 2000.

————. *By Different Paths To Common Outcomes.* York, ME: Stenhouse, 1998.

————. "Introducing a New Storybook to Young Readers." *The Reading Teacher 45* (1991): 264-273.

————. *An Observation Survey.* Portsmouth, NH: Heinemann, 1993.

Cunningham, Patricia. *Phonics They Use: Words for Reading and Writing.* New York: HarperCollins, 1995.

DeFord, Diane E., Carol A. Lyons, and Gay Su Pinnell, eds. *Bridges to Literacy: Learning From Reading Recovery.* Portsmouth, NH: Heinemann, 1991.

DeFord, Diane E., Carol A. Lyons, and Gay Su Pinnell. *Partners in Learning: Teachers and Children in Reading Recovery.* New York: Teachers College Press, 1993.

Fielding, Linda and Cathy Roller. "Making Difficult Books Accessible and Easy Books Acceptable." *The Reading Teacher 45* (1992): 678–685.

Fountas, Irene C. and Gay Su Pinnell. *Guided Reading: Good First Teaching For All Children.* Portsmouth, NH: Heinemann, 1996.

————. *Matching Books to Readers.* Portsmouth, NH: Heinemann, 1999.

Fountas, Irene C. and Gay Su Pinnell, eds. *Voices on Word Matters.* Portsmouth, NH: Heinemann, 1999.

Gentry, J. Richard. *My Kid Can't Spell.* Portsmouth, NH: Heinemann, 1997.

Goodman, Kenneth, Yetta Goodman, and Wendy J. Hood. *The Whole Language Evaluation Book.* Portsmouth, NH: Heinemann, 1989.

Hall, Nigel and Anne Robinson. *Looking at Literacy*. London, England: David Fulton, 1995.

Henry, Jim. *Fresh Takes on Using Journals to Teach Beginning Writers*. New York: Scholastic, 1998.

Holdaway, Don. *The Foundations of Literacy*. Sydney, Australia: Ashton Scholastic, 1979.

Kobrin, Beverly. *Eyeopeners II*. New York: Scholastic, 1995.

Laminack, Lester L. and Katie Wood. *Spelling in Use*. Urbana, IL: National Council of Teachers of English, 1996.

Learning Media, Ministry of Education. *Reading in the Junior Classes*. Wellington, New Zealand: Ministry of Education. Katonah, NY: Richard C. Owen, 1991.

————. *Reading For Life: The Learner as a Reader*. Wellington, New Zealand: Ministry of Education. Katonah, NY: Richard C. Owen, 1997.

Leslie, Lauren and JoAnne Caldwell. *Qualitative Reading Inventory II*. New York: HarperCollins, 1995.

Lynch, Judy. *Easy Lessons for Teaching Word Families*. New York, Scholastic, 1998.

McGill-Franzen, Anne. "'I Could Read the Words!': Selecting Good Books For Inexperienced Readers." *The Reading Teacher* 46 (1993): 424–426.

Mooney, Margaret. *Reading To, With, and By Children*. Katonah, NY: Richard C. Owen, 1990.

————. *Developing Life-Long Readers*. Katonah, NY: Richard C. Owen, 1988.

Payne, Carleen D. and Mary B. Schulman. *Getting the Most Out of Morning Message and Other Shared Writing Lessons*. New York: Scholastic, 1998.

Peterson, Barbara. "Selecting Books For Beginning Readers" in DeFord, D. E., Lyons, C.A., & Pinnell, G.S. (eds.). *Bridges to Literacy: Learning From Reading Recovery* (119–147). Portsmouth, NH: Heinemann, 1991.

Pinnell, Gay Su and Irene C. Fountas. *Word Matters: Teaching Phonics and Spelling in the Reading/Writing Classroom*. Portsmouth, NH: Heinemann, 1998.

Powell, Debbie and David Hornsby. *Learning Phonics and Spelling in a Whole Language Classroom*. New York: Scholastic, 1993.

Snowball, Diane and Faye Bolton. *Spelling K–8*. York, ME: Stenhouse, 1999.

Stahl, Steven A., Jean Osborn, and Fran Lehr. *Beginning to Read: Thinking and Learning About Print, A Summary*. Champaign, IL: University of Illinois, 1990.

Strickland, Dorothy. *Teaching Phonics Today: A Primer For Educators*. Newark, DE: International Reading Association, 1998.

Traill, Leanna. *Highlight My Strengths*. Crystal Lake, IL: Rigby, 1995.

Vygotsky, Lev. *Thought and Language*. Cambridge, MA: M. I. T. Press, 1962.

————. *Mind in Society: The Development of Higher Psychological Processes*. Cambridge, MA: Harvard University Press, 1978.

Wagstaff, Janiel M. *Teaching Reading and Writing with Word Walls*. New York: Scholastic, 1999.

————. *Phonics That Work!: New Strategies for the Reading/Writing Classroom*. New York: Scholastic, 1994.

Wright Group. *Story Box, Level 1—Teacher's Guide*. Bothell, WA: Wright Group, 1990.

Zemelman, Steven, Harvey Daniels, and Arthur Hyde. *Best Practice: New Standards for Teaching and Learning in America's Schools*. Portsmouth, NH: Heinemann, 1993.

Publisher Information

Annie's Home Tools for Teaching
2784 Shady Ridge Drive
Columbus, OH 43231
614-882-1879

Resources such as magnetic boards and easels;
whiteboard; magnetic letters and punctuation

Celebration Press
4350 Equity Drive
P.O. Box 2649
Columbus, OH 43216-2649
800-552-2259

Collection of fiction and nonfiction chapter books
for guided reading and independent reading grades
3–5; Development Reading Assessment package

Childwood
8873 Woodbank Drive
Bainbridge Island, WA 98110
800-362-9825

Magnetic manipulatives for storytelling and
reproducible mini books; includes activities for
integrating literature, language, science, and math

Creative Teaching Press
Abrams & Company Publishers, Inc.
61 Mattatuck Heights
Waterbury, CT 06705
800-227-9120

Range of books to support shared, guided, and
independent reading; easy content area books

Dominie Press, Inc.
1949 Kellogg Avenue
Carlsbad, CA 92008
800-232-4570
www.dominie.com

Range of leveled books to support shared, guided,
and independent reading; old familiar tale;
beginning easy chapter books

Edukits, Inc.
1089 Memorex Drive
Santa Clara, CA 95050
800-433-8548

Resources such as magnetic letters; magnetic
chalkboards; whiteboards

Fairfax County Public Schools
FCPS Department of General Services
Office of Supply Operations
6800B Industrial Road
Springfield, VA 22151
703-658-3640

Range of books to support emergent guided
reading

Felt Education Products
Storytellers, Inc.
19900 Stough Farm Road
Cornelius, NC 28031
888-470-FELT

Washable storyboards; hand puppets; felt fairy
tales; nursery rhymes; alphabets

Friends of Early Literacy
University of Maine Center For Early Literacy
College of Education & Human Development
5766 Shibles Hall
Orono, ME 04469-5766
207-581-2438

Range of books to support emergent guided
reading

Great Source Education Group
181 Ballardvale Street
Wilmington, MA 01887
800-289-4490

Language reference books for first, second, and
third grades and upper grade levels

HarperCollins Publishers Order Department
1000 Keystone Industrial Park
Scranton, PA 18512-4621
800-242-7737
www.harperchildrens.com/schoolhouse

Range of books for guided and independent reading; I Can Read series; Let's-Read-and-Find-Out Science

Houghton Mifflin
222 Berkeley Street
Boston, MA 02116-3764
800-733-2828
www.schooldirect.com

Wide range of tradebooks for shared, guided, and independent reading; alphabet books; manipulative letter cards with plastic trays

Kaeden Books
P.O. Box 16190
Rocky River, OH 44116
800-890-READ

Leveled books for guided and independent reading; math and science texts

McCracken Educational Services, Inc.
P.O. Box 3588
Blaine, WA 98231
800-447-1462

Books for shared, guided, and independent reading; poetry posters; manipulative materials

Markerboard People
2300 Spikes Lane
Lansing, MI 48906
800-828-3375

Whiteboards, chalkboards, markers, erasers

Modern Curriculum
4350 Equity Drive
P.O. Box 2649
Columbus, OH 43216
800-321-3106
www.pearsonlearning.com

Range of leveled books for shared, guided and independent reading; early chapter books; interactive phonics and word study CD-ROMs

Mondo Publishing
One Plaza Road
Greenvale, NY 11548
800-242-3650

Range of books for shared, guided, and independent reading; includes fiction and nonfiction titles.

Newbridge Educational Publishing
P.O. Box 6002
Delran, NJ 08370-6002
800-867-0307
www. newbridgeonline.com

Range of books for shared, guided, and independent reading; includes many content area subject titles

Ohio State University Keep Books™
1929 Kenny Road, Suite 100
Columbus, OH 43210
614-292-2909

Inexpensive little storybooks developed for young readers to read and keep at home

Outside the Box, Inc.
P.O. Box 16751
Seattle, WA 98116
800-808-4199

Beginning books for shared, guided, and independent reading

Oxford University Press Education
Box 1550
Woodstock, IL 60098
888-551-5454

Range of leveled books for shared, guided, and independent reading

Pacific Learning
P.O. Box 2723
Huntington Beach, CA 92647-0723
800-279-0737

Range of books to support shared, guided and independent reading

Peguis Publishers
100–318 McDermot Avenue
Winnipeg, Manitoba Canada R3A0A2
800-667-9673

Non-fiction, primary books for shared, guided, and independent reading; content-related topics; teacher professional books

Pioneer Valley Educational Press Inc.
P.O. Box 9375
North Amherst, MA 01059
413-367-9817
www.pvep.com

Range of books to support emergent guided reading

Primary Concepts
Box 100043
Berkeley, CA 94709
800-660-8646

Alphabet and word-building tiles; books and storytelling objects for literature and math

Rand McNally
P.O. Box 1906
Skokie, IL 60076-8906
800-678-7263

Nonfiction primary books for shared, guided, and independent reading; content-related topics

Resources for Reading
P.O. Box 9
La Honda, CA 94020-0009
800-278-7323
www.abcstuff.com

Magnetic letters; magnetic chalk and white boards

Richard C. Owen Publisher, Inc.
P.O. Box 585
Katonah, NY 10536
914-232-3903
www.rcowen.com

Range of books for shared, guided, and independent reading

Rigby
P.O. Box 797
Crystal Lake, IL 60039-0797
800-822-8661
www.rigby.com

Range of books for shared, guided, and independent reading; content area subject titles; letter books; phonics and phonemic awareness materials

Sadlier-Oxford
A Division of William H. Sadlier, Inc.
9 Pine Street
New York, NY 10005-1002
800-221-5175
www.sadlier-oxford.com

Range of books for shared, guided, and independent reading; includes fiction and nonfiction titles

Scholastic, Inc.
2931 East McCarty Street
Jefferson City, MO 65101
800-724-6527
www.scholastic.com

Range of books for shared, guided, and independent reading; old and new favorite tales; Hello Readers; easy chapter books; wide range of content and subject titles

Scott Foresman
1900 East Lake Avenue
Glenview, IL 60025
800-792-0550

*Range of books for shared, guided, and
independent reading*

Seedling Publications, Inc.
4079 Overlook Drive East
Columbus, OH 43214-2931
614-451-2412
www.seedlingpub.com

*Leveled beginning books for guided and
independent reading*

Shortland Publications, Inc.
50 South Steele Street, Suite 755
Denver, CO 80209-9927
800-775-9995
www.shortland.com

*Range of books for guided and independent
reading; includes narrative, procedural, plays,
nonfiction, and traditional stories or innovations
on a tale*

Steck-Vaughn Company
P.O. Box 690789
Orlando, FL 32819-0789
800-531-5015
www.steck-vaughn.com

*Range of books for shared, guided, and
independent reading; some titles leveled; wide
range of topic titles; family literacy program*

Sundance
P.O. Box 1326
Littleton, MA 01460
800-343-8204
www.sundancepub.com

*Wide range of leveled books for guided and
independent reading; content-related topics*

Teacher's Bag
P.O. Box 241
Edmond, OK 73083
888-824-7224

*Pointers for reading the room; manipulatives;
laminated letters; story stampers for teacher-made
books*

Troll Communications
100 Corporate Drive
Mahwah, NJ 07430
800-929-8765
www.troll.com

*Range of books for shared, guided, and
independent reading; wide range of content and
subject titles*

Wikki Stix Company
2432 West Peoria Avenue, Suite 1188
Phoenix, AZ 85029
800-869-4554

*Nontoxic, waxed yarn for highlighting text and
forming letters*

Wright Group
19201-120th Avenue, N. E.
Bothell, WA 98011
800-648-2970
www.wrightgroup.com

*Range of book titles for shared, guided, and
independent reading; old and new favorite tales;
content area and real-world topic titles; letter
books; phonics and phonemic awareness materials*

Leveled Books for Guided Reading

We've include a listing of book titles that we use to support guided reading instruction in the classroom. We leveled them according to our four broad stages of reading development—emergent, progressing, transitional, and fluent—to help you select appropriate texts for your readers. We also provide Reading Recovery® levels and levels from *Guided Reading: Good First Teaching for All Children* (Fountas and Pinnell, 1996); however, not all titles listed in the appendix will carry these two levels.

Please note that Reading Recovery® is a registered servicemark of the Ohio State University. Reading Recovery® book levels are from a book list created by the Reading Recovery Council of North America; this list includes books from numerous publishers since a premise of the program is that children be provided with a wide range of texts. One publisher's book list alone is not sufficient to implement a Reading Recovery® program. Levels are subject to change as they are periodically tested and reevaluated.

The chart on the next page lists comparable book levels and equivalents for *Guided Reading: Making It Work*; Reading Recovery®; *Guided Reading: Good First Teaching*; Basal Reading Series; and *DRA Testing*.

Book Level and Equivalence Grid

Guided Reading: Making It Work Level	Reading Recovery®	Guided Reading: Good First Teaching		Basal Reading Series Level	DRA Testing Level
		Level	Grade		
Emergent	1	K,1	1	Readiness	A, 1, 2
	2	K,1	1		
	3	K,1	1	PP1	3
	4				
	5	D	1	PP2	4
	6				
Progressing	7	E	1	PP3	6–8
	8				
	9	F	1	Primer	10
	10				
	11	G	1		12
	12				
Transitional	13	H	1	Grade 1	14
	14				
	15	I	1, 2		16
	16				
	17				
	18	J	2	Grade 2	18–20
	19				
Fluent	20	K	2		
		L	2		24–28
		M	2, 3		
		N	3	Grade 3	30
		O	3		34–38
Advanced Fluent		P	3, 4		
		Q	4	Grade 4	40
		R	4		
		S	4	Grade 5	44

Title	Level	RR–GR Level	Words	Publisher	Series/Author
1 is One	Progressing	7–8*/E	82	Mondo	Bookshop
Abiyoyo	Fluent		250+	Scholastic	Seeger, Pete
Abracadabra	Transitional	18/L	372	Celebration Press	Reading Unlimited
Adventures of Ali Baba Bernstein	Fluent	O	250+	Scholastic	Hurwitz, Joanna
Afternoon on the Amazon	Fluent	L	250+	Random House	Pope Osborne, Mary
Aladdin and the Magic Lamp	Fluent	22*/J	250+	Dominie Press	Traditional Tales
Aldo Ice Cream	Fluent	O	250+	Penguin	Hurwitz, Joanna
Alexander and the Wind-up Mouse	Fluent	L	250+	Scholastic	Guided Reading Program
Alfie's Gift	Fluent	L	250+	Rigby	Literacy 2000
Alison Wendlebury	Fluent	J	250+	Rigby	Literacy Tree
Alison's Puppy	Fluent	K	250+	Hyperion	Bauer, Marion
All About	Transitional	17/J	259	Modern Curriculum	Ready Readers
All About You	Transitional	G	250+	Scholastic	Anholt, Catherine L.
All By Myself	Progressing	8/E	157	Golden	Mayer, Mercer
All Fall Down	Emergent	3/C	72	Oxford Univ. Press	Cat on the Mat Series
All Through the Week With Cat and Dog	Emergent	3/C	91	Creative Teaching	Learn to Read
Along Came Greedy Cat	Progressing	11/G	166	Pacific Learning	Ready to Read
Along Comes Jake	Emergent	6/D	86	Wright Group	Sunshine
Amalia and the Grasshopper	Transitional	I	250+	Scholastic	Guided Reading Program
Amanda's Bear	Progressing	12/G	154	Dominie Press	Reading Corners
Amazing Rescues	Fluent		250+	Random House	Shea, George
Amber Brown Goes Fourth	Fluent	N	250+	Scholastic	Danziger, Paula
Amber Brown Is Not a Crayon	Fluent	N	250+	Scholastic	Danziger, Paula
Amber Brown Sees Red	Fluent	N	250+	Scholastic	Danziger, Paula
Amber Brown Wants Extra Credit	Fluent	N	250+	Scholastic	Danziger, Paula
Amelia Bedelia	Fluent	L	250+	Harper & Row	Parish, Peggy
Amelia Bedelia Helps Out	Fluent	L	250+	Avon Camelot	Parish, Peggy
Amelia Bedelia and the Surprise Shower	Fluent	L	250+	HarperTrophy	Parish, Peggy
Amelia Bedelia Goes Camping	Fluent	L	250+	Avon Camelot	Parish, Peggy
And Billy Went Out to Play	Progressing	10–11/I	227	Mondo	Bookshop
Andi's Wool	Transitional	14/H	107	Richard C. Owen	Books For Young Learners
Animal Babies	Progressing	8/E	114	Children's Press	Rookie Reader
Animal Builders	Transitional	17/F	217	Sundance	AlphaKids
Animal Champions	Fluent		250+	Modern Curriculum	First Chapters
Animal Diggers	Transitional	16/F	262	Sundance	AlphaKids
Animal Feet	Transitional		164	Scholastic	Reading Discovery
Animal Habitats	Emergent	3/C	73	Sundance	Little Red Readers
Animal Homes	Emergent	2/B	48	Sundance	Little Red Readers
Animal Skeletons	Progressing	8/C	115	Sundance	AlphaKids
Animal Tracks	Fluent	L		Scholastic	Dorros, Arthur
Animals at the Zoo	Emergent		35	Fairfax County	Books for Budding Readers
Animals at the Zoo	Progressing	10/F	158	Troll	First Start
Animals of the Ice and Snow	Fluent	R	250+	Rigby	Literacy 2000
Ant and the Dove, The	Transitional	14–16/I	173	Steck-Vaughn	New Way
Ant and the Grasshopper, The	Transitional	15*/I	231	Dominie Press	Aesop's Fables

*Tentatively leveled

Title	Level	RR–GR Level	Words	Publisher	Series/Author
Ants	Emergent	B	16	Newbridge	Discovery Links
Ants and the Grasshopper	Progressing	12–13/G	144	Steck-Vaughn	New Way
Ants Go Marching, The	Progressing			Wright Group	Song Box
Apples and Pumpkins	Transitional	I	185	Scholastic	Guided Reading Program
Armies of Ants	Fluent	O	250+	Scholastic	Retan, Walter
Art	Progressing	12/E	238	Sundance	AlphaKids
Art Lesson, The	Transitional	20/M	246	Putnam	dePaola, Tommi
Arthur Writes a Story	Fluent		250+	Little, Brown	Brown, Marc
Arthur's First Sleepover	Fluent		250+	Little, Brown	Brown, Marc
Arthur's Reading Race	Transitional		250+	Random House	Brown, Marc
Artist, The	Progressing	9/F	83	Richard C. Owen	Books For Young Learners
As Fast as a Fox	Emergent	5/D	69	Modern Curriculum	Ready Readers
Ask Nicely	Progressing	10/F	110	Rigby	Literacy 2000
At My School	Emergent	B	43	University of Maine	Little Books for Early Readers
At the Beach	Progressing	8/E	84	Oxford Univ. Press	Oxford Reading Tree
At the Fair	Emergent	4/D	116	Sundance	Little Red Readers
At the Farm	Emergent	2/C	52	Sundance	Little Red Readers
At the Horse Show	Emergent	6/D	24	Richard C. Owen	Books For Young Learners
At the Park	Emergent	4/D	91	Sundance	Little Red Readers
At the Playground	Emergent	4/C	86	Sundance	Little Red Readers
At the Playground	Emergent	B	51	University of Maine	Little Books for Early Readers
At the Pool	Progressing	8/E	87	Oxford Univ. Press	Oxford Reading Tree
At the Wildlife Park	Emergent	2/B	34	Sundance	Little Red Readers
At the Zoo	Emergent	2/B	40	Rigby	PM Starters
At the Zoo	Emergent	3/ C	73	Sundance	Little Red Readers
Away Went the Hat	Transitional	15,15,18/I	260	Steck-Vaughn	New Way
Awful Waffles	Progressing	16–17/G	296	Seedling	Williams, Deborah Holt
Baby	Emergent	A	28	University of Maine	Little Books for Early Readers
Baby Chimp	Emergent	1/A	14	Wright Group	Twig
Baby Hippo	Emergent	6/D	117	Rigby	PM Extensions
Baby Owls, The	Emergent	4/C	90	Rigby	PM Extensions
Baby Sister For Frances, A	Fluent	K	250+	Scholastic	Hoban, Russell
Bad Luck of King Fred	Fluent	N	250+	Rigby	Literacy Tree
Bags, Cans, Pots, and Pans	Emergent	4/C	56	Modern Curriculum	Ready Readers
Bakery, The	Transitional	13/E	196	Sundance	AlphaKids
Ball Game, The	Emergent	D	46	Scholastic	Guided Reading Program
Balloons	Emergent	2*/B	55	Pioneer Valley	Early Emergent/Set 2
Barry the Bravest Saint Bernard	Fluent		250+	Random House	Hall, Lynn
Bath Day For Brutus	Transitional	18/K	348	Sundance	Little Red Readers
Bath For a Beagle	Emergent	5/D	102	Troll	First Start
Bath For Patches, A	Progressing	8/E	89	Dominie Press	Carousel Readers
Bath, The	Emergent	1/A	14	Modern Curriculum	Ready Readers
Bathwater Gang	Fluent		250+	Little, Brown	Spinnelli, Jerry
Bats	Fluent	M	250+	Rigby	Literacy 2000
Bats	Transitional			Scholastic	Reading Discovery

* Tentatively leveled

Title	Level	RR–GR Level	Words	Publisher	Series/Author
Beaks and Feet	Progressing	11/D	244	Sundance	AlphaKids
Bear Lived in A Cave, A	Emergent	4/D	102	Sundance	Little Red Readers
Bear Shadow	Transitional	18/J	489	Simon & Schuster	Asch, Frank
Bear's Bargain	Transitional	J	250+	Scholastic	Asch, Frank
Bear, The	Emergent	2/B	17	Dominie Press	Carousel Earlybirds
Bears in the Night	Emergent	5/D	108	Random House	Berenstain, Stan & Jan
Bears on Hemlock Mountain, The	Fluent	M	250+	Aladdin	Dalgliesh, Alice
Beauregard the Cat	Fluent	20–22*/M	876	Mondo	Bookshop
Beautiful Bugs	Progressing	F	69	Scholastic	Guided Reading Program
Bedtime For Frances	Fluent	K	250+	Scholastic	Guided Reading Program
Bedtime Story, A	Progressing	12*/K	335	Mondo	Bookshop
Beekeeper, The	Fluent	M	250+	Rigby	Literacy 2000
Ben's Pets	Emergent	3/C	30	Modern Curriculum	Ready Readers
Ben's Teddy Bear	Emergent	5/D	68	Rigby	PM Story Books
Ben's Treasure Hunt	Emergent	5/D	72	Rigby	PM Story Books
Best Birthday Mole Ever Had	Progressing	8/E	252	Modern Curriculum	Ready Readers
Best Clown in Town	Fluent		250+	Dominie Press	Chapter Books
Best Places, The	Emergent	6/D	68	Modern Curriculum	Ready Readers
Best Way to Play, The	Fluent	K	250+	Scholastic	Cosby, Bill
Betsy the Babysitter	Progressing	10/F	115	Troll	First Start
Big Al	Fluent	L	250+	Scholastic	Guided Reading Program
Big and Little	Emergent	2/B	40	Dominie Press	Carousel Earlybirds
Big Bed, The	Transitional	16/I	346	Pacific Learning	Ready to Read
Big Block of Chocolate	Transitional			Scholastic	Redhead, Janice S.
Big Box, The	Progressing	11/G	183	Steck-Vaughn	New Way
Big Dog, The	Transitional	14/E	324	Sundance	AlphaKids
Big Red Fire Engine	Progressing	12/G	158	Troll	First Start
Big Things	Emergent	2/A	33	Rigby	PM Starters
Biggest Bear, The	Fluent		250+	Houghton Mifflin	Ward, Lynd
Biggest Cake in the World, The	Progressing	9/F	120	Pacific Learning	Ready to Read
Biggest Fish, The	Transitional	I	254	Rigby	PM Story Books
Bike Ride, The	Emergent	5*/D	100	Pioneer Valley	Emergent/Set 1
Bike, The	Emergent	1/A	14	Wright Group	Twig
Billy Goats Gruff	Transitional	18*	250+	Dominie Press	Traditional Tales
Billy Goats Gruff	Progressing	10/F	381	Ladybird	Read It Yourself
Bird's Eye View	Transitional	K	393	Rigby	PM Story Books
Birds	Transitional		156	Scholastic	Reading Discovery
Birthday Bird, The	Progressing	11/F	82	Richard C. Owen	Books for Young Learners
Birthday Cake, The	Emergent	1/A	22	Wright Group	Sunshine
Birthday Cakes	Emergent	4/B	95	Sundance	AlphaKids
Birthday Candles	Emergent	3/C	52	Dominie Press	Carousel Readers
Birthday In the Woods, A	Progressing	13–14/F	199	Seedling	Salem, Lynn
Birthday Party, A	Emergent	2/3*/C	47	Pioneer Valley	Early Emergent/Set 1
Birthday, The	Emergent	A	23	University of Maine	Little Books for Early Readers
Blackbird's Nest	Progressing	12/G	71	Pacific Learning	Ready to Read

Tentatively leveled

Title	Level	RR–GR Level	Words	Publisher	Series/Author
Blind Man and the Elephant, The	Fluent	K	250+	Scholastic	Backstein, Karen
Blocks	Emergent	3*/C	60	Pioneer Valley	Early Emergent/Set 1
Blueberries For Sal	Fluent	M	250+	Scholastic	McCloskey, Robert
Blueberries From Maine	Emergent	A	28	University of Maine	Little Books for Early Readers
BMX Billy	Progressing	11/G	93	Rigby	Literacy 2000
Bo and Peter	Emergent	C		Scholastic	Franco, Betsy
Bobbie's Airplane	Progressing	7/E	64	Oxford Univ. Press	Oxford Reading Tree
Book Week	Progressing	8/E	71	Oxford Univ. Press	Oxford Reading Tree
Boots	Emergent	C	57	Scholastic	Schreiber, A. & Doughty, A.
Boots For Toots	Emergent	4/C	41	Pacific Learning	Ready to Read
Box Car Children Mystery Bookstore	Fluent	O	250+	Albert Whitman	Warner, Gertrude Chandler
Box Car Children Mystery of the Missing Cat	Fluent	O	250+	Albert Whitman	Warner, Gertrude Chandler
Box Car Children Schoolhouse Mystery	Fluent	O	250+	Albert Whitman	Warner, Gertrude Chandler
Box Car Children Snowbound Mystery	Fluent	O	250+	Albert Whitman	Warner, Gertrude Chandler
Box Car Children, The	Fluent	O	250+	Albert Whitman	Warner, Gertrude Chandler
Boy Who Cried Wolf, The	Fluent	L	250+	Rigby	Literacy 2000
Boy Who Cried Wolf, The	Transitional	18*/K	460	Dominie Press	Aesop's Fables
Brave Little Tailor	Transitional	18/K	250+	Rigby	PM Traditional Tales & Plays
Bravest Dog Ever, The True Story of Balto	Fluent	L	50+	Random House	Standiford, Natalie
Bread	Emergent	6/D	69	Wright Group	Sunshine
Bread, Bread, Bread	Progressing	F	95	Scholastic	Guided Reading Program
Breakfast With John	Emergent	5/C	29	Richard C. Owen	Books For Young Learners
Bringing the Rain to Kapiti Plain	Fluent		250+	Dial	Aardema, Verna
Brith the Terrible	Fluent	M	250+	Rigby	Literacy 2000
Bruno's Birthday	Progressing	8/E	32	Rigby	Literacy 2000
Brutus Learns to Fetch	Progressing	9/10*	155	Sundance	Little Red Readers
Bubble Gum	Emergent	2/B	21	Dominie Press	Carousel Readers
Bull's-Eye!	Progressing	8/F	87	Oxford Univ. Press	Oxford Reading Tree
Bully Brothers Making the Grade	Fluent		250+	Scholastic	Thaler, Mike
Bumblebee	Emergent	6/D	53	Pacific Learning	Ready to Read
Bumper Cars, The	Emergent	4/C	94	Rigby	PM Extensions
Bus Ride, The	Emergent	3/C	164	Celebration Press	Little Celebrations
Bush Bunyip, The	Fluent	J	396	Mondo	Bookshop
Busy Beavers, The	Transitional	I	362	Rigby	PM Story Books
Butterfly	Emergent	3/B	39	Sundance	AlphaKids
Butterfly, the Bird, the Beetle, and Me, The	Transitional	15/F	200	Sundance	AlphaKids
Buzzzzzz Said the Bee	Progressing	G	62	Scholastic	Guided Reading Program
By the Stream	Progressing	8/E	73	Oxford Univ. Press	Oxford Reading Tree
Cabbage Princess, The	Fluent	K	250+	Rigby	Literacy 2000
Cabin in the Hills	Transitional	J	349	Rigby	PM Story Books
Cam Jansen and Mystery of UFO	Fluent	L	250+	Puffin Books	Adler, David A.
Cam Jansen and Mystery of Monster Movie	Fluent	L	250+	Puffin Books	Adler, David A.
Cam Jansen and Mystery of the Dinosaur Bones	Fluent	L	250+	Puffin Books	Adler, David A.
Camp Knock Knock	Fluent	K	250+	Dell	Duffey, Betsy
Camping	Progressing	7*/D	64	Kaeden	Hooker, Karen

Tentatively leveled

B

C

Title	Level	RR–GR Level	Words	Publisher	Series/Author
Camping With Claudine	Fluent	K	250+	Rigby	Literacy 2000
Can Do, Jenny Archer	Fluent	M	250+	Little, Brown	Conford, Ellen
Can I Have a Dinosaur?	Fluent	L	250+	Rigby	Literacy 2000
Can I Have a Lick?	Emergent	4 /C	69	Dominie Press	Carousel Readers
Can You See Me?	Emergent	1/A	34	Sundance	AlphaKids
Canoe Diary	Fluent		250+	Pacific Learning	Orbit Chapter Books
Caps For Sale	Transitional	20/K	675	HarperCollins	Slobodkina, Esphyr
Car Ride, The	Emergent	2/A	41	Sundance	Little Red Readers
Careful Crocodile, The	Transitional	I	271	Rigby	PM Story Books
Carla's Breakfast	Progressing	12/G	225	Kaeden	Harper, Leslie
Carla's Ribbon	Progressing	11/G	212	Kaeden	Harper, Leslie
Carnival, The	Progressing	9/F	82	Oxford Univ. Press	Oxford Reading Tree
Carrot Seed, The	Progressing	12/G	101	HarperCollins	Krauss, Ruth
Case for Jenny Archer, A	Fluent	M	250+	Little, Brown	Conford, Ellen
Cass Becomes a Star	Fluent	L	250+	Rigby	Literacy 2000
Cat and Dog	Emergent	3/C	71	Creative Teaching	Learn to Read
Cat Chat	Progressing	9/F	85	Modern Curriculum	Ready Readers
Cat Concert	Transitional	J	250+	Rigby	Literacy Tree
Cat in the Tree, A	Progressing	9/F	79	Oxford Univ. Press	Oxford Reading Tree
Cat On the Mat	Emergent	2/B	37	Oxford Univ. Press	Wildsmith, Brian
Cat Talk	Fluent		250+	Pacific Learning	Orbit Chapter Books
Cat That Broke the Rules, The	Progressing	11/G	192	Modern Curriculum	Ready Readers
Cat Who Loved Red, The	Emergent	6/D	63	Seedling	Salem, L. & Stewart, J.
Cat With No Tail, The	Transitional	15/I	137	Richard C. Owen	Books For Young Learners
Cat, The	Emergent	A	42	University of Maine	Little Books for Early Readers
Catch That Frog	Progressing	8/E	131	Celebration Press	Reading Unlimited
Caterpillars	Transitional	19–20*/M	114	Mondo	Bookshop
Cats and Kittens	Progressing	9/F	51	Celebration Press	Reading Unlimited
Cement Tent	Progressing	12/G	358	Troll	First Start
Chair For My Mother, A	Fluent	M	250+	Scholastic	Williams, Vera
Changing Caterpillar, The	Progressing	12/G	56	Richard C. Owen	Books for Young Learners
Changing Land, The	Transitional	16/I	64	Pacific Learning	Ready to Read
Chase, The	Progressing	8/F	85	Oxford Univ. Press	Oxford Reading Tree
Chasing Tornadoes	Fluent		250+	Modern Curriculum	First Chapters
Chick and the Duckling, The	Emergent	6/D	112	Macmillan	Ginsburg, Mirra
Chicken in the Middle of the Road	Transitional	16–18*/J	478	Mondo	Bookshop
Chicken Little	Transitional	20/L	250+	Rigby	Traditional Tales
Chicken Little	Fluent		250+	William Morrow	Kellogg, Steven
Chicken Soup With Rice	Transitional	20/M	250+	Scholastic	Sendak, Maurice
Chickens	Progressing	12*/G	105	Mondo	Bookshop
Chickens	Progressing	8/D	23	Richard C. Owen	Books For Young Learners
Children of Sierra Leone, The	Transitional	16/J	142	Richard C. Owen	Books for Young Learners
Chinese New Year	Emergent	6/D	33	Pacific Learning	Ready to Read
Chocolate Touch	Fluent		250+	Dell	Catling, Patrick Skene
Choosing a Puppy	Progressing	7/E	158	Rigby	PM Extensions

Tentatively leveled

Title	Level	RR–GR Level	Words	Publisher	Series/Author
Cinderella	Transitional	18*/ I	580	Dominie Press	Traditional Tales
Cinderella	Fluent		250+	Scholastic	Wegman, William
Circus Train, The	Emergent	1/A	48	Sundance	Little Red Readers
City Mouse, Country Mouse	Emergent	4/D	87	Creative Teaching	Learn to Read
City Mouse-Country Mouse	Fluent	J	250+	Scholastic	Guided Reading Program
City Sounds	Progressing	G	142	Scholastic	Guided Reading Program
Claudine's Concert	Fluent	L	250+	Rigby	Literacy 2000
Clean House For Mole and Mouse, A	Transitional	H	201	Scholastic	Guided Reading Program
Clifford the Big Red Dog	Transitional	18/K	241	Scholastic	Bridwell, Norman
Clifford the Small Red Puppy	Transitional	18/K	499	Scholastic	Bridwell, Norman
Cloudy With a Chance of Meatballs	Transitional	M	250+	Atheneum	Barrett, Judi
Coaching Ms. Parker	Fluent		250+	Aladdin	Heymsfeld, Carla
Coat Full of Bubbles, A	Progressing	10/G	72	Richard C. Owen	Books For Young Learners
Cold Day, The	Progressing	9/F	80	Oxford Univ. Press	Oxford Reading Tree
Collections	Progressing	E		Scholastic	Guided Reading Program
Commander Toad In Space	Fluent		250+	Scholastic	Yolen, Jane
Coo Coo Caroo	Progressing	12/G	79	Richard C. Owen	Books For Young Learners
Cook-Out, The	Progressing	9/E	78	Oxford Univ. Press	Oxford Reading Tree
Cookie's Week	Progressing	10/F	84	Scholastic	Ward, Cindy
Cooking Pot, The	Progressing	10/F	132	Wright Group	Sunshine
Cooking Thanksgiving Dinner	Emergent	5*	126	Pioneer Valley	Emergent/Set 2
Cool Off	Emergent	3–4*/C	37	Mondo	Bookshop
Copycat	Emergent	4 /C	54	Wright Group	Story Box
Costumes	Emergent	3/C	23	Oxford Univ. Press	Oxford Reading Tree
Cow in the Garden, The	Progressing	8/E	158	Steck-Vaughn	New Way
Cow Up a Tree	Transitional	13/H	215	Rigby	Read Along
Cows in the Garden	Progressing	11/G	163	Rigby	PM Story Books
Coyote Plants a Peach Tree	Transitional	16/I	233	Richard C. Owen	Books For Young Learners
Crabbing Time	Transitional	15/I	76	Richard C. Owen	Books For Young Learners
Crazy Cats	Emergent	A	42	University of Maine	Little Books for Early Readers
Crazy Quilt, The	Progressing	11/G	148	Celebration Press	Little Celebrations
Crosby Crocodile's Disguise	Transitional	K	250+	Rigby	Literacy Tree
Cross Country Race, The	Transitional	14 /H	246	Rigby	PM Story Books
Crow and the Pitcher, The	Transitional	15*/I	265	Dominie Press	Aesop's Fables
Crunchy Munchy	Progressing	12*/G	189	Mondo	Bookshop
Curious George and the Ice Cream	Fluent	J	250	Scholastic	Rey, Margaret and H. A.
Dad	Emergent	1/A	24	Rigby	PM Starters
Dad's Headache	Progressing	10/F	86	Wright Group	Sunshine
Dad's Shirt	Emergent	6/F	38	Dominie Press	Joy Readers
Dan the Flying Man	Emergent	4/C	60	Wright Group	Read Togethers
Dark, Dark Tale, A	Progressing	10/F	115	Penguin	Brown, Ruth
Dear Zoo	Progressing	9 /F	115	Macmillan	Campbell, Rod
Debra's Dog	Transitional	14/H	157	Rigby	Tadpoles
Dee and Me	Progressing	12/G	189	Modern Curriculum	Ready Readers
Desert Run	Fluent		250+	Pacific Learning	Orbit Chapter Books

* *Tentatively leveled*

Title	Level	RR–GR Level	Words	Publisher	Series/Author
Desert, The	Emergent	3/C	34	Dominie Press	Carousel Readers
Did You Say "Fire"?	Progressing	11/G	158	Pacific Learning	Ready to Read
Digging Dinosaurs	Fluent		250+	Modern Curriculum	First Chapters
Digging To China	Transitional	13/H	108	Richard C. Owen	Books For Young Learners
Dinosaur Chase, The	Transitional	I	240	Rigby	PM Story Books
Dinosaur Girl	Fluent	N	250+	Rigby	Literacy Tree
Dinosaur Who Lived in My Backyard, The	Transitional	H	250+	Scholastic	Guided Reading Program
Dinosaurs Galore	Progressing	4–5/D	34	Seedling	Eaton, A. & Kennedy, J.
Dive In!	Progressing	9/F	133	Modern Curriculum	Ready Readers
Doctor DeSoto Goes to Africa	Fluent		250+	HarperCollins	Steig, William
Doctor Has the Flu, The	Transitional	13/H	106	Modern Curriculum	Ready Readers
Dog	Emergent	A		Scholastic	Guided Reading Program
Dog at School	Progressing	10/F	94	Richard C. Owen	Books For Young Learners
Dogs	Emergent	1/A	34	Sundance	AlphaKids
Dogstar	Transitional	J	250+	Rigby	Literacy 2000
Don't Be Late!	Emergent	D	112	Scholastic	Guided Reading Program
Don't Forget the Bacon	Transitional	20/M	174	Puffin Books	Hutchins, Pat
Don't Panic!	Progressing	8/E	122	Wright Group	Book Bank
Don't Splash Me!	Emergent	1/A	24	Rigby	Windmill
Don't You Laugh at Me!	Progressing	7/E	167	Wright Group	Sunshine
Donkey	Fluent	M	250+	Rigby	Literacy 2000
Doorbell Rang, The	Transitional	17/J	283	Scholastic	Hutchins, Pat
Double Trouble	Fluent	M	250+	Rigby	Literacy 2000
Down at the River	Progressing	8/E	51	Pacific Learning	Ready to Read
Down on the Ice	Fluent		250+	Pacific Learning	Orbit Chapter Books
Dragon Feet	Transitional	15/K	153	Richard C. Owen	Books For Young Learners
Dragon Flies	Progressing	11/G	53	Richard C. Owen	Books For Young Learners
Dragon Hunt, The	Progressing	9/F	53	Steck-Vaughn	New Way
Dragon's Birthday, The	Fluent	L	250+	Rigby	Literacy 2000
Dragon's Lunch	Progressing	9/F	85	Modern Curriculum	Ready Readers
Dragon, The	Transitional	15/F	374	Sundance	AlphaKids
Drawbridge	Progressing	7/E	29	Richard C. Owen	Books For Young Learners
Dream, The	Progressing	9/F	54	Oxford Univ. Press	Oxford Reading Tree
Dreams	Progressing	8 /E	93	Wright Group	Book Bank
Dressed Up Sammy	Progressing	7/E	91	Kaeden	Urmston, K. & Evans, K.
Dressing Up	Emergent	1/A	12	Rigby	PM Starters
Drought Maker, The	Fluent	M	250+	Rigby	Literacy 2000
Duck in the Gun, The	Fluent	M	250+	Rigby	Literacy 2000
Duckling, The	Transitional	14/E	405	Sundance	AlphaKids
Each Peach Pear Plum	Progressing	11/G	115	Penguin	Ahlberg, A. & J.
Early One Morning	Transitional	13/E	240	Sundance	AlphaKids
Edgar Badger's Balloon Day	Transitional	18–20/I–J	864	Mondo	Bookshop
Egyptians	Fluent		250+	Gareth Stevens	Allard, Denise
Eight Friends In All	Emergent	6/D	64	Modern Curriculum	Ready Readers
Elves and Shoemaker, The	Progressing	10	317	Ladybird	Read It Yourself

Tentatively leveled

Title	Level	RR–GR Level	Words	Publisher	Series/Author
Elves and Shoemaker, The	Transitional	18/K	622	Steck-Vaughn	New Way
Elves and the Shoemaker, The	Transitional	14/E	251	Sundance	AlphaKids
Elves and the Shoemaker, The	Transitional	18/K	300	Rigby	PM Traditional Tales & Plays
Emily Can't Sleep	Emergent	6*	124	Pioneer Valley	Emergent/Set 2
Emily's Babysitter	Emergent	4*/C	67	Pioneer Valley	Emergent/Set 1
Emma's Problem	Transitional	13/H	190	Rigby	Literacy 2000
Enjoy! Enjoy!	Transitional	17/F	268	Sundance	AlphaKids
Enormous Crocodile, The	Fluent	N	250+	Puffin Books	Dahl, Roald
Enormous Turnip, The	Transitional	14/H	431	Ladybird	Read It Yourself
Enormous Watermelon, The	Transitional	14/H	304	Rigby	Traditional Tales
Excuses, Excuses	Progressing	8/E	104	Rigby	Tadpoles
Exploring the Titantic	Fluent		250+	Scholastic/Madison	Ballard, Robert D.
Fall	Emergent	A	22	University of Maine	Little Books for Early Readers
Fall Harvest	Emergent	A	16	University of Maine	Little Books for Early Readers
Family Work and Fun	Emergent	3/4*	38	Sundance	Little Red Readers
Fantail, Fantail	Emergent	5/D	67	Pacific Learning	Ready to Read
Farm Concert, The	Emergent	5/D	74	Wright Group	Story Box
Farm in Spring	Emergent	5/D	69	Rigby	PM Starters
Farm, A	Emergent	A	28	University of Maine	Little Books for Early Readers
Farm, The	Emergent	1/A	14	Modern Curriculum	Ready Readers
Farm, The	Emergent	A	28	University of Maine	Little Books for Early Readers
Farmer and His Two Lazy Sons, The	Transitional	17*/J	250	Dominie Press	Aesop's Fables
Farmer and the Skunk	Progressing	8/E	127	Peguis	Tiger Cub
Farmer Had a Pig	Progressing	11/G	149	Peguis	Tiger Cub
Farmer Joe's Hat Day	Transitional	17/J	406	Scholastic	Richards/Zimmerman
Father Bear Comes Home	Transitional	19/I	331	HarperCollins	Minarik, E. H.
Father Bear Goes Fishing	Emergent	5/D	98	Rigby	PM Story Books
Father Who Walked on Hands	Transitional	18/K	344	Rigby	Literacy 2000
Fern and Bert	Transitional	14/H	375	Modern Curriculum	Ready Readers
Fiddle and the Gun, The	Fluent	M	250+	Rigby	Literacy 2000
Fire, Fire	Progressing	8/E	164	Rigby	PM Story Books
Fireflies	Fluent		250	Atheneum	Brinckloe, Julie
First Day of School	Emergent	6/D	60	Dominie Press	Carousel Earlybirds
Fishing	Emergent	4/C	63	Rigby	PM Starters
Fishing	Emergent	B	41	University of Maine	Little Books for Early Readers
Fishing	Progressing	7/D	48	Kaeden	Yukish, J.
Five Little Dinosaurs	Progressing	8/E	113	Modern Curriculum	Ready Readers
Five Little Ducks	Emergent	5	164	Random House	Raffi
Five Little Monkeys	Progressing	8*/F	81	Mondo	Bookshop
Five Little Monkeys Going to the Zoo	Progressing	8–9/E	201	Seedling	Cutteridge's 1st Grade, V.
Five Little Monkeys Jumping on the Bed	Progressing	8/E	200	Clarion	Christelow, Eileen
Five True Dog Stories	Fluent	M	250+	Scholastic	Davidson, Margaret
Five True Horse Stories	Fluent	M	250+	Scholastic	Davidson, Margaret
Flatfoot Fox	Fluent		250+	Scholastic	Clifford, Eth
Flip Flop	Progressing	11/G	70	Richard C. Owen	Books For Young Learners

* Tentatively leveled

Title	Level	RR–GR Level	Words	Publisher	Series/Author
Flip's Trick	Transitional	14/H	134	Modern Curriculum	Ready Readers
Floating and Sinking	Progressing	11/D	220	Sundance	AlphaKids
Floppy the Hero	Progressing	9/F	74	Oxford Univ. Press	Oxford Reading Tree
Floppy's Bath	Progressing	8/E	55	Oxford Univ. Press	Oxford Reading Tree
Flossie and the Fox	Fluent	O	250+	Scholastic	McKissack, Patricia
Flying and Floating	Emergent	3/B	64	Sundance	Little Red Readers
Flying Fish, The	Transitional	14/H	215	Rigby	PM Extensions
Forgetful Fred	Progressing	7/E	78	Rigby	Tadpoles
Four Getters and Arf, The	Progressing	11/G	123	Celebration Press	Little Celebrations
Four Ice Creams	Emergent	4/C	61	Rigby	PM Starters
Fox and the Little Red Hen	Transitional	19/L	400	Rigby	PM Traditional Tales & Plays
Fox and His Friends	Transitional	18/J	417	Scholastic	Marshall, E. & Marshall, J.
Fox and the Crow, The	Progressing	9/D	201	Sundance	AlphaKids
Fox and the Crow, The	Transitional	17*	250+	Dominie Press	Aesop's Fables
Fox, The	Emergent	4/C	24	Richard C. Owen	Books For Young Learners
Franklin and the Tooth Fairy	Fluent		250+	Scholastic	Bourgeois, P. & Clark, B.
Franklin Goes to School	Fluent	K	250+	Scholastic	Bourgeois, P. & Clark, B.
Franklin Has a Sleepover	Fluent		250+	Scholastic	Bourgeois, P. & Clark, B.
Franklin Plays the Game	Fluent	J	250+	Scholastic	Bourgeois, P. & Clark, B.
Freddie the Frog	Emergent	6/D	132	Troll	First Start
Free to Fly	Progressing	8–9/E	96	Seedling	Gibson, Kathleen
Friend For Little White Rabbit	Progressing	8/E	113	Rigby	PM Story Books
Friendly Snowman	Progressing	11/F	134	Troll	First Start
Friends	Emergent	5*/D	57	Mondo	Bookshop
Friends	Emergent		42	Fairfax County	Books for Budding Readers
Friends	Progressing	12/G	195	Celebration Press	Reading Unlimited
Frog and the Fly, The	Emergent	5/D	33	Oxford Univ. Press	Cat on the Mat Series
Frog and Toad Are Friends	Transitional	19/K	250+	HarperCollins	Lobel, Arnold
Frog and Toad Together	Transitional	19/K	250+	HarperCollins	Lobel, Arnold
Frog Prince, The	Fluent	21*	572	Dominie Press	Traditional Tales
Frog Prince, The	Transitional	20/H	908	Wright Group	Sunshine
Frog Princess, The	Transitional	18/K	206	Rigby	Literacy Tree
Frogs	Fluent	N	1440	Mondo	Bookshop
Frogs	Transitional		190	Scholastic	Reading Discovery
Fruit Salad	Emergent	1/A	22	Sundance	AlphaKids
Fruit Salad	Emergent	2*/B	15	Pioneer Valley	Early Emergent/Set 2
Fun at Camp	Transitional	13/H	178	Troll	First Start
Fun Place to Eat, A	Progressing	7/E	90	Modern Curriculum	Ready Readers
Fun With Hats	Emergent	2*/B	38	Mondo	Bookshop
Fun With Mo and Toots	Emergent	3/C	41	Pacific Learning	Ready to Read
Funny Faces and Funny Places	Emergent	6/D	45	Modern Curriculum	Ready Readers
Funny Man, A	Progressing	E	244	Scholastic	Guided Reading Program
Funny Old Man and the Funny Old Woman, The	Transitional	16–18*/M	562	Mondo	Bookshop
Gabby Is Hungry	Emergent	4*/C	78	Pioneer Valley	Emergent/Set 1
Gail and Me	Fluent	L	250+	Rigby	Literacy 2000

Tentatively leveled

Title	Level	RR–GR Level	Words	Publisher	Series/Author
Gecko's Story	Progressing	12/F	61	Richard C. Owen	Books for Young Learners
George and Martha	Fluent	L	250+	Houghton Mifflin	Marshall, James
George Shrinks	Transitional	H	114	Scholastic	Guided Reading Program
George's Show and Tell	Emergent	5*	133	Pioneer Valley	Emergent/Set 2
Get Lost, Becka!	Progressing	8/E	102	School Zone	Start to Read
Getting Ready	Emergent	B	29	University of Maine	Little Books for Early Readers
Getting Ready For School	Emergent	3/4*	39	Sundance	Little Red Readers
Ghost	Emergent	1/A	26	Wright Group	Story Box
Giant Gingerbread Man, The	Progressing	9/D	243	Sundance	AlphaKids
Giant's Job, The	Transitional	13–14/H	180	Seedling	Stewart, J. & Salem, L.
Giant, The	Emergent	1/A	20	Dominie Press	Joy Readers
Gifts For Dad	Transitional	14/H	178	Kaeden	Urmston, K. & Evans, K.
Gingerbread Boy, The	Progressing	10–11/F	137	Steck-Vaughn	New Way
Gingerbread Man, The	Transitional	I	250+	Scholastic	Guided Reading Program
Gingerbread Man, The	Transitional	15 /J	535	Rigby	PM Traditional Tales & Plays
Gingerbread Man, The	Transitional	15*/I	534	Dominie Press	Traditional Tales
Glasses	Emergent	1/A	24	Sundance	AlphaKids
Goha and His Donkey	Transitional	15/I	114	Richard C. Owen	Books For Young Learners
Going For a Ride	Emergent	B	40	University of Maine	Little Books for Early Readers
Going For a Ride	Emergent	3*/C	52	Pioneer Valley	Early Emergent/Set 1
Going Shopping	Emergent	5/B	105	Sundance	AlphaKids
Going Shopping	Emergent		45	Fairfax County	Books for Budding Readers
Going to McDonald's	Emergent		43	Fairfax County	Books for Budding Readers
Going to The Beach	Emergent	5/C	75	Dominie Press	Carousel Readers
Going to the Beach	Emergent	3/4*	44	Sundance	Little Red Readers
Going Up and Down	Emergent	2*/B	51	Pioneer Valley	Early Emergent/Set 1
Golden Goose, The	Fluent	M	250+	Rigby	Literacy 2000
Goldilocks and the Three Bears	Transitional	17/H	250+	Rigby	PM Traditional Tales & Plays
Good Catch!, A	Progressing	6–7/E	191	Steck-Vaughn	New Way
Good Old Mom	Emergent	4/C	34	Oxford Univ. Press	Oxford Reading Tree
Good-bye Summer, Hello Fall	Transitional	14/H	169	Modern Curriculum	Ready Readers
Good-bye, Zoo	Emergent	6/D	48	Modern Curriculum	Ready Readers
Goodnight, Little Bug	Emergent	6/D	54	Modern Curriculum	Ready Readers
Gooey Chewy Contest, The	Fluent	22*/N	1512	Mondo	Bookshop
Grandmother	Progressing	7/E	60	Dominie Press	Joy Readers
Grandpa Comes to Stay	Transitional	18–20*/K	1,083	Mondo	Bookshop
Grandpa's Candy Store	Emergent	6/F	25	Richard C. Owen	Books For Young Learners
Grandpa's House	Emergent	2/A	47	Sundance	AlphaKids
Grandpa, Grandma and the Tractor	Transitional	14/H	220	Modern Curriculum	Ready Readers
Grandpa, Grandpa	Progressing	11/G	122	Wright Group	Read-Togethers
Great Black Heroes: Five Brave Explorers	Fluent	P	250+	Scholastic	Hudson, Wade
Great Day	Progressing	10/D	162	Sundance	AlphaKids
Greedy Cat	Progressing	11/G	166	Pacific Learning	Ready to Read
Greedy Cat and the Birthday Cake	Fluent		250	Pacific Learning	Orbit Chapter Books
Greedy Cat is Hungry	Emergent	6/D	103	Pacific Learning	Ready to Read

* Tentatively leveled

Title	Level	RR–GR Level	Words	Publisher	Series/Author
Greedy Goat, The	Transitional	19/L	451	Mondo	Bookshop
Greedy Gray Octopus, The	Progressing	12/G	195	Rigby	Tadpoles
Green	Progressing	12/E	174	Sundance	AlphaKids
Green Dragons	Transitional	K	250+	Rigby	PM Story Books
Green Eyes	Progressing	10/F	111	Rigby	Literacy 2000
Green Footprints	Progressing	7/E	42	Rigby	Literacy 2000
Gregory, The Terrible Eater	Fluent	L	250+	Scholastic	Weinman, Sharmat
Growing Tomatoes	Progressing	8/C	92	Sundance	AlphaKids
Grumpy Elephant	Progressing	7/E	100	Wright Group	Story Box
Haddie's Caps	Emergent	6/D	90	Modern Curriculum	Ready Readers
Hairy Bear	Progressing	11/G	109	Wright Group	Read-Togethers
Hannah's Halloween	Emergent	A	14	University of Maine	Little Books for Early Readers
Happy Birthday, Martin Luther King	Fluent	L	250+	Scholastic	Marzollo, Jean
Hard at Work	Emergent	2*/B	66	Pioneer Valley	Early Emergent/Set 2
Hare and the Tortoise, The	Fluent	K	250+	Rigby	Literacy 2000
Hats Around the World	Emergent	B	59	Scholastic	Charlesworth, Liza
Have You Seen My Cat?	Emergent	2/B	93	Scholastic	Carle, Eric
Have You Seen My Duckling?	Emergent	2/B	28	Scholastic	Tafuri, Nancy
Headache, The	Emergent	2/B	20	Oxford Univ. Press	Oxford Reading Tree
Heather's Book	Transitional	18/K	469	Modern Curriculum	Ready Readers
Helen Keller	Fluent	P	250+	Dell	Graff, S. & P.
Hello Creatures!	Fluent	K	250+	Rigby	Literacy 2000
Help Me	Emergent	5*/D	107	Pioneer Valley	Emergent/Set 1
Henny Penny	Transitional	I	582	Scholastic	Guided Reading Program
Henry	Progressing	8/E	77	Richard C. Owen	Books For Young Learners
Henry and Beezus	Fluent	O	250+	Avon Books	Cleary, Beverly
Henry and Mudge and the Forever Sea	Fluent	J	250+	Aladdin	Rylant, Cynthia
Henry and Mudge in Puddle Trouble	Fluent	J	250+	Aladdin	Rylant, Cynthia
Henry and Mudge in the Green Time	Fluent	J	250+	Aladdin	Rylant, Cynthia
Henry and Mudge, The First Book	Fluent	J	250+	Aladdin	Rylant, Cynthia
Henry and Ribsy	Fluent	O	250+	Avon Books	Cleary, Beverly
Henry Huggins	Fluent	O	250+	Avon Books	Cleary, Beverly
Here Is…	Emergent	2/B	49	Dominie Press	Carousel Earlybirds
Hermit Crab, The	Progressing	12/G	119	Wright Group	Sunshine
Hide and Seek	Emergent	5/D	108	Rigby	PM Extensions
Hide and Seek	Emergent	D	63	Scholastic	Guided Reading Program
Hill of Fire	Fluent	20/L	1099	HarperCollins	Lewis, T. P.
Hogboggit	Emergent	6/D	65	Pacific Learning	Ready to Read
Hoketichee and the Manatee	Transitional	15/I	113	Richard C. Owen	Books For Young Learners
Home For Little Teddy, A	Emergent	5/D	53	Rigby	PM Extensions
Honk!	Emergent	2*/B	36	Mondo	Bookshop
Hooray For the Golly Sisters	Fluent	K	250+	HarperTrophy	Byers, Betsy
Horace	Emergent	5/D	56	Wright Group	Story Box
Horrible Big Black Bug, The	Emergent	6/D	50	Rigby	Tadpoles
House That Stood on Booker Hill, The	Transitional	17/J	324	Modern Curriculum	Ready Readers

Tentatively leveled

Title	Level	RR–GR Level	Words	Publisher	Series/Author
How Far Will I Fly?	Progressing	F	94	Scholastic	Guided Reading Program
How Fire Came to Earth	Transitional	19 /K	250+	Rigby	Literacy 2000
How Have I Grown?	Progressing	G	235	Scholastic	Guided Reading Program
How Many Fish?	Emergent	B	30	Scholastic	Gossett, R. & Ballinger, M.
How Many Pets?	Emergent	5*/D	37	Mondo	Bookshop
How Much Is That Guinea Pig in the Window?	Fluent	L	250+	Scholastic	Guided Reading Program
How the Chick Tricked the Fox	Progressing	12/G	167	Modern Curriculum	Ready Readers
How The Mouse Got Brown Teeth	Transitional	16*/I	460	Mondo	Bookshop
How to Draw a Dinosaur	Transitional	16/F	229	Sundance	AlphaKids
How Turtle Raced Beaver	Transitional	17/J	182	Rigby	Literacy 2000
Huberta the Hiking Hippo	Fluent	L	250+	Rigby	Literacy 2000
Humphrey	Fluent	O	250+	Rigby	Literacy Tree
Hungry Sea Star, The	Transitional	14/I	69	Richard C. Owen	Books For Young Learners
Hungry, Hungry Sharks	Fluent	L	250+	Random House	Cole, Joanna
Hunt For Clues, A	Progressing	12/G	157	Modern Curriculum	Ready Readers
I Am	Emergent	A		Scholastic	Guided Reading Program
I Am Thankful	Emergent	1/A	42	Dominie Press	Carousel Earlybirds
I Can Do It	Transitional	13*/I	200	Mondo	Bookshop
I Can Draw	Emergent	4/C	75	Dominie Press	Carousel Earlybirds
I Can Make Music	Emergent	2/B	41	Sundance	Little Red Readers
I Can Read	Emergent	2/B	38	Pacific Learning	Ready to Read
I Can See	Emergent	A		Scholastic	Guided Reading Program
I Can Swim	Emergent	6/D	61	Modern Curriculum	Ready Readers
I Can Wash	Emergent	4/C	66	Dominie Press	Carousel Earlybirds
I Can Write. Can You?	Emergent	2/B	30	Seedling	Stewart, J. & Salem, L.
I Can't Find My Roller Skates	Emergent	5/B	73	Sundance	AlphaKids
I Eat Leaves	Emergent	3*/C	47	Mondo	Bookshop
I Got a Goldfish	Progressing	8/E	92	Modern Curriculum	Ready Readers
I Like	Emergent	A		Scholastic	Guided Reading Program
I Like	Emergent	3/C	24	Rigby	Literacy 2000
I Like Balloons	Emergent	1/A	27	Dominie Press	Reading Corners
I Like Painting	Emergent	4*	68	Sundance	Little Red Readers
I Like Shapes	Emergent	B	21	Scholastic	Armstrong, Shane
I Like to Count	Emergent	3/C	40	Modern Curriculum	Ready Readers
I Like to Eat	Emergent	1/A	41	Dominie Press	Reading Corners
I Like to Help	Emergent	B	46	University of Maine	Little Books for Early Readers
I Like to Paint	Emergent	1/A	29	Dominie Press	Reading Corners
I Like to Play	Emergent	3/C	50	Dominie Press	Carousel Readers
I Like to Read	Emergent	B	49	University of Maine	Little Books for Early Readers
I Love Bugs	Emergent	4*/C	40	Mondo	Bookshop
I Love Camping	Emergent	2*/B	34	Pioneer Valley	Early Emergent/Set 2
I Love Camping	Progressing	8/E	83	Dominie Press	Carousel Readers
I Love Mud and Mud Loves Me	Emergent	D	121	Scholastic	Guided Reading Program
I Love My Family	Emergent	3/B	31	Wright Group	Sunshine
I Love the Beach	Fluent	M	250+	Rigby	Literacy 2000

* Tentatively leveled

Title	Level	RR–GR Level	Words	Publisher	Series/Author
I Paint	Emergent	2/A	22	Rigby	Literacy Tree
I Read	Emergent	1/A	38	Dominie Press	Reading Corners
I See	Emergent	2*/B	29	Mondo	Bookshop
I Shop With My Daddy	Progressing	G	131	Scholastic	Guided Reading Program
I Was Walking Down the Road	Transitional	H	299	Scholastic	Guided Reading Program
I Went Walking	Emergent	4/C	105	Harcourt Brace	Williams, Sue
I'm a Big Brother	Progressing		79	Fairfax County	Books for Budding Readers
I'm a Caterpillar	Progressing	G	169	Scholastic	Guided Reading Program
I'm a Good Reader	Transitional	13/H	188	Dominie Press	Carousel Readers
I'm Brave	Emergent	2/A	35	Sundance	AlphaKids
I'm Hungry	Emergent	D	84	Scholastic	Guided Reading Program
I'm King of the Mountain	Progressing	12/G	285	Pacific Learning	Ready to Read
I'm On the Phone	Transitional	13/E	241	Sundance	AlphaKids
I'm So Hungry and Other Plays	Fluent		250+	Pacific Learning	Orbit Chapter Books
Ice Cream	Emergent	1/A	41	Sundance	AlphaKids
In My Garden	Emergent	3/C	36	Dominie Press	Carousel Readers
In My School	Emergent	A	27	University of Maine	Little Books for Early Readers
In the City	Emergent	C	45	Scholastic	Pasternac, Susana
In the Clouds	Fluent	M	250+	Rigby	Literacy 2000
In the Forest	Emergent	B		Scholastic	Guided Reading Program
In the Woods	Emergent	2*/B	48	Mondo	Bookshop
Insects	Transitional	14/E	256	Sundance	AlphaKids
Insects	Transitional	J	171	Scholastic	Maclulich, Carolyn
Inside School	Emergent	A	35	University of Maine	Little Books for Early Readers
Is It Time?	Emergent	C	52	Scholastic	Reading Discovery
Is This a Monster?	Emergent	5*/C	93	Mondo	Bookshop
Is Tomorrow My Birthday?	Progressing	E	87	Scholastic	Guided Reading Program
It Came Through the Wall	Fluent	20–22*/O	1182	Mondo	Bookshop
Itchy, Itchy Chicken Pox	Progressing	F	131	Scholastic	Guided Reading Program
Jack and Chug	Transitional	I	337	Rigby	PM Story Books
Jack's Seed	Emergent		56	Fairfax County	Books for Budding Readers
Jake	Emergent	A	35	University of Maine	Little Books for Early Readers
Jake Can Play	Emergent	B	42	University of Maine	Little Books for Early Readers
James is Hiding	Emergent	1/A	24	Rigby	Windmill
Jan and the Jacket	Progressing	7/E	74	Oxford Univ. Press	Oxford Reading Tree
Jessica in the Dark	Transitional	I	362	Rigby	PM Story Books
Jigaree, The	Progressing	7/E	128	Wright Group	Story Box
Jim's Visit to Kim	Progressing	12/G	149	Modern Curriculum	Ready Readers
Joe and the BMX Bike	Progressing	8/E	91	Oxford Univ. Press	Oxford Reading Tree
Joe and the Mouse	Progressing	10/F	138	Oxford Univ. Press	Oxford Reading Tree
Johnny Appleseed	Fluent		250+	Scholastic	Kellogg, Steven
Jolly Roger, the Pirate	Emergent	6/D	138	Rigby	PM Extensions
Jonathan Buys a Present	Transitional	J	353	Rigby	PM Story Books
Jordan is Hiding	Emergent	A	24	University of Maine	Little Books for Early Readers
Josephina Story Quilt	Fluent	L	250+	HarperTrophy	Coerr, Eleanor

Tentatively leveled

Title	Level	RR–GR Level	Words	Publisher	Series/Author
Julian's Glorious Summer	Fluent	N	250+	Random House	Cameron, Ann
Jump the Broom	Transitional	15/L	119	Richard C. Owen	Books For Young Learners
Junie B. Jones and the Stupid Smelly Bus	Fluent	M	250+	Random House	Park, Barbara
Junie B. Jones and the Yucky Blucky Fruit Cake	Fluent	M	250+	Random House	Park, Barbara
Just a Seed	Progressing	E	74	Scholastic	Guided Reading Program
Just Like Grandpa	Progressing	8/E	81	Rigby	Literacy Tree
Just Like Me	Progressing	7/E	138	Children's Press	Rookie Reader
Just Like Us	Progressing	7/E	55	Modern Curriculum	Ready Readers
Just One Guinea Pig	Transitional	I	339	Rigby	PM Story Books
Kangaroos	Transitional		155	Scholastic	Reading Discovery
Kate's Skates	Progressing		80	Scholastic	Reading Discovery
Katie Did It	Progressing	7/G	105	Children's Press	Rookie Reader
Katy and the Big Snow	Fluent	L	250+	Scholastic	Guided Reading Program
Katydids	Progressing	7/E	20	Richard C. Owen	Books For Young Learners
Keep the Lights Burning, Abbie	Fluent	K	250+	Scholastic	Guided Reading Program
Kenny and the Little Kickers	Fluent	J	250+	Scholastic	Mareollo, Claudio
King Beast's Birthday	Fluent	L	250+	Rigby	Literacy 2000
King Kong and the Flower Fairy	Fluent		250+	Rigby	Literacy Tree
King Midas and the Golden Touch	Fluent	22*/J	562	Dominie Press	Traditional Tales
Lad Who Went To The North Wind, The	Transitional	20*/J	796	Mondo	Bookshop
Last One Picked	Transitional	13/E	329	Sundance	AlphaKids
Late For Soccer	Progressing	11/F	185	Rigby	PM Story Books
Lazy Mary	Emergent	6/D	191	Wright Group	Story Box
Legs	Emergent	A		Scholastic	Guided Reading Program
Let's Get Moving	Fluent	M	250+	Rigby	Literacy 2000
Let's Move	Emergent	2/B	29	Modern Curriculum	Ready Readers
Let's Play Ball	Emergent	B	40	University of Maine	Little Books for Early Readers
Library, The	Emergent	6*/D	96	Pioneer Valley	Emergent/Set 1
Library, The	Emergent	3/C	33	Dominie Press	Carousel Readers
Lines	Transitional	13/E	262	Sundance	AlphaKids
Lion and the Mouse, The	Progressing	10/F	115	Steck-Vaughn	New Way
Lion's Tail, The	Progressing	9/F	147	Celebration Press	Reading Unlimited
Lionel and Amelia	Transitional	20*/L	702	Mondo	Bookshop
Little and Big	Emergent	2*	57	Sundance	Little Red Readers
Little Bear	Fluent	J	1664	HarperCollins	Minarik, E. H.
Little Bear's Friend	Fluent	J	250+	HarperTrophy	Minarik, E. H.
Little Bear's Visit	Fluent	J	250+	HarperTrophy	Minarik, E. H.
Little Bulldozer Helps Again	Progressing	9/F	197	Rigby	PM Extensions
Little Cousins' Visit, The	Emergent	5*/C	123	Pioneer Valley	Emergent/Set 1
Little Dinosaur Escapes	Fluent	J	389	Rigby	PM Story Books
Little Girl and Her Beetle, The	Transitional	15/I	250+	Rigby	Literacy 2000
Little Monkey	Progressing	11/D	315	Sundance	AlphaKids
Little Mouse's Trail Tale	Transitional	13*/I	349	Mondo	Bookshop
Little Pig	Emergent	4/C	63	Wright Group	Story Box
Little Red Hen	Emergent	2/B	87	Wright Group	Windmill

* Tentatively leveled

Title	Level	RR–GR Level	Words	Publisher	Series/Author
Little Red Hen, The	Transitional	15	250+	Scholastic	Easy to Read
Little Red Hen, The	Transitional	16/I	416	Rigby	PM Traditional Tales & Plays
Little Red Hen, The	Transitional	13*/H	375	Dominie Press	Traditional Tales
Little Red Riding Hood	Transitional	17/J	250+	Rigby	PM Traditional Tales & Plays
Little Sister	Emergent	C	40	Scholastic	Mitchell, Robin
Little Spider, The	Fluent	L	250+	Rigby	Literacy 2000
Living and Non Living	Emergent	2/A	30	Sundance	AlphaKids
Lizard Loses His Tail	Emergent	5/D	54	Rigby	PM Story Books
Lobstering	Emergent	A	14	University of Maine	Little Books for Early Readers
Lonely Giant, The	Transitional	18/K	449	Rigby	Literacy 2000
Lonely Troll, The	Transitional	17/F	518	Sundance	AlphaKids
Look at Conor	Emergent	A	27	University of Maine	Little Books for Early Readers
Look at Kyle	Emergent	B	46	University of Maine	Little Books for Early Readers
Look at Me	Emergent	A	17	University of Maine	Little Books for Early Readers
Look at the Ocean, A	Emergent	B	50	University of Maine	Little Books for Early Readers
Look At This	Emergent	2/B	57	Dominie Press	Carousel Earlybirds
Look For Me	Emergent	5/D	71	Wright Group	Story Box
Look-Alike Animals	Transitional	I	132	Scholastic	Guided Reading Program
Looking for Fang	Emergent	5/B	185	Sundance	AlphaKids
Looking After Chicks	Transitional	15/F	327	Sundance	AlphaKids
Loose Laces	Transitional	17/L	209	Celebration Press	Reading Unlimited
Lost at the Fun Park	Progressing	9/F	192	Rigby	PM Extensions
Lost in the Fog	Emergent	5/D	59	Modern Curriculum	Ready Readers
Lost Mother, The	Emergent	6/C	108	Sundance	AlphaKids
Lots and Lots of Stairs	Emergent	B	33	University of Maine	Little Books for Early Readers
Lots of Caps	Transitional	15/I	205	Steck-Vaughn	New Way
Lottie Goat and Donny Goat	Transitional	13/H	145	Modern Curriculum	Ready Readers
Loudest Sneeze, The	Transitional	16/F	255	Sundance	AlphaKids
Lucky Baseball Bat, The	Fluent	M	250+	Little, Brown	Christopher, Matt
Lucky Day For Little Dinosaur, A	Progressing	8/F	135	Rigby	PM Extensions
Lucky Duck, The	Progressing	7/E	73	Modern Curriculum	Ready Readers
Lucky Feather, The	Fluent	L	250+	Rigby	Literacy 2000
Lucky Goes to Dog School	Progressing	7/E	127	Rigby	PM Story Books
Lunch	Emergent	A		Scholastic	Guided Reading Program
Lunch at the Zoo	Emergent	B	64	Scholastic	Reading Discovery
Lydia and Her Garden	Progressing	11/G	88	Oxford Univ. Press	Oxford Reading Tree
Lydia and Her Kitten	Progressing	12/G	77	Oxford Univ. Press	Oxford Reading Tree
Lydia and the Ducks	Progressing	11/G	87	Oxford Univ. Press	Oxford Reading Tree
Lydia and the Present	Progressing	9/F	77	Oxford Univ. Press	Oxford Reading Tree
Magic Fish, The	Transitional	J	250+	Scholastic	Guided Reading Program
Mai-Li's Surprise	Progressing	7/F	61	Richard C. Owen	Books For Young Learners
Mailbox, The	Emergent	3/B	46	Sundance	AlphaKids
Mailman Mario and His Boris-Busters	Fluent		250+	Dominie Press	Chapter Books
Make a Wish, Molly	Fluent	O	250+	Dell	Cohen, Barbara
Making a Memory	Emergent	D	53	Scholastic	Guided Reading Program

Tentatively leveled

Title	Level	RR–GR Level	Words	Publisher	Series/Author
Making Butter	Emergent	4/B	106	Sundance	AlphaKids
Making Concrete	Progressing	9/D	134	Sundance	AlphaKids
Making Lunch	Emergent	5/B	131	Sundance	AlphaKids
Making Mountains	Emergent	B	35	Scholastic	Ballinger, M. & Gossett, R.
Marcella	Fluent	L	250+	Rigby	Literacy 2000
Mario's Mayan Journey	Fluent	22–24*/P	1021	Mondo	Bookshop
Marvin Redpost: Why Pick on Me?	Fluent	L	250+	Random House	Sachar, Louis
Me	Emergent	1/A	24	Rigby	PM Starters
Meanies	Progressing	8/F	158	Wright Group	Story Box
Meeka	Emergent		42	Fairfax County	Books for Budding Readers
Meeka Goes Swimming	Progressing		65	Fairfax County	Books for Budding Readers
Meet Mr. Cricket	Progressing	8/E	86	Dominie Press	Carousel Readers
Merry Go Round, The	Emergent	4/C	66	Dominie Press	Teacher's Choice
Merry-Go-Round, The	Emergent	3/C	84	Rigby	PM Story Books
Mess, A	Emergent	6/D	34	Modern Curriculum	Ready Readers
Message on a Rocket	Progressing	12/E	174	Sundance	AlphaKids
Messages	Progressing	F	79	Scholastic	Guided Reading Program
Messy Mark	Progressing	9/F	180	Troll	First Start
Michael in the Hospital	Progressing	8/E	91	Oxford Univ. Press	Oxford Reading Tree
Midnight Pig	Fluent	P	250+	Rigby	Literacy Tree
Midnight Rescue	Fluent	N	250+	Rigby	Literacy Tree
Mike's First Haircut	Progressing	9/G	136	Troll	First Start
Mike's New Bike	Progressing	9/F	183	Troll	First Start
Miss Geneva's Lantern	Fluent	22–24*/P	1691	Mondo	Bookshop
Miss Nelson Is Missing!	Transitional	20/L	598	Scholastic	Allard, Harry
Miss Rumphius	Fluent		250+	Puffin Books	Cooney, Barbara
Missing Necklace, The	Transitional	14/H	231	Celebration Press	Reading Unlimited
Misty of Chincoteague	Fluent		250+	Scholastic	Henry, Marguerite
Mitch to the Rescue	Transitional	I	302	Rigby	PM Story Books
Mitten, The	Fluent	M	250+	Scholastic	Brett, Jan
Molly's Pilgrim	Fluent	M	250+	Dell	Cohen, Barbara
Mom Can Fix Anything	Emergent	4/D	74	Creative Teaching	Science II
Mom's Haircut	Transitional	13/H	99	Rigby	Literacy 2000
Mom's Secret	Transitional	H	141	Scholastic	Guided Reading Program
Monkey and Fire	Transitional	18 /J	372	Rigby	Literacy Tree
Monkey See, Monkey Do	Progressing	F	89	Scholastic	Guided Reading Program
Monkeys	Emergent	B	27	Scholastic	Canizares, S. & Chanko, P.
Monster Bus	Transitional	13/H	103	Dominie Press	Monster Bus Series
Monster Bus Goes on a Hot Air Balloon Trip	Transitional	16/I	254	Dominie Press	Monster Bus Series
Monster Bus Goes to the Races	Transitional	13 /H	158	Dominie Press	Monster Bus Series
Monster Bus Goes to Yellowstone Park	Transitional	15/I	259	Dominie Press	Monster Bus Series
Monster Math Picnic	Progressing	F		Scholastic	Guided Reading Program
Monster Math School Time	Progressing	G	120	Scholastic	Guided Reading Program
Monsters	Emergent	3/B	93	Sundance	AlphaKids
Moon, The	Emergent	6/D	139	Dominie Press	Joy Readers

* Tentatively leveled

Title	Level	RR–GR Level	Words	Publisher	Series/Author
More Spaghetti, I Say!	Transitional	H	250+	Scholastic	Guided Reading Program
More Stories Julian Tells	Fluent	N	250+	Random House	Cameron, Ann
Mountain Gorillas	Fluent	P	330	Wright Group	Wonder World
Mouse Soup	Transitional	J	1350	Scholastic	Guided Reading Program
Mouse's Baby Blanket	Emergent	6/D	68	Seedling	Swerdlow, Beverly Brown
Moving	Emergent	3/B	56	Sundance	Little Red Readers
Mr. Cricket Finds a Friend	Progressing	11/G	134	Dominie Press	Carousel Readers
Mr. Cricket Takes a Vacation	Progressing	8/E	165	Dominie Press	Carousel Readers
Mr. Cricket's New Home	Progressing	10/F	121	Dominie Press	Carousel Readers
Mr. Grindy's Shoes	Transitional	15	211	Wright Group	Sunshine
Mr. McCready's Cleaning Day	Transitional	H	119	Scholastic	Guided Reading Program
Mr. Pepperpot's Pet	Transitional	K	250+	Rigby	Literacy 2000
Mr. Putter and Tabby Bake The Cake	Fluent	J	250+	Harcourt Brace	Rylant, Cynthia
Mr. Putter and Tabby Pick The Pears	Fluent	J	250+	Harcourt Brace	Rylant, Cynthia
Mr. Putter and Tabby Pour The Tea	Fluent	J	250+	Harcourt Brace	Rylant, Cynthia
Mr. Putter and Tabby Walk The Dog	Fluent	J	250+	Harcourt Brace	Rylant, Cynthia
Mr. Wolf Leaves Town	Progressing	10/D	211	Sundance	AlphaKids
Mr. Wolf Tries Again	Progressing	9/D	215	Sundance	AlphaKids
Mrs. Murphy's Crows	Transitional	14/H	122	Richard C. Owen	Books For Young Learners
Mrs. Wishy-Washy	Progressing	8/E	102	Wright Group	Story Box
Mrs. Wishy-Washy's Tub	Emergent	B	38	Wright Group	Story Box
Much Ado About Aldo	Fluent	O	250+	Puffin Books	Hurwitz, Joanna
Muggie Maggie	Fluent	O	250+	Avon Camelot	Cleary, Beverly
My Baby Sister	Emergent	2/A	50	Sundance	AlphaKids
My Backyard	Emergent	A	14	University of Maine	Little Books for Early Readers
My Bike	Progressing	8/D	108	Pacific Learning	Ready to Read
My Brother Wants to Be Like Me	Progressing	8/D	62	Kaeden	Mader, Jan
My Bug Box	Progressing	7/E	98	Richard C. Owen	Books For Young Learners
My Cat Muffin	Emergent	B	35	Scholastic	Gardner, Marjory
My Cats	Emergent	A		Scholastic	Guided Reading Program
My Circus Family	Emergent	3*/C	42	Mondo	Bookshop
My Dad's Truck	Progressing	E	57	Scholastic	Guided Reading Program
My Dog	Emergent	2/3*/C	79	Pioneer Valley	Early Emergent/Set 1
My Dog's The Best	Progressing	F	175	Scholastic	Guided Reading Program
My Father	Transitional	I	194	Scholastic	Guided Reading Program
My Five Senses	Emergent		59	Fairfax County	Books for Budding Readers
My Fort	Emergent	A	17	University of Maine	Little Books for Early Readers
My Friends	Progressing	G	152	Scholastic	Guided Reading Program
My Grandpa	Progressing	9*/F	75	Mondo	Bookshop
My Home	Emergent	2/B	56	Wright Group	Sunshine
My House	Emergent	1/A	40	Dominie Press	Carousel Earlybirds
My Little Brother	Emergent	3/C	59	Wright Group	Windmill
My Little Brother Ben	Emergent	5/D	35	Richard C. Owen	Books For Young Learners
My Little Dog	Emergent	4/C	90	Rigby	PM Starters
My Little Sister	Emergent	5/D	44	Dominie Press	Joy Readers

Tentatively leveled

Title	Level	RR–GR Level	Words	Publisher	Series/Author
My Lost Top	Progressing	7/E	70	Modern Curriculum	Ready Readers
My Lunch	Emergent	2/3*/C	70	Pioneer Valley	Early Emergent/Set 1
My Mom	Emergent	B	40	University of Maine	Little Books for Early Readers
My Monster and Me	Emergent	2/B	37	Modern Curriculum	Ready Readers
My New Bike	Emergent		33	Fairfax County	Books for Budding Readers
My New School	Progressing		63	Fairfax County	Books for Budding Readers
My Shadow	Progressing	10/F	116	Modern Curriculum	Ready Readers
My Shadow	Progressing	8/E	116	Pacific Learning	Ready to Read
My Shells	Transitional	16/F	276	Sundance	AlphaKids
My Sloppy Tiger	Transitional	16/I	217	Wright Group	Sunshine
My Street	Transitional	16/F	284	Sundance	AlphaKids
My Toys	Emergent	A	28	University of Maine	Little Books for Early Readers
Nate the Great	Fluent	K	250+	Dell	Sharmat, Marjorie Weinman
Nate the Great and the Sticky Case	Fluent	K	250+	Dell	Sharmat, Marjorie Weinman
Nathan and Nicholas Alexander	Fluent	K	250+	Scholastic	Guided Reading Program
Nelson the Baby Elephant	Transitional	J	350	Rigby	PM Story Books
Nesting Place	Transitional	K	356	Rigby	PM Story Books
New Baby Calf, The	Transitional	H	240	Scholastic	Guided Reading Program
New Cat, The	Emergent	2/B	29	Pacific Learning	Ready to Read
New Dog, A	Emergent	6/D	52	Oxford Univ. Press	Oxford Reading Tree
New York City Buildings	Progressing	12/F	59	Richard C. Owen	Books For Young Learners
Nick's Glasses	Progressing	7/E	51	Pacific Learning	Ready to Read
Nicky Upstairs and Down	Progressing	12/G	179	Penguin	Ziefert, Harriet
Nicole Helps Grandma	Emergent	B	35	University of Maine	Little Books for Early Readers
Night Walk	Progressing	9/F	51	Richard C. Owen	Books For Young Learners
No Dogs Allowed	Progressing	10/F	73	Richard C. Owen	Books For Young Learners
No Luck	Progressing	10/F	120	Seedling	Stewart, J. & Salem, L.
No One Is Going To Nashville	Fluent	O	250+	Bullseye Books	Jukes, Mavis
No Recess	Emergent		61	Fairfax County	Books for Budding Readers
No Singing Today	Progressing	12–13*/H	419	Mondo	Bookshop
No Trouble At All	Fluent	O	250+	Rigby	Literacy Tree
No Way, Winky Blue!	Fluent	24*/P	4053	Mondo	Bookshop
Noisy Nora	Transitional	I	204	Scholastic	Guided Reading Program
Not Enough Water	Progressing	D	84	Scholastic	Reading Discovery
Not-So-Jolly Roger	Fluent		250+	Penguin	Scieszka, Jon
Notes From Mom	Progressing	10/F	99	Seedling	Salem, L. & Stewart, J.
Notes to Dad	Progressing	9/F	114	Seedling	Stewart, J. & Salem, L.
Nothing In the Mailbox	Progressing	9/F	73	Richard C. Owen	Books For Young Learners
Octopus Goes to School	Emergent	4/C	42	Seedling	Bordelon, Carolyn
Octopuses and Squids	Fluent	N	328	Wright Group	Wonder World
Off to Squintum's/The Four Musicians	Fluent	20–22*/N	1268	Mondo	Bookshop
Oh No!	Emergent	5*/E	127	Mondo	Bookshop
Oh, No, Sherman!	Progressing	7/E	66	Seedling	Erickson, Betty
Oh, What a Daughter!	Fluent	L	250+	Rigby	Literacy 2000
Old Man's Mitten, The	Transitional	19*/I	378	Mondo	Bookshop

* Tentatively leveled

Title	Level	RR–GR Level	Words	Publisher	Series/Author
Old Train, The	Progressing	11/F	68	Richard C. Owen	Books For Young Learners
Old Tuatara	Emergent	4/C	33	Pacific Learning	Ready to Read
Old Woman Who Lived in a Vinegar Bottle, The	Transitional	18*/M	1161	Mondo	Bookshop
On the Playground	Emergent		44	Fairfax County	Books for Budding Readers
On Top of Spaghetti	Progressing	11/G	105	Celebration Press	Little Celebrations
On Vacation	Emergent	4/D	88	Sundance	Little Red Readers
Once When I Was Ship Wrecked	Fluent	L	250	Rigby	Literacy 2000
One Cold Wet Night	Emergent	6/D	134	Wright Group	Story Box
One For You, One For Me	Emergent	C	27	Scholastic	Blaxland, Wendy
One Frog, One Fly	Emergent		26	Scholastic	Reading Discovery
One Hot Summer Night	Progressing	10*/I	126	Mondo	Bookshop
One Pig, Two Pigs	Emergent	2 /B	142	Peguis	Tiger Cub
One Sock, Two Socks	Progressing	12/H	285	Dominie Press	Reading Corners
Our Dog Sam	Emergent	5/C	56	Rigby	Literacy Tree
Our House Had a Mouse	Progressing	8/E	102	Seedling	Worthington, Denise
Our Polliwogs	Transitional	15/I	91	Richard C. Owen	Books For Young Learners
Our Teacher, Miss Pool	Emergent	6/D	62	Pacific Learning	Ready to Read
Over the Bridge	Emergent	3/B	50	Sundance	Little Red Readers
Paco's Garden	Progressing	12/G	120	Richard C. Owen	Books For Young Learners
Paint My Room!	Transitional	14/E	317	Sundance	AlphaKids
Pancakes for Breakfast	Emergent	5*/C	108	Pioneer Valley	Emergent/Set 1
Pancakes!	Progressing	10/F	106	Modern Curriculum	Ready Readers
Papa's Spaghetti	Progressing	12/G	248	Rigby	Literacy 2000
Paper Bag Trail	Progressing	E	67	Scholastic	Guided Reading Program
Party, The	Emergent	3/B	61	Sundance	AlphaKids
Party, The	Emergent	5/D	29	Modern Curriculum	Ready Readers
Pat's New Puppy	Progressing	7/E	88	Celebration Press	Reading Unlimited
Pat's Perfect Pizza	Emergent	3/C	37	Modern Curriculum	Ready Readers
Patchwork Quilt	Fluent		250+	Scholastic	Flournoy, Valerie
Paul Bunyan	Fluent		250+	William Morrow	Kellogg, Steven
Paul's Day at School	Emergent	B	38	University of Maine	Little Books for Early Readers
Pecos Bill	Fluent		250+	William Morrow	Kellogg, Steven
Pee Wee Scouts: Cookies and Crutches	Fluent	L	250+	Dell	Delton, Judy
Pepper Sees Me	Emergent	A	28	University of Maine	Little Books for Early Readers
Pet For Me, A	Emergent	3*/C	73	Pioneer Valley	Early Emergent/Set 1
Pet For Me, A	Progressing	8/C	145	Sundance	AlphaKids
Pet Shop, The	Emergent	4/C	32	Oxford Univ. Press	Oxford Reading Tree
Pete Little	Progressing	12/G	222	Rigby	PM Story Books
Peter the Pumpkin Eater	Fluent		250+	Rigby	Literacy Tree
Pheasant and Kingfisher	Transitional	18–20*/L	910	Mondo	Bookshop
Pie, Pie, Beautiful Pie	Fluent		250+	Rigby	Literacy Tree
Pig William's Midnight Walk	Transitional	14/H	354	Wright Group	Book Bank
Pigs Peek	Emergent	4/C	28	Richard C. Owen	Books For Young Learners
Pioneer Cat	Fluent	N	250+	Random House	Hooks, William H.
Pip and the Little Monkey	Progressing	10/F	111	Oxford Univ. Press	Oxford Reading Tree

Tentatively leveled

Title	Level	RR–GR Level	Words	Publisher	Series/Author
Pip at the Zoo	Progressing	9/F	69	Oxford Univ. Press	Oxford Reading Tree
Pizza Day	Emergent		63	Fairfax County	Books For Budding Readers
Places	Emergent	3/4/C	88	Sundance	Little Red Readers
Plants	Emergent	5/B	122	Sundance	AlphaKids
Play Ball!	Emergent	5/D	30	Richard C. Owen	Books For Young Learners
Play Ball, Sherman	Progressing	8–9/F	88	Seedling	Erickson, Betty
Playground, The	Emergent	3*/C	108	Pioneer Valley	Early Emergent/Set 1
Playing	Emergent	1/A	31	Sundance	AlphaKids
Playing in the Snow	Emergent	3*/C	61	Pioneer Valley	Early Emergent/Set 1
Pocket Full of Acorns, A	Fluent		250+	Dominie Press	Chapter Books
Polly's Shop	Progressing	7/E	130	Modern Curriculum	Ready Readers
Pony Named Shawnee, A	Fluent	24*/P	3075	Mondo	Bookshop
Pot of Gold, The	Transitional	16/I	266	Celebration Press	Reading Unlimited
Potato Harvest Time	Emergent	A	33	University of Maine	Little Books for Early Readers
Praying Mantis, The	Progressing	8/D	46	Pacific Learning	Ready to Read
Predators	Transitional	16/F	283	Sundance	AlphaKids
Present From Aunt Skidoo, The	Fluent	M	250+	Rigby	Literacy 2000
Princess and the Pea	Transitional	17*/I	304	Dominie Press	Traditional Tales
Princess and the Wise Woman, The	Transitional	18/K	320	Modern Curriculum	Ready Readers
Prize For Purry	Fluent	K	250+	Rigby	Literacy 2000
PS I Love You, Gramps	Fluent		250+	Rigby	Literacy Tree
Pterosaur's Long Flight	Transitional	I	301	Rigby	PM Story Books
Pumpkin House, The	Transitional	J	250+	Rigby	Literacy 2000
Pumpkin Patch, The	Emergent		51	Fairfax County	Books for Budding Readers
Puppets	Fluent	K	250+	Rigby	Literacy Tree
Puppy Who Wanted a Boy, The	Fluent	L	250+	Scholastic	Guided Reading Program
Push!	Emergent	5/D	21	Oxford Univ. Press	Oxford Reading Tree
Quack!	Progressing	7/E	54	Modern Curriculum	Ready Readers
Quackers, the Troublesome Duck	Fluent		250+	Modern Curriculum	First Chapters
Rabbit Stew	Fluent	L	250+	Rigby	Literacy 2000
Rabbits	Fluent	M	250+	Rigby	Literacy Tree
Race to Green End, The	Transitional	K	506	Rigby	PM Story Books
Race, The	Emergent	2/B	34	Rigby	Windmill
Rain	Emergent	4/B	140	Sundance	AlphaKids
Rain, Rain	Emergent	5/D	58	Pacific Learning	Ready to Read
Raindrops	Emergent	C	66	Scholastic	Gay, Sandy
Rainforest Plants	Progressing	10/D	145	Sundance	AlphaKids
Ralph S. Mouse	Fluent	O	250+	Avon Books	Cleary, Beverly
Ramona and Her Father	Fluent	O	250+	Avon Books	Cleary, Beverly
Ramona Quimby, Age 8	Fluent	O	250+	Avon Books	Cleary, Beverly
Ramona the Brave	Fluent	O	250+	Avon Books	Cleary, Beverly
Ramona the Pest	Fluent	O	250+	Avon Books	Cleary, Beverly
Rapunzel	Fluent	L	250+	Rigby	Literacy 2000
Raven's Gift	Transitional	20/L	160	Richard C. Owen	Books For Young Learners
Red and I Visit the Vet	Progressing	10/F	196	Modern Curriculum	Ready Readers

* Tentatively leveled

Title	Level	RR–GR Level	Words	Publisher	Series/Author
Red Rose, The	Progressing	7/E	127	Wright Group	Story Box
Red Socks and Yellow Socks	Progressing	12/G	155	Wright Group	Sunshine
Red Tailed Hawk, The	Transitional	19/L	199	Richard C. Owen	Books For Young Learners
Rescuing Nelson	Transitional	J	369	Rigby	PM Story Books
Riding to Craggy Rock	Transitional	K	386	Rigby	PM Story Books
River Runners	Fluent	N	250+	Rigby	Literacy Tree
Roads and Bridges	Progressing	11/D	253	Sundance	AlphaKids
Robert and the Rocket	Transitional	H		Scholastic	Guided Reading Program
Roberto's Snack	Emergent	4*		Pioneer Valley	Emergent/Set 2
Rope Swing, The	Progressing	7/E	77	Oxford Univ. Press	Oxford Reading Tree
Rosa at the Zoo	Transitional	13/H	135	Pacific Learning	Ready to Read
Rosie's House	Fluent	K	250+	Rigby	Literacy 2000
Rosie's Walk	Progressing	9/F	32	Scholastic	Hutchins, Pat
Rough-Face Girl, The	Fluent		250+	Scholastic	Martin, Rafe
Roy and the Parakeet	Progressing	8/E	74	Oxford Univ. Press	Oxford Reading Tree
Roy at the Fun Park	Progressing	11/G	111	Oxford Univ. Press	Oxford Reading Tree
Royal Drum, The	Transitional	20*/L	526	Mondo	Bookshop
Rummage Sale, The	Progressing	8/E	81	Oxford Univ. Press	Oxford Reading Tree
Rumpelstiltskin	Fluent	23*/J	940	Dominie Press	Traditional Tales
Rush, Rush, Rush	Progressing	8/E	52	Modern Curriculum	Ready Readers
Sally and the Sparrows	Progressing	7/E	151	Rigby	PM Extensions
Sally's Space Ship	Progressing	7/E	87	Modern Curriculum	Ready Readers
Sam's Glasses	Fluent	M	250+	Rigby	Literacy 2000
Sam's Mask	Progressing	7/E	36	Pacific Learning	Ready to Read
Sammy at the Farm	Emergent	6/C	83	Kaeden	Urmston, K. & Evans, K.
Sammy Gets a Ride	Progressing	10/F	91	Kaeden	Evans, K. & Urmston, K.
Sammy's Supper	Transitional	16/I	293	Celebration Press	Reading Unlimited
Sandwiches	Emergent	2/A	59	Sundance	AlphaKids
Sarah and the Barking Dog	Transitional	I	328	Rigby	PM Story Books
Sarah and Will	Progressing	10/D	258	Sundance	AlphaKids
Saturday Mornings	Emergent	5–6*/D	63	Mondo	Bookshop
Saving the Yellow Eye	Fluent		250+	Pacific Learning	Orbit Chapter Books
Say It, Sign It	Progressing	G	169	Scholastic	Guided Reading Program
Scare and Dare	Progressing	9/D	281	Sundance	AlphaKids
Scarecrow, The	Emergent	5/D	97	Sundance	Little Red Readers
School Bus Ride, The	Progressing	10/11*	160	Sundance	Little Red Readers
Schoolyard Mystery	Fluent	L	250+	Scholastic	Guided Reading Program
Sea Animals	Transitional	15/16*	326	Sundance	Little Red Readers
Sea Star, A	Progressing	7/E	82	Modern Curriculum	Ready Readers
Seat Belt Song, The	Transitional	K	505	Rigby	PM Story Books
Sebastian	Progressing	9/D	158	Sundance	AlphaKids
Sebastian Gets the Hiccups	Progressing	12/E	320	Sundance	AlphaKids
Sebastian's Special Present	Transitional	15/F	300	Sundance	AlphaKids
Secret Soup	Progressing	8/E	51	Rigby	Literacy Tree
Seesaw, The	Emergent	4*/C	100	Pioneer Valley	Emergent/Set 1

Tentatively leveled

Title	Level	RR–GR Level	Words	Publisher	Series/Author
Selfish Giant, The	Fluent	L	250+	Rigby	Literacy 2000
Shadow Puppets	Progressing	7/C	162	Sundance	AlphaKids
Shadows	Emergent		46	Fairfax County	Books for Budding Readers
Shark In a Sack	Emergent	4/C	65	Wright Group	Sunshine
Shark Lady: The Adventures of Eugenia Clark	Fluent	N	250+	Scholastic	McGovern, Ann
Sharks	Transitional	13/H	155	Modern Curriculum	Ready Readers
Sharks	Transitional		228	Scholastic	Reading Discovery
Sheeba	Fluent		250+	Dominie Press	Chapter Books
Shell Shopping	Progressing	9/F	145	Modern Curriculum	Ready Readers
Shintaro's Umbrella	Transitional	16/I	101	Richard C. Owen	Books For Young Learners
Shoes	Progressing	8/D	79	Wright Group	Book Bank
Shopping	Emergent	4/C	78	Sundance	Little Red Readers
Shorty	Fluent	M	250+	Rigby	Literacy 2000
Shoveling Snow	Progressing	F	109	Scholastic	Guided Reading Program
Show and Tell	Progressing	8/C	213	Sundance	AlphaKids
Sick in Bed	Progressing	9/F	109	Sundance	Little Red Readers
Sing a Song	Progressing	7/E	154	Wright Group	Story Box
Skates for Luke	Transitional	I	346	Rigby	PM Story Books
Ski School	Emergent	A	34	University of Maine	Little Books for Early Readers
Skipper's Birthday	Progressing	8/E	64	Oxford Univ. Press	Oxford Reading Tree
Skipper's Idea	Progressing	10/F	81	Oxford Univ. Press	Oxford Reading Tree
Skipper's Laces	Progressing	9/F	66	Oxford Univ. Press	Oxford Reading Tree
Sky Is Falling Down, The	Emergent	5/D	101	Dominie Press	Joy Readers
SkyFire	Fluent	J	250+	Scholastic	Asch, Frank
Sleeping Animals	Emergent	6/C	193	Sundance	AlphaKids
Slugs and Snails	Fluent	J	426	Mondo	Bookshop
Small Baby Raccoon, A	Progressing	11/G	104	Modern Curriculum	Ready Readers
Smile! said Dad	Emergent	6/D	66	Pacific Learning	Ready to Read
Smile, The	Emergent	6/D	53	Pacific Learning	Ready to Read
Smokey the Dragon	Fluent		250+	Dominie Press	Chapter Books
Snake's Dinner	Progressing	7/C	156	Sundance	AlphaKids
Snakes	Transitional		227	Scholastic	Reading Discovery
Snow Goes To Town	Fluent	L	250+	Rigby	Literacy 2000
Snowman, The	Progressing	8/E	76	Oxford Univ. Press	Oxford Reading Tree
Snowy Day, The	Transitional	18/J	319	Scholastic	Keats, Ezra Jack
Snowy Gets a Wash	Progressing	8/F	181	Rigby	PM Extensions
Soccer at the Park	Progressing	8/F	131	Rigby	PM Extensions
Sock Gobbler, The	Fluent		250+	Pacific Learning	Orbit Chapter Books
Socks Off!	Progressing	10/D	178	Sundance	AlphaKids
Sooty	Progressing	12/E	218	Sundance	AlphaKids
Space Aliens in Our School	Emergent	5/D	45	Dominie Press	Joy Readers
Space Travel	Transitional	15/F	225	Sundance	AlphaKids
Sparrows, The	Progressing	11/F	60	Richard C. Owen	Books For Young Learners
Spider and the King, The	Fluent	L	250+	Rigby	Literacy 2000
Spider Man	Fluent	M	250+	Rigby	Literacy 2000

* Tentatively leveled

Title	Level	RR–GR Level	Words	Publisher	Series/Author
Spiders	Fluent	M	447	Mondo	Bookshop
Spirit of Hope	Fluent	22*/N	878	Mondo	Bookshop
Splash!	Emergent		32	Fairfax County	Books for Budding Readers
Splashing Dad	Emergent	2/3*/C	37	Pioneer Valley	Early Emergent/Set 1
Spots!	Progressing	8/E	53	Oxford Univ. Press	Oxford Reading Tree
Springs	Emergent	6/C	128	Sundance	AlphaKids
Squanto and the First Thanksgiving	Fluent	L	250+	Steck-Vaughn	Celso, Teresa
Starfish	Transitional	17/F	241	Sundance	AlphaKids
Staying Alive	Transitional	17/F	296	Sundance	AlphaKids
Staying With Grandma Norma	Progressing	10/F	168	Seedling	Salem, L. & Stewart, J.
Steve's Room	Progressing	12/G	171	Modern Curriculum	Ready Readers
Stew For Igor's Mom, A	Progressing	12/G	162	Modern Curriculum	Ready Readers
Stone Soup	Transitional	J	932	Scholastic	Guided Reading Program
Stone Soup	Transitional	17/J	250+	Rigby	PM Traditional Tales & Plays
Stop That Rabbit	Progressing	12/G	168	Troll	First Start
Storm Chasers: Tracking Twisters	Fluent		250+	Grossett & Dunlap	Herman, Gayle
Storm, The	Progressing	11/G	75	Richard C. Owen	Books For Young Learners
Story of Hungbu and Nolbu, The	Fluent	K	802	Mondo	Bookshop
Story of the White House	Fluent		250+	Scholastic	Waters, Kate
Story Time	Emergent	C	32	Modern Curriculum	Emergent/Set 2
Strange Creatures	Fluent		250+	Pacific Learning	Orbit Chapter Books
Strange Plants	Emergent	5/E	30	Richard C. Owen	Books For Young Learners
Strawberry Jam	Progressing	8/E	77	Oxford Univ. Press	Oxford Reading Tree
Strongest Animal, The	Progressing	7/F	58	Richard C. Owen	Books For Young Learners
Stubborn Goat, The	Progressing	11/D	222	Sundance	AlphaKids
Sugar Cakes Cyril	Fluent	22*/N	4022	Mondo	Bookshop
Suki and the Case of the Lost Bunnies	Transitional	18/K	529	Modern Curriculum	Ready Readers
Summer at Cove Lake	Progressing	11/G	288	Modern Curriculum	Ready Readers
Sunday Horse	Fluent	O	250+	Rigby	Literacy Tree
Sunflowers	Emergent	4/E	33	Richard C. Owen	Books For Young Learners
Super Pig's Adventure	Progressing	8–9/E	133	Steck-Vaughn	New Way
Susie Goes Shopping	Progressing	10/F	194	Troll	First Start
Swing, Swing, Swing	Emergent	C	93	Scholastic	Tuchman, Gail
T-Shirt Triplets, The	Transitional	19/L	344	Rigby	Literacy 2000
T-Shirts	Progressing	9/F	112	Pacific Learning	Ready to Read
Tadpoles and Frogs	Emergent	5/B	41	Sundance	AlphaKids
Taking Care of Rosie	Progressing	7/E	61	Seedling	Salem, L. & Stewart, J.
Taking Pictures	Emergent	6/C	137	Sundance	AlphaKids
Tale of the Turnip, The	Transitional	16/I	250+	Rigby	PM Traditional Tales & Plays
Tale of Veruschka Babuschka, The	Fluent	M	250+	Rigby	Literacy 2000
Tar Beach	Fluent			Scholastic	Ringgold, Faith
Tarantula	Progressing	11/D	140	Sundance	AlphaKids
Tarantulas Are Spiders	Progressing	9*/F	39	Mondo	Bookshop
Teach Us, Amelia Bedelia	Fluent	L	250+	Scholastic	Guided Reading Program
Teasing Dad	Progressing	9/F	158	Rigby	PM Extensions

Tentatively leveled

Title	Level	RR–GR Level	Words	Publisher	Series/Author
Ted's Red Sled	Emergent	6/D	69	Modern Curriculum	Ready Readers
Teeny Tiny Woman, The	Fluent	J	369	Scholastic	Seuling, Barbara
Terrific Shoes	Emergent	3/C	19	Modern Curriculum	Ready Readers
Thank You, Nicky!	Progressing	10/F	119	Penguin	Ziefert, Harriet
That Fly	Emergent	3/C	29	Modern Curriculum	Ready Readers
That Cat!	Progressing	12/G	146	Modern Curriculum	Ready Readers
That Pig Can't Do a Thing	Progressing	10/F	83	Modern Curriculum	Ready Readers
That's a Laugh! Four Funny Fables	Fluent	M	250+	Rigby	Literacy 2000
There Are Spots On…	Emergent	A	14	University of Maine	Little Books for Early Readers
There's a Mouse In the House	Emergent	2*/B	42	Mondo	Bookshop
Things on Wheels	Emergent	3/C	69	Sundance	Little Red Readers
Things to Read	Emergent	A	18	University of Maine	Little Books for Early Readers
Things to See in Maine	Emergent	A	14	University of Maine	Little Books for Early Readers
This Game	Emergent	2/B	63	Dominie Press	Carousel Earlybirds
This is Lobstering	Emergent	A	27	University of Maine	Little Books for Early Readers
This is the Place For Me	Transitional	I	250+	Scholastic	Guided Reading Program
Thomas Had a Temper	Progressing	8/C	137	Sundance	AlphaKids
Three Bears	Transitional	17/K	873	Scholastic	Galdone, Paul
Three Billy Goats Gruff, The	Progressing	11	387	Scholastic	Blair, Susan
Three Billy Goats Gruff, The	Progressing	8/E	123	Modern Curriculum	Ready Readers
Three Billy Goats Gruff, The	Transitional	16/I	450	Rigby	PM Traditional Tales & Plays
Three Little Pigs, The	Progressing	8/C	272	Sundance	AlphaKids
Three Little Pigs, The	Progressing		159	Fairfax County	Books for Budding Readers
Three Little Pigs, The	Transitional	16/I	523	Rigby	PM Traditional Tales & Plays
Three Little Pigs, The	Transitional	13/H	276	Celebration Press	Reading Unlimited
Three Little Pigs, The	Transitional	13/H	392	Steck-Vaughn	New Way
Three Little Pigs, The	Transitional	13/H	346	Dominie Press	Reading Corners
Three Little Witches	Progressing	12/G	189	Troll	First Start
Three Sillies, The	Fluent	L	250+	Rigby	Literacy 2000
Three Wishes, The	Transitional	18–20/L	717	Mondo	Bookshop
Tickling	Emergent	4/B	74	Sundance	AlphaKids
Tiger Dave	Progressing	12/G	33	Richard C. Owen	Books For Young Learners
Time For a Change	Emergent	4/C	31	Pacific Learning	Ready to Read
Tiny and the Big Wave	Progressing	8/F	163	Rigby	PM Extensions
Titch	Progressing	12/G	121	Penguin	Hutchins, Pat
Toby and B. J.	Transitional	I	307	Rigby	PM Story Books
Toby and the Accident	Transitional	J	329	Rigby	PM Story Books
Toby and the Big Red Van	Transitional	I	291	Rigby	PM Story Books
Toby and the Big Tree	Transitional	I	298	Rigby	PM Story Books
Too Busy	Emergent	3/B	50	Sundance	AlphaKids
Too High!	Emergent	5/D	66	Modern Curriculum	Ready Readers
Too Many Animals	Progressing	7/C	111	Sundance	AlphaKids
Too Many Bones	Progressing	12/G	125	Steck-Vaughn	New Way
Too Many Puppies	Transitional	I		Scholastic	Guided Reading Program
Tortillas	Progressing	E	71	Scholastic	Guided Reading Program

* Tentatively leveled

Title	Level	RR–GR Level	Words	Publisher	Series/Author
Toy Farm, The	Transitional	I	311	Rigby	PM Story Books
Transportation Museum, The	Emergent	4/C	79	Sundance	Little Red Readers
Trash or Treasure	Transitional	14/E	298	Sundance	AlphaKids
Treasure Hunting	Fluent	M	250+	Rigby	Literacy 2000
Tree Can Be…, A	Progressing	E	74	Scholastic	Guided Reading Program
Tree Fell Over the River, A	Emergent	3*/C	72	Sundance	Little Red Readers
Tree, The	Emergent	6/C	94	Sundance	AlphaKids
Trees Belong to Everyone	Fluent	L	250+	Rigby	Literacy 2000
Tricking Tracy	Progressing	9/F	125	Rigby	Tadpoles
Trip, The	Progressing	7/E	108	Modern Curriculum	Ready Readers
Trolley Ride, The	Emergent	4/C	87	Rigby	Tadpoles
Trouble With Herbert, The	Transitional	18–20*/L	1830	Mondo	Bookshop
Trucks	Emergent	A	35	University of Maine	Little Books for Early Readers
Tubes In My Ears: My Trip to the Hospital	Fluent	K	658	Mondo	Bookshop
Turtle Nest	Transitional	13/H	84	Richard C. Owen	Books For Young Learners
Twins	Emergent	4/B	76	Sundance	AlphaKids
Two Foolish Cats	Fluent	K	250+	Rigby	Literacy Tree
Two Little Dogs	Progressing	7/E	74	Wright Group	Story Box
Two Ogres, The	Progressing	9/F	116	Dominie Press	Joy Readers
Two Points	Emergent	2/B	40	Seedling	Kennedy, J. & Eaton, A.
Ugly Duckling, The	Transitional	18/K	452	Rigby	PM Traditional Tales & Plays
Uncle Tease	Fluent		250+	Rigby	Literacy Tree
Under My Sombrero	Progressing	9/F	79	Richard C. Owen	Books For Young Learners
Until We Got Princess	Progressing	10*/E	94	Mondo	Bookshop
Up and Down	Emergent	B	25	University of Maine	Little Books for Early Readers
Up In a Tree	Emergent	4/C	47	Wright Group	Sunshine
Vacation, The	Emergent	4*/C	94	Pioneer Valley	Emergent/Set 1
Very Big	Emergent	6/D	49	Modern Curriculum	Ready Readers
Very Greedy Dog, The	Transitional	14*/H	228	Dominie Press	Aesop's Fables
Very Hungry Caterpillar	Transitional	18/H	237	Scholastic	Carle, Eric
Very Strong Baby, The	Progressing	8/E	74	Dominie Press	Joy Readers
Very Thin Cat of Alloway Road, The	Fluent	L	250+	Rigby	Literacy 2000
Victor and the Kite	Progressing	10/F	84	Oxford Univ. Press	Oxford Reading Tree
Victor and the Martian	Transitional	14/H	109	Oxford Univ. Press	Oxford Reading Tree
Victor and the Sail-cart	Progressing	12/H	91	Oxford Univ. Press	Oxford Reading Tree
Victor the Champion	Progressing	12/G	102	Oxford Univ. Press	Oxford Reading Tree
Victor the Hero	Transitional	13/H	103	Oxford Univ. Press	Oxford Reading Tree
Video Game	Progressing	7/C	115	Sundance	AlphaKids
Visit to the Doctor, A	Emergent	A	22	University of Maine	Little Books for Early Readers
Wake Me in Spring	Progressing	E	250+	Scholastic	Guided Reading Program
Walking in the Jungle	Emergent	5/6*	113	Sundance	Little Red Readers
Washing Our Dog	Progressing	7/C	120	Sundance	AlphaKids
Waterfight, The	Progressing	8/E	64	Oxford Univ. Press	Oxford Reading Tree
Way I Go To School, The	Emergent	2/B	53	Rigby	PM Starters
We are Twins	Emergent	A	24	University of Maine	Little Books for Early Readers

Tentatively leveled

Title	Level	RR–GR Level	Words	Publisher	Series/Author
We Can Make Pizza	Emergent	A	30	University of Maine	Little Books for Early Readers
We Go To School	Emergent	2/B	27	Dominie Press	Carousel Earlybirds
We Like Fruit	Emergent	A		Scholastic	Guided Reading Program
We Went to the Movies	Emergent		26	Fairfax County	Books for Budding Readers
We Went to the Zoo	Emergent	2/B	32	Sundance	Little Red Readers
Weather	Emergent	C	54	Scholastic	Chanko, P. & Moreton, D.
Weather Watching	Transitional	15/F	196	Sundance	AlphaKids
Week With Aunt Bea, A	Emergent	5*/D	62	Mondo	Bookshop
Wet Grass	Transitional	14/H	188	Wright Group	Story Box
Whales	Fluent	N	1617	Mondo	Bookshop
What a Bad Dog!	Emergent	6/D	52	Oxford Univ. Press	Oxford Reading Tree
What a Dog!	Progressing	9/F	134	Troll	First Start
What a Mess!	Progressing	11/G	124	Steck-Vaughn	New Way
What a School	Progressing	10/F	100	Seedling	Salem, L. & Stewart, J.
What Are Purple Elephants Good For?	Transitional	13/H	136	Dominie Press	Reading Corners
What Can She Do?	Emergent	A	21	University of Maine	Little Books for Early Readers
What Comes Out at Night?	Emergent	2/B	48	Sundance	Little Red Readers
What Do Insects Do?	Emergent	A	24	Scholastic	Canizares, S. & Chanko, P.
What Do You Like?	Emergent	B	52	University of Maine	Little Books for Early Readers
What Does Greedy Cat Like?	Emergent	3/C	35	Pacific Learning	Ready to Read
What Has Stripes?	Emergent	C	28	Scholastic	Ballinger, Margaret
What I Like at School	Emergent	3/C	64	Sundance	Little Red Readers
What I'd Like to Be	Progressing	9/10*/F	112	Sundance	Little Red Readers
What is Big?	Emergent	D	72	Scholastic	Guided Reading Program
What Is Green?	Emergent	2/B	30	Dominie Press	Carousel Readers
What is It?	Emergent		31	Fairfax County	Books for Budding Readers
What is That? said the Cat	Progressing	F	118	Scholastic	Guided Reading Program
What Is This?	Emergent	A	23	University of Maine	Little Books for Early Readers
What People Do	Transitional	14/H	148	Sundance	Little Red Readers
What's For Dinner?	Emergent	3/B	38	Sundance	AlphaKids
What's For Dinner?	Progressing	7/E	115	Seedling	Salem, L. & Stewart, J.
What's That Noise?	Emergent	4/B	102	Sundance	AlphaKids
What's This? What's That?	Emergent	2/A	35	Sundance	AlphaKids
When Goldilocks Went to the House of the Bears	Emergent	6*/F	156	Mondo	Bookshop
When I Grow Up	Progressing	12/E	227	Sundance	AlphaKids
When the Circus Comes to Town	Emergent	2/A	40	Sundance	Little Red Readers
When the King Rides By	Fluent	17/J	247	Mondo	Bookshop
When the Truck Got Stuck	Fluent		250+	Pacific Learning	Orbit Chapter Books
When We Are Big	Progressing	7/E	123	Modern Curriculum	Ready Readers
Where Are the Car Keys?	Emergent	2/B	36	Rigby	Windmill
Where Are We Going?	Transitional	13/E	255	Sundance	AlphaKids
Where are We?	Emergent	2*/B	72	Pioneer Valley	Early Emergent/Set 1
Where Are You Going, Aja Rose?	Emergent	6/D	100	Wright Group	Sunshine
Where Can a Hippo Hide?	Emergent	5/D	41	Modern Curriculum	Ready Readers
Where Does the Teacher Sleep?	Emergent	4/C	50	Seedling	Gibson, K.

* Tentatively leveled

W

Title	Level	RR–GR Level	Words	Publisher	Series/Author
Where is Hannah?	Emergent	5/D	141	Rigby	PM Extensions
Where is Miss Pool?	Emergent	6/D	55	Pacific Learning	Ready to Read
Where is My Teacher?	Emergent	B	43	University of Maine	Little Books for Early Readers
Where is She?	Emergent	A	35	University of Maine	Little Books for Early Readers
Where Jeans Come From	Transitional	18/K	351	Modern Curriculum	Ready Readers
Where's My Pencil?	Progressing		86	Fairfax County	Books for Budding Readers
Where's the Baby?	Emergent	6/C	138	Sundance	AlphaKids
Which Hat Today?	Progressing	E	94	Scholastic	Guided Reading Program
Which Way Jack?	Fluent		250+	Rigby	Literacy Tree
Whipping Boy, The	Fluent	O	250+	Troll	Fleischman, Sid
Who Can?	Emergent	2*/B	35	Mondo	Bookshop
Who Cried Pie?	Emergent	5/D	86	Troll	First Start
Who Helps You?	Emergent		33	Fairfax County	Books for Budding Readers
Who is the Tallest?	Progressing	7/C	89	Sundance	AlphaKids
Who Lives in a Tree?	Emergent	B	46	Scholastic	Guided Reading Program
Who Lives in the Artic?	Emergent	B	48	Scholastic	Guided Reading Program
Who Lives in the Sea?	Emergent	2*/B	69	Mondo	Bookshop
Who Made That?	Emergent	3/C	31	Modern Curriculum	Ready Readers
Who Stole the Cookies From the Cookie Jar?	Progressing	G	153	Scholastic	Guided Reading Program
Who Will Be My Mother?	Progressing	8/E	156	Wright Group	Story Box
Who Will Help?	Emergent	2/B	20	Dominie Press	Carousel Readers
Who's Afraid of the Big Bad Bully?	Fluent	K	250+	Scholastic	Slater, Teddy
Who's in the Shed?	Transitional	16/ I	202	Rigby	Traditional Tales
Whose Mouse Are You?	Transitional	13/H	98	Scholastic	Guided Reading Program
Willie the Slowpoke	Progressing	11/G	125	Troll	First Start
Willy's Hats	Progressing	7–8/E	65	Seedling	Salem, L. & Stewart, J.
Winter is Here!	Emergent	D	55	Scholastic	Guided Reading Program
Wish Fish	Fluent		250+	Rigby	Literacy Tree
Witch's Haircut, The	Progressing	12/G	135	Wright Group	Windmill
Wobbly Tooth, The	Emergent	6/D	102	Rigby	Literacy Tree
Wobbly Tooth, The	Progressing	10/E	74	Oxford Univ. Press	Oxford Reading Tree
Wonder Women of Sports	Fluent		250+	Grosset & Dunlap	Kramer, S. A.
Worm Rap	Progressing	10/D	249	Sundance	AlphaKids
Worms Are Everywhere	Emergent		66	Fairfax County	Books for Budding Readers
Yes, I Can!	Emergent	5/D	45	Modern Curriculum	Ready Readers
Yes, Ma'am	Transitional	14/H	125	Wright Group	Read Togethers
You Can Play Soccer	Emergent		37	Fairfax County	Books for Budding Readers
You Can't Eat Your Chicken Pox, Amber Brown	Fluent	N	250+	Scholastic	Danziger, Paula
You'll Soon Grow Into Them, Titch	Transitional	14*/H	191	Rigby	Hutchins, Pat
Zack's House	Emergent	6*	114	Pioneer Valley	Emergent/Set 2
Zippers	Emergent	3/C	21	Richard C. Owen	Books For Young Learners
Zoe at the Fancy Dress Ball	Fluent	J	250+	Rigby	Literacy 2000
Zoe's Birthday Presents	Emergent	6*	83	Pioneer Valley	Emergent/Set 1
Zoo in Willy's Bed, The	Progressing	8/E	81	Seedling	Sturnman Gorman, Kate
Zoo Looking	Progressing	7*/G	149	Mondo	Bookshop

* Tentatively leveled

Title	Level	RR–GR Level	Words	Publisher	Series/Author
All Fall Down	Emergent	3/C	72	Oxford Univ. Press	Cat on the Mat Series
All Through the Week With Cat and Dog	Emergent	3/C	91	Creative Teaching	Learn to Read
Along Comes Jake	Emergent	6/D	86	Wright Group	Sunshine
Animal Habitats	Emergent	3/C	73	Sundance	Little Red Readers
Animal Homes	Emergent	2/B	48	Sundance	Little Red Readers
Animals at the Zoo	Emergent		35	Fairfax County	Books for Budding Readers
Ants	Emergent	B	16	Newbridge	Discovery Links
As Fast as a Fox	Emergent	5/D	69	Modern Curriculum	Ready Readers
At My School	Emergent	B	43	University of Maine	Little Books for Early Readers
At the Fair	Emergent	4/D	116	Sundance	Little Red Readers
At the Farm	Emergent	2/C	52	Sundance	Little Red Readers
At the Horse Show	Emergent	6/D	24	Richard C. Owen	Books For Young Learners
At the Park	Emergent	4/D	91	Sundance	Little Red Readers
At the Playground	Emergent	B	51	University of Maine	Little Books for Early Readers
At the Playground	Emergent	4/C	86	Sundance	Little Red Readers
At the Wildlife Park	Emergent	2/B	34	Sundance	Little Red Readers
At the Zoo	Emergent	3/C	73	Sundance	Little Red Readers
At the Zoo	Emergent	2/B	40	Rigby	PM Starters
Baby	Emergent	A	28	University of Maine	Little Books for Early Readers
Baby Chimp	Emergent	1/A	14	Wright Group	Twig
Baby Hippo	Emergent	6/D	117	Rigby	PM Extensions
Baby Owls, The	Emergent	4/C	90	Rigby	PM Extensions
Bags, Cans, Pots, and Pans	Emergent	4/C	56	Modern Curriculum	Ready Readers
Ball Game, The	Emergent	D	46	Scholastic	Guided Reading Program
Balloons	Emergent	2*/B	55	Pioneer Valley	Early Emergent/Set 2
Bath For a Beagle	Emergent	5/D	102	Troll	First Start
Bath, The	Emergent	1/A	14	Modern Curriculum	Ready Readers
Bear Lived in A Cave, A	Emergent	4/D	102	Sundance	Little Red Readers
Bear, The	Emergent	2/B	17	Dominie Press	Carousel Earlybirds
Bears in the Night	Emergent	5/D	108	Random House	Berenstain, Stan & Jan
Ben's Pets	Emergent	3/C	30	Modern Curriculum	Ready Readers
Ben's Teddy Bear	Emergent	5/D	68	Rigby	PM Story Books
Ben's Treasure Hunt	Emergent	5/D	72	Rigby	PM Story Books
Best Places, The	Emergent	6/D	68	Modern Curriculum	Ready Readers
Big and Little	Emergent	2/B	40	Dominie Press	Carousel Earlybirds
Big Things	Emergent	2/A	33	Rigby	PM Starters
Bike Ride, The	Emergent	5*/D	100	Pioneer Valley	Emergent/Set 1
Bike, The	Emergent	1/A	14	Wright Group	Twig
Birthday Cake, The	Emergent	1/A	22	Wright Group	Sunshine
Birthday Cakes	Emergent	4/B	95	Sundance	AlphaKids
Birthday Candles	Emergent	3/C	52	Dominie Press	Carousel Readers
Birthday Party, A	Emergent	2/3*/C	47	Pioneer Valley	Early Emergent/Set 1
Birthday, The	Emergent	A	23	University of Maine	Little Books for Early Readers
Blocks	Emergent	3*/C	60	Pioneer Valley	Early Emergent/Set 1
Blueberries From Maine	Emergent	A	28	University of Maine	Little Books for Early Readers

*Tentatively leveled

Title	Level	RR–GR Level	Words	Publisher	Series/Author
Bo and Peter	Emergent	C	45	Scholastic	Franco, Betsy
Boots	Emergent	C	57	Scholastic	Schreiber, A. & Doughty, A.
Boots For Toots	Emergent	4/C	41	Pacific Learning	Ready to Read
Bread	Emergent	6/D	69	Wright Group	Sunshine
Breakfast With John	Emergent	5/C	29	Richard C. Owen	Books For Young Learners
Bubble Gum	Emergent	2/B	21	Dominie Press	Carousel Readers
Bumblebee	Emergent	6/D	53	Pacific Learning	Ready to Read
Bumper Cars, The	Emergent	4/C	94	Rigby	PM Extensions
Bus Ride, The	Emergent	3/C	164	Celebration Press	Little Celebrations
Butterfly	Emergent	3/B	39	Sundance	AlphaKids
Can I Have a Lick?	Emergent	4/C	69	Dominie Press	Carousel Readers
Can You See Me?	Emergent	1/A	34	Sundance	AlphaKids
Car Ride, The	Emergent	2/A	41	Sundance	Little Red Readers
Cat and Dog	Emergent	3/C	71	Creative Teaching	Learn to Read
Cat On the Mat	Emergent	2/B	37	Oxford Univ. Press	Wildsmith, Brian
Cat Who Loved Red, The	Emergent	6/D	63	Seedling	Salem, L. & Stewart, J.
Cat, The	Emergent	A	42	University of Maine	Little Books for Early Readers
Chick and the Duckling, The	Emergent	6/D	112	Macmillan	Ginsburg, Mirra
Chinese New Year	Emergent	6/D	33	Pacific Learning	Ready to Read
Circus Train, The	Emergent	1/A	48	Sundance	Little Red Readers
City Mouse, Country Mouse	Emergent	4/D	87	Creative Teaching	Learn to Read
Cooking Thanksgiving Dinner	Emergent	5*	126	Pioneer Valley	Emergent/Set 2
Cool Off	Emergent	3–4*/C	37	Mondo	Bookshop
Copycat	Emergent	4/C	54	Wright Group	Story Box
Costumes	Emergent	3/C	23	Oxford Univ. Press	Oxford Reading Tree
Crazy Cats	Emergent	A	42	University of Maine	Little Books for Early Readers
Dad	Emergent	1/A	24	Rigby	PM Starters
Dad's Shirt	Emergent	6/F	38	Dominie Press	Joy Readers
Dan the Flying Man	Emergent	4/C	60	Wright Group	Read Togethers
Desert, The	Emergent	3/C	34	Dominie Press	Carousel Readers
Dog	Emergent	A		Scholastic	Guided Reading Program
Dogs	Emergent	1/A	34	Sundance	AlphaKids
Don't Be Late!	Emergent	D	112	Scholastic	Guided Reading Program
Don't Splash Me!	Emergent	1/A	24	Rigby	Windmill
Dressing Up	Emergent	1/A	12	Rigby	PM Starters
Eight Friends In All	Emergent	6/D	64	Modern Curriculum	Ready Readers
Emily Can't Sleep	Emergent	6*	124	Pioneer Valley	Emergent/Set 2
Emily's Babysitter	Emergent	4*/C	67	Pioneer Valley	Emergent/Set 1
Fall	Emergent	A	22	University of Maine	Little Books for Early Readers
Fall Harvest	Emergent	A	16	University of Maine	Little Books for Early Readers
Family Work and Fun	Emergent	3/4*	38	Sundance	Little Red Readers
Fantail, Fantail	Emergent	5/D	67	Pacific Learning	Ready to Read
Farm Concert, The	Emergent	5/D	74	Wright Group	Story Box
Farm in Spring	Emergent	5/D	69	Rigby	PM Starters
Farm, A	Emergent	A	28	University of Maine	Little Books for Early Readers

*Tentatively leveled

Title	Level	RR–GR Level	Words	Publisher	Series/Author
Farm, The	Emergent	A	28	University of Maine	Little Books for Early Readers
Farm, The	Emergent	1/A	14	Modern Curriculum	Ready Readers
Father Bear Goes Fishing	Emergent	5/D	98	Rigby	PM Story Books
First Day of School	Emergent	6/D	60	Dominie Press	Carousel Earlybirds
Fishing	Emergent	B	41	University of Maine	Little Books for Early Readers
Fishing	Emergent	4/C	63	Rigby	PM Starters
Five Little Ducks	Emergent	5	164	Random House	Raffi
Flying and Floating	Emergent	3/B	64	Sundance	Little Red Readers
Four Ice Creams	Emergent	4/C	61	Rigby	PM Starters
Fox, The	Emergent	4/C	24	Richard C. Owen	Books For Young Learners
Freddie the Frog	Emergent	6/D	132	Troll	First Start
Friends	Emergent	5*/D	57	Mondo	Bookshop
Friends	Emergent		42	Fairfax County	Books for Budding Readers
Frog and the Fly, The	Emergent	5/D	33	Oxford Univ. Press	Cat on the Mat Series
Fruit Salad	Emergent	1/A	22	Sundance	AlphaKids
Fruit Salad	Emergent	2*/B	15	Pioneer Valley	Early Emergent/Set 2
Fun With Hats	Emergent	2*/B	38	Mondo	Bookshop
Fun With Mo and Toots	Emergent	3/C	41	Pacific Learning	Ready to Read
Funny Faces and Funny Places	Emergent	6/D	45	Modern Curriculum	Ready Readers
Gabby Is Hungry	Emergent	4*/C	78	Pioneer Valley	Emergent/Set 1
George's Show and Tell	Emergent	5*	133	Pioneer Valley	Emergent/Set 2
Getting Ready	Emergent	B	29	University of Maine	Little Books for Early Readers
Getting Ready For School	Emergent	3/4*	39	Sundance	Little Red Readers
Ghost	Emergent	1/A	26	Wright Group	Story Box
Giant, The	Emergent	1/A	20	Dominie Press	Joy Readers
Glasses	Emergent	1/A	24	Sundance	AlphaKids
Going For a Ride	Emergent	3*/C	52	Pioneer Valley	Early Emergent/Set 1
Going For a Ride	Emergent	B	40	University of Maine	Little Books for Early Readers
Going Shopping	Emergent	5/B	105	Sundance	AlphaKids
Going Shopping	Emergent		45	Fairfax County	Books for Budding Readers
Going to McDonald's	Emergent		43	Fairfax County	Books for Budding Readers
Going to The Beach	Emergent	5/C	75	Dominie Press	Carousel Readers
Going to the Beach	Emergent	3/4*	44	Sundance	Little Red Readers
Going Up and Down	Emergent	2*/B	51	Pioneer Valley	Early Emergent/Set 1
Good Old Mom	Emergent	4/C	34	Oxford Univ. Press	Oxford Reading Tree
Good-bye, Zoo	Emergent	6/D	48	Modern Curriculum	Ready Readers
Goodnight, Little Bug	Emergent	6/D	54	Modern Curriculum	Ready Readers
Grandpa's Candy Store	Emergent	6/F	25	Richard C. Owen	Books For Young Learners
Grandpa's House	Emergent	2/A	47	Sundance	AlphaKids
Greedy Cat is Hungry	Emergent	6/D	103	Pacific Learning	Ready to Read
Haddie's Caps	Emergent	6/D	90	Modern Curriculum	Ready Readers
Hannah's Halloween	Emergent	A	14	University of Maine	Little Books for Early Readers
Hard at Work	Emergent	2*/B	66	Pioneer Valley	Early Emergent/Set 2
Hats Around the World	Emergent	B	59	Scholastic	Charlesworth, Liza
Have You Seen My Cat?	Emergent	2/B	93	Scholastic	Carle, Eric

*Tentatively leveled

Title	Level	RR–GR Level	Words	Publisher	Series/Author
Have You Seen My Duckling?	Emergent	2/B	28	Scholastic	Tafuri, Nancy
Headache, The	Emergent	2/B	20	Oxford Univ. Press	Oxford Reading Tree
Help Me	Emergent	5*/D	107	Pioneer Valley	Emergent/Set 1
Here Is…	Emergent	2/B	49	Dominie Press	Carousel Earlybirds
Hide and Seek	Emergent	D	63	Scholastic	Guided Reading Program
Hide and Seek	Emergent	5/D	108	Rigby	PM Extensions
Hogboggit	Emergent	6/D	65	Pacific Learning	Ready to Read
Home For Little Teddy, A	Emergent	5/D	53	Rigby	PM Extensions
Honk!	Emergent	2*/B	36	Mondo	Bookshop
Horace	Emergent	5/D	56	Wright Group	Story Box
Horrible Big Black Bug, The	Emergent	6/D	50	Rigby	Tadpoles
How Many Fish?	Emergent	B	30	Scholastic	Gossett, R. & Ballinger, M.
How Many Pets?	Emergent	5*/D	37	Mondo	Bookshop
I Am	Emergent	A		Scholastic	Guided Reading Program
I Am Thankful	Emergent	1/A	42	Dominie Press	Carousel Earlybirds
I Can Draw	Emergent	4/C	75	Dominie Press	Carousel Earlybirds
I Can Make Music	Emergent	2/B	41	Sundance	Little Red Readers
I Can Read	Emergent	2/B	38	Pacific Learning	Ready to Read
I Can See	Emergent	A		Scholastic	Guided Reading Program
I Can Swim	Emergent	6/D	61	Modern Curriculum	Ready Readers
I Can Wash	Emergent	4/C	66	Dominie Press	Carousel Earlybirds
I Can Write. Can You?	Emergent	2/B	30	Seedling	Stewart, J. & Salem, L.
I Can't Find My Roller Skates	Emergent	5/B	73	Sundance	AlphaKids
I Eat Leaves	Emergent	3*/C	47	Mondo	Bookshop
I Like	Emergent	3/C	24	Rigby	Literacy 2000
I Like	Emergent	A		Scholastic	Guided Reading Program
I Like Balloons	Emergent	1/A	27	Dominie Press	Reading Corners
I Like Painting	Emergent	4*	68	Sundance	Little Red Readers
I Like Shapes	Emergent	B	21	Scholastic	Armstrong, Shane
I Like to Count	Emergent	3/C	40	Modern Curriculum	Ready Readers
I Like to Eat	Emergent	1/A	41	Dominie Press	Reading Corners
I Like to Help	Emergent	B	46	University of Maine	Little Books for Early Readers
I Like to Paint	Emergent	1/A	29	Dominie Press	Reading Corners
I Like to Play	Emergent	3/C	50	Dominie Press	Carousel Readers
I Like to Read	Emergent	B	49	University of Maine	Little Books for Early Readers
I Love Bugs	Emergent	4*/C	40	Mondo	Bookshop
I Love Camping	Emergent	2*/B	34	Pioneer Valley	Early Emergent/Set 2
I Love Mud and Mud Loves Me	Emergent	D	121	Scholastic	Guided Reading Program
I Love My Family	Emergent	3/B	31	Wright Group	Sunshine
I Paint	Emergent	2/A	22	Rigby	Literacy Tree
I Read	Emergent	1/A	38	Dominie Press	Reading Corners
I See	Emergent	2*/B	29	Mondo	Bookshop
I Went Walking	Emergent	4/C	105	Harcourt Brace	Williams, Sue
I'm Brave	Emergent	2/A	35	Sundance	AlphaKids
I'm Hungry	Emergent	D	84	Scholastic	Guided Reading Program

*Tentatively leveled

Title	Level	RR–GR Level	Words	Publisher	Series/Author
Ice Cream	Emergent	1/A	41	Sundance	AlphaKids
In My Garden	Emergent	3/C	36	Dominie Press	Carousel Readers
In My School	Emergent	A	27	University of Maine	Little Books for Early Readers
In the City	Emergent	C	45	Scholastic	Pasternac, Susana
In the Forest	Emergent	B		Scholastic	Guided Reading Program
In the Woods	Emergent	2*/B	48	Mondo	Bookshop
Inside School	Emergent	A	35	University of Maine	Little Books for Early Readers
Is It Time?	Emergent	C	52	Scholastic	Reading Discovery
Is This a Monster?	Emergent	5*/C	93	Mondo	Bookshop
Jack's Seed	Emergent		56	Fairfax County	Books for Budding Readers
Jake	Emergent	A	35	University of Maine	Little Books for Early Readers
Jake Can Play	Emergent	B	42	University of Maine	Little Books for Early Readers
James is Hiding	Emergent	1/A	24	Rigby	Windmill
Jolly Roger, the Pirate	Emergent	6/D	138	Rigby	PM Extensions
Jordan is Hiding	Emergent	A	24	University of Maine	Little Books for Early Readers
Lazy Mary	Emergent	6/D	191	Wright Group	Story Box
Legs	Emergent	A		Scholastic	Guided Reading Program
Let's Move	Emergent	2/B	29	Modern Curriculum	Ready Readers
Let's Play Ball	Emergent	B	40	University of Maine	Little Books for Early Readers
Library, The	Emergent	6*/D	96	Pioneer Valley	Emergent/Set 1
Library, The	Emergent	3/C	33	Dominie Press	Carousel Readers
Little and Big	Emergent	2*	57	Sundance	Little Red Readers
Little Cousins' Visit, The	Emergent	5*/C	123	Pioneer Valley	Emergent/Set 1
Little Pig	Emergent	4/C	63	Wright Group	Story Box
Little Red Hen	Emergent	2/B	87	Wright Group	Windmill
Little Sister	Emergent	C	40	Scholastic	Mitchell, Robin
Living and Non Living	Emergent	2/A	30	Sundance	AlphaKids
Lizard Loses His Tail	Emergent	5/D	54	Rigby	PM Story Books
Lobstering	Emergent	A	14	University of Maine	Little Books for Early Readers
Look at Conor	Emergent	A	27	University of Maine	Little Books for Early Readers
Look at Kyle	Emergent	B	46	University of Maine	Little Books for Early Readers
Look at Me	Emergent	A	17	University of Maine	Little Books for Early Readers
Look at the Ocean, A	Emergent	B	50	University of Maine	Little Books for Early Readers
Look At This	Emergent	2/B	57	Dominie Press	Carousel Earlybirds
Look For Me	Emergent	5/D	71	Wright Group	Story Box
Looking for Fang	Emergent	5/B	185	Sundance	AlphaKids
Lost in the Fog	Emergent	5/D	59	Modern Curriculum	Ready Readers
Lost Mother, The	Emergent	6/C	108	Sundance	AlphaKids
Lots and Lots of Stairs	Emergent	B	33	University of Maine	Little Books for Early Readers
Lunch	Emergent	A		Scholastic	Guided Reading Program
Lunch at the Zoo	Emergent	B	64	Scholastic	Reading Discovery
Mailbox, The	Emergent	3/B	46	Sundance	AlphaKids
Making a Memory	Emergent	D	53	Scholastic	Guided Reading Program
Making Butter	Emergent	4/B	106	Sundance	AlphaKids
Making Lunch	Emergent	5/B	131	Sundance	AlphaKids

*Tentatively leveled

Title	Level	RR–GR Level	Words	Publisher	Series/Author
Making Mountains	Emergent	B	35	Scholastic	Ballinger, M. & Gossett, R.
Me	Emergent	1/A	24	Rigby	PM Starters
Meeka	Emergent		42	Fairfax County	Books for Budding Readers
Merry Go Round, The	Emergent	4/C	66	Dominie Press	Teacher's Choice
Merry-Go-Round, The	Emergent	3/C	84	Rigby	PM Story Books
Mess, A	Emergent	6/D	34	Modern Curriculum	Ready Readers
Mom Can Fix Anything	Emergent	4/D	74	Creative Teaching	Science II
Monkeys	Emergent	B	27	Scholastic	Canizares, S. & Chanko, P.
Monsters	Emergent	3/B	93	Sundance	AlphaKids
Moon, The	Emergent	6/D	139	Dominie Press	Joy Readers
Mouse's Baby Blanket	Emergent	6/D	68	Seedling	Swerdlow, Beverly Brown
Moving	Emergent	3/B	56	Sundance	Little Red Readers
Mrs. Wishy-Washy's Tub	Emergent	B	38	Wright Group	Story Box
My Baby Sister	Emergent	2/A	50	Sundance	AlphaKids
My Backyard	Emergent	A	14	University of Maine	Little Books for Early Readers
My Cat Muffin	Emergent	B	35	Scholastic	Gardner, Marjory
My Cats	Emergent	A		Scholastic	Guided Reading Program
My Circus Family	Emergent	3*/C	42	Mondo	Bookshop
My Dog	Emergent	2/3*/C	79	Pioneer Valley	Early Emergent/Set 1
My Five Senses	Emergent		59	Fairfax County	Books for Budding Readers
My Fort	Emergent	A	17	University of Maine	Little Books for Early Readers
My Home	Emergent	2/B	56	Wright Group	Sunshine
My House	Emergent	1/A	40	Dominie Press	Carousel Earlybirds
My Little Brother	Emergent	3/C	59	Wright Group	Windmill
My Little Brother Ben	Emergent	5/D	35	Richard C. Owen	Books For Young Learners
My Little Dog	Emergent	4/C	90	Rigby	PM Starters
My Little Sister	Emergent	5/D	44	Dominie Press	Joy Readers
My Lunch	Emergent	2/3*/C	70	Pioneer Valley	Early Emergent/Set 1
My Mom	Emergent	B	40	University of Maine	Little Books for Early Readers
My Monster and Me	Emergent	2/B	37	Modern Curriculum	Ready Readers
My New Bike	Emergent		33	Fairfax County	Books for Budding Readers
My Toys	Emergent	A	28	University of Maine	Little Books for Early Readers
New Cat, The	Emergent	2/B	29	Pacific Learning	Ready to Read
New Dog, A	Emergent	6/D	52	Oxford Univ. Press	Oxford Reading Tree
Nicole Helps Grandma	Emergent	B	35	University of Maine	Little Books for Early Readers
No Recess	Emergent		61	Fairfax County	Books for Budding Readers
Octopus Goes to School	Emergent	4/C	42	Seedling	Bordelon, Carolyn
Oh No!	Emergent	5*/E	127	Mondo	Bookshop
Old Tuatara	Emergent	4/C	33	Pacific Learning	Ready to Read
On the Playground	Emergent		44	Fairfax County	Books for Budding Readers
On Vacation	Emergent	4/D	88	Sundance	Little Red Readers
One Cold Wet Night	Emergent	6/D	134	Wright Group	Story Box
One For You, One For Me	Emergent	C	27	Scholastic	Blaxland, Wendy
One Frog, One Fly	Emergent		26	Scholastic	Reading Discovery
One Pig, Two Pigs	Emergent	2/B	142	Peguis	Tiger Cub

*Tentatively leveled

Title	Level	RR–GR Level	Words	Publisher	Series/Author
Our Dog Sam	Emergent	5/C	56	Rigby	Literacy Tree
Our Teacher, Miss Pool	Emergent	6/D	62	Pacific Learning	Ready to Read
Over the Bridge	Emergent	3/B	50	Sundance	Little Red Readers
Pancakes for Breakfast	Emergent	5*/C	108	Pioneer Valley	Emergent/Set 1
Party, The	Emergent	5/D	29	Modern Curriculum	Ready Readers
Party, The	Emergent	3/B	61	Sundance	AlphaKids
Pat's Perfect Pizza	Emergent	3/C	37	Modern Curriculum	Ready Readers
Paul's Day at School	Emergent	B	38	University of Maine	Little Books for Early Readers
Pepper Sees Me	Emergent	A	28	University of Maine	Little Books for Early Readers
Pet For Me, A	Emergent	3*/C	73	Pioneer Valley	Early Emergent/Set 1
Pet Shop, The	Emergent	4/C	32	Oxford Univ. Press	Oxford Reading Tree
Pigs Peek	Emergent	4/C	28	Richard C. Owen	Books For Young Learners
Pizza Day	Emergent		63	Fairfax County	Books For Budding Readers
Places	Emergent	3/4/C	88	Sundance	Little Red Readers
Plants	Emergent	5/B	122	Sundance	AlphaKids
Play Ball!	Emergent	5/D	30	Richard C. Owen	Books For Young Learners
Playground, The	Emergent	3*/C	108	Pioneer Valley	Early Emergent/Set 1
Playing	Emergent	1/A	31	Sundance	AlphaKids
Playing in the Snow	Emergent	3*/C	61	Pioneer Valley	Early Emergent/Set 1
Potato Harvest Time	Emergent	A	33	University of Maine	Little Books for Early Readers
Pumpkin Patch, The	Emergent		51	Fairfax County	Books for Budding Readers
Push!	Emergent	5/D	21	Oxford Univ. Press	Oxford Reading Tree
Race, The	Emergent	2/B	34	Rigby	Windmill
Rain	Emergent	4/B	140	Sundance	AlphaKids
Rain, Rain	Emergent	5/D	58	Pacific Learning	Ready to Read
Raindrops	Emergent	C	66	Scholastic	Gay, Sandy
Roberto's Snack	Emergent	4*		Pioneer Valley	Emergent/Set 2
Sammy at the Farm	Emergent	6/C	83	Kaeden	Urmston, K. & Evans, K.
Sandwiches	Emergent	2/A	59	Sundance	AlphaKids
Saturday Mornings	Emergent	5–6*/D	63	Mondo	Bookshop
Scarecrow, The	Emergent	5/D	97	Sundance	Little Red Readers
Seesaw, The	Emergent	4*/C	100	Pioneer Valley	Emergent/Set 1
Shadows	Emergent		46	Fairfax County	Books for Budding Readers
Shark In a Sack	Emergent	4/C	65	Wright Group	Sunshine
Shopping	Emergent	4/C	78	Sundance	Little Red Readers
Ski School	Emergent	A	34	University of Maine	Little Books for Early Readers
Sky Is Falling Down, The	Emergent	5/D	101	Dominie Press	Joy Readers
Sleeping Animals	Emergent	6/C	193	Sundance	AlphaKids
Smile! said Dad	Emergent	6/D	66	Pacific Learning	Ready to Read
Smile, The	Emergent	6/D	53	Pacific Learning	Ready to Read
Space Aliens in Our School	Emergent	5/D	45	Dominie Press	Joy Readers
Splash!	Emergent		32	Fairfax County	Books for Budding Readers
Splashing Dad	Emergent	2/3*/C	37	Pioneer Valley	Early Emergent/Set 1
Springs	Emergent	6/C	128	Sundance	AlphaKids
Story Time	Emergent	C	32	Modern Curriculum	Emergent/Set 2

*Tentatively leveled

Title	Level	RR–GR Level	Words	Publisher	Series/Author
Strange Plants	Emergent	5/E	30	Richard C. Owen	Books For Young Learners
Sunflowers	Emergent	4/E	33	Richard C. Owen	Books For Young Learners
Swing, Swing, Swing	Emergent	C	93	Scholastic	Tuchman, Gail
Tadpoles and Frogs	Emergent	5/B	41	Sundance	AlphaKids
Taking Pictures	Emergent	6/C	137	Sundance	AlphaKids
Ted's Red Sled	Emergent	6/D	69	Modern Curriculum	Ready Readers
Terrific Shoes	Emergent	3/C	19	Modern Curriculum	Ready Readers
That Fly	Emergent	3/C	29	Modern Curriculum	Ready Readers
There Are Spots On…	Emergent	A	14	University of Maine	Little Books for Early Readers
There's a Mouse In the House	Emergent	2*/B	42	Mondo	Bookshop
Things on Wheels	Emergent	3/C	69	Sundance	Little Red Readers
Things to Read	Emergent	A	18	University of Maine	Little Books for Early Readers
Things to See in Maine	Emergent	A	14	University of Maine	Little Books for Early Readers
This Game	Emergent	2/B	63	Dominie Press	Carousel Earlybirds
This is Lobstering	Emergent	A	27	University of Maine	Little Books for Early Readers
Tickling	Emergent	4/B	74	Sundance	AlphaKids
Time For a Change	Emergent	4/C	31	Pacific Learning	Ready to Read
Too Busy	Emergent	3/B	50	Sundance	AlphaKids
Too High!	Emergent	5/D	66	Modern Curriculum	Ready Readers
Transportation Museum, The	Emergent	4/C	79	Sundance	Little Red Readers
Tree Fell Over the River, A	Emergent	3*/C	72	Sundance	Little Red Readers
Tree, The	Emergent	6/C	94	Sundance	AlphaKids
Trolley Ride, The	Emergent	4/C	87	Rigby	Tadpoles
Trucks	Emergent	A	35	University of Maine	Little Books for Early Readers
Twins	Emergent	4/B	76	Sundance	AlphaKids
Two Points	Emergent	2/B	40	Seedling	Kennedy, J. & Eaton, A.
Up and Down	Emergent	B	25	University of Maine	Little Books for Early Readers
Up In a Tree	Emergent	4/C	47	Wright Group	Sunshine
Vacation, The	Emergent	4*/C	94	Pioneer Valley	Emergent/Set 1
Very Big	Emergent	6/D	49	Modern Curriculum	Ready Readers
Visit to the Doctor, A	Emergent	A	22	University of Maine	Little Books for Early Readers
Walking in the Jungle	Emergent	5/6*	113	Sundance	Little Red Readers
Way I Go To School, The	Emergent	2/B	53	Rigby	PM Starters
We are Twins	Emergent	A	24	University of Maine	Little Books for Early Readers
We Can Make Pizza	Emergent	A	30	University of Maine	Little Books for Early Readers
We Go To School	Emergent	2/B	27	Dominie Press	Carousel Earlybirds
We Like Fruit	Emergent	A		Scholastic	Guided Reading Program
We Went to the Movies	Emergent		26	Fairfax County	Books for Budding Readers
We Went to the Zoo	Emergent	2/B	32	Sundance	Little Red Readers
Weather	Emergent	C	54	Scholastic	Chanko, P. & Moreton, D.
Week With Aunt Bea, A	Emergent	5*/D	62	Mondo	Bookshop
What a Bad Dog!	Emergent	6/D	52	Oxford Univ. Press	Oxford Reading Tree
What Can She Do?	Emergent	A	21	University of Maine	Little Books for Early Readers
What Comes Out at Night?	Emergent	2/B	48	Sundance	Little Red Readers
What Do Insects Do?	Emergent	A	24	Scholastic	Canizares, S. & Chanko, P.

*Tentatively leveled

Title	Level	RR–GR Level	Words	Publisher	Series/Author
What Do You Like?	Emergent	B	52	University of Maine	Little Books for Early Readers
What Does Greedy Cat Like?	Emergent	3/C	35	Pacific Learning	Ready to Read
What Has Stripes?	Emergent	C	28	Scholastic	Ballinger, Margaret
What I Like at School	Emergent	3/C	64	Sundance	Little Red Readers
What is Big?	Emergent	D	72	Scholastic	Guided Reading Program
What Is Green?	Emergent	2/B	30	Dominie Press	Carousel Readers
What is It?	Emergent		31	Fairfax County	Books for Budding Readers
What Is This?	Emergent	A	23	University of Maine	Little Books for Early Readers
What's For Dinner?	Emergent	3/B	38	Sundance	AlphaKids
What's That Noise?	Emergent	4/B	102	Sundance	AlphaKids
What's This? What's That?	Emergent	2/A	35	Sundance	AlphaKids
When Goldilocks Went to the House of the Bears	Emergent	6*/F	156	Mondo	Bookshop
When the Circus Comes to Town	Emergent	2/A	40	Sundance	Little Red Readers
Where Are the Car Keys?	Emergent	2/B	36	Rigby	Windmill
Where are We?	Emergent	2*/B	72	Pioneer Valley	Early Emergent/Set 1
Where Are You Going, Aja Rose?	Emergent	6/D	100	Wright Group	Sunshine
Where Can a Hippo Hide?	Emergent	5/D	41	Modern Curriculum	Ready Readers
Where Does the Teacher Sleep?	Emergent	4/C	50	Seedling	Gibson, K.
Where is Hannah?	Emergent	5/D	141	Rigby	PM Extensions
Where is Miss Pool?	Emergent	6/D	55	Pacific Learning	Ready to Read
Where is My Teacher?	Emergent	B	43	University of Maine	Little Books for Early Readers
Where is She?	Emergent	A	35	University of Maine	Little Books for Early Readers
Where's the Baby?	Emergent	6/C	138	Sundance	AlphaKids
Who Can?	Emergent	2*/B	35	Mondo	Bookshop
Who Cried Pie?	Emergent	5/D	86	Troll	First Start
Who Helps You?	Emergent		33	Fairfax County	Books for Budding Readers
Who Lives in a Tree?	Emergent	B	46	Scholastic	Guided Reading Program
Who Lives in the Artic?	Emergent	B	48	Scholastic	Guided Reading Program
Who Lives in the Sea?	Emergent	2*/B	69	Mondo	Bookshop
Who Made That?	Emergent	3/C	31	Modern Curriculum	Ready Readers
Who Will Help?	Emergent	2/B	20	Dominie Press	Carousel Readers
Winter is Here!	Emergent	D	55	Scholastic	Guided Reading Program
Wobbly Tooth, The	Emergent	6/D	102	Rigby	Literacy Tree
Worms Are Everywhere	Emergent		66	Fairfax County	Books for Budding Readers
Yes, I Can!	Emergent	5/D	45	Modern Curriculum	Ready Readers
You Can Play Soccer	Emergent		37	Fairfax County	Books for Budding Readers
Zack's House	Emergent	6*	114	Pioneer Valley	Emergent/Set 2
Zippers	Emergent	3/C	21	Richard C. Owen	Books For Young Learners
Zoe's Birthday Presents	Emergent	6*	83	Pioneer Valley	Emergent/Set 1
1 is One	Progressing	7–8*/E	82	Mondo	Bookshop
All By Myself	Progressing	8/E	157	Golden	Mayer, Mercer
Along Came Greedy Cat	Progressing	11/G	166	Pacific Learning	Ready to Read
Amanda's Bear	Progressing	12/G	154	Dominie Press	Reading Corners
And Billy Went Out to Play	Progressing	10–11/I	227	Mondo	Bookshop
Animal Babies	Progressing	8/E	114	Children's Press	Rookie Reader

* Tentatively leveled

Title	Level	RR–GR Level	Words	Publisher	Series/Author
Animal Skeletons	Progressing	8/C	115	Sundance	AlphaKids
Animals at the Zoo	Progressing	10/F	158	Troll	First Start
Ants and the Grasshopper	Progressing	12–13/G	144	Steck-Vaughn	New Way
Ants Go Marching, The	Progressing			Wright Group	Song Box
Art	Progressing	12/E	238	Sundance	AlphaKids
Artist, The	Progressing	9/F	83	Richard C. Owen	Books For Young Learners
Ask Nicely	Progressing	10/F	110	Rigby	Literacy 2000
At the Beach	Progressing	8/E	84	Oxford Univ. Press	Oxford Reading Tree
At the Pool	Progressing	8/E	87	Oxford Univ. Press	Oxford Reading Tree
Awful Waffles	Progressing	16–17/G	296	Seedling	Williams, Deborah Holt
Bath For Patches, A	Progressing	8 /E	89	Dominie Press	Carousel Readers
Beaks and Feet	Progressing	11/D	244	Sundance	AlphaKids
Beautiful Bugs	Progressing	F	69	Scholastic	Guided Reading Program
Bedtime Story, A	Progressing	12*/K	335	Mondo	Bookshop
Best Birthday Mole Ever Had	Progressing	8/E	252	Modern Curriculum	Ready Readers
Betsy the Babysitter	Progressing	10/F	115	Troll	First Start
Big Box, The	Progressing	11/G	183	Steck-Vaughn	New Way
Big Red Fire Engine	Progressing	12/G	158	Troll	First Start
Biggest Cake in the World, The	Progressing	9 /F	120	Pacific Learning	Ready to Read
Billy Goats Gruff	Progressing	10 /F	381	Ladybird	Read It Yourself
Birthday Bird, The	Progressing	11/F	82	Richard C. Owen	Books for Young Learners
Birthday In the Woods, A	Progressing	13–14/F	199	Seedling	Salem, Lynn
Blackbird's Nest	Progressing	12/G	71	Pacific Learning	Ready to Read
BMX Billy	Progressing	11/G	93	Rigby	Literacy 2000
Bobbie's Airplane	Progressing	7/E	64	Oxford Univ. Press	Oxford Reading Tree
Book Week	Progressing	8/E	71	Oxford Univ. Press	Oxford Reading Tree
Bread, Bread, Bread	Progressing	F	95	Scholastic	Guided Reading Program
Bruno's Birthday	Progressing	8/E	32	Rigby	Literacy 2000
Brutus Learns to Fetch	Progressing	9/10*	155	Sundance	Little Red Readers
Bull's-Eye!	Progressing	8/F	87	Oxford Univ. Press	Oxford Reading Tree
Buzzzzzz Said the Bee	Progressing	G	62	Scholastic	Guided Reading Program
By the Stream	Progressing	8/E	73	Oxford Univ. Press	Oxford Reading Tree
Camping	Progressing	7*/D	64	Kaeden	Hooker, Karen
Carla's Breakfast	Progressing	12 /G	225	Kaeden	Harper, Leslie
Carla's Ribbon	Progressing	11/G	212	Kaeden	Harper, Leslie
Carnival, The	Progressing	9/F	82	Oxford Univ. Press	Oxford Reading Tree
Carrot Seed, The	Progressing	12/G	101	HarperCollins	Krauss, Ruth
Cat Chat	Progressing	9/F	85	Modern Curriculum	Ready Readers
Cat in the Tree, A	Progressing	9/F	79	Oxford Univ. Press	Oxford Reading Tree
Cat That Broke the Rules, The	Progressing	11/G	192	Modern Curriculum	Ready Readers
Catch That Frog	Progressing	8/E	131	Celebration Press	Reading Unlimited
Cats and Kittens	Progressing	9/F	51	Celebration Press	Reading Unlimited
Cement Tent	Progressing	12/G	358	Troll	First Start
Changing Caterpillar, The	Progressing	12/G	56	Richard C. Owen	Books for Young Learners
Chase, The	Progressing	8/F	85	Oxford Univ. Press	Oxford Reading Tree

*Tentatively leveled

Title	Level	RR–GR Level	Words	Publisher	Series/Author
Chickens	Progressing	8/D	23	Richard C. Owen	Books For Young Learners
Chickens	Progressing	12*/G	105	Mondo	Bookshop
Choosing a Puppy	Progressing	7/E	158	Rigby	PM Extensions
City Sounds	Progressing	G	142	Scholastic	Guided Reading Program
Coat Full of Bubbles, A	Progressing	10/G	72	Richard C. Owen	Books For Young Learners
Cold Day, The	Progressing	9/F	80	Oxford Univ. Press	Oxford Reading Tree
Collections	Progressing	E		Scholastic	Guided Reading Program
Coo Coo Caroo	Progressing	12/G	79	Richard C. Owen	Books For Young Learners
Cook-Out, The	Progressing	9/E	78	Oxford Univ. Press	Oxford Reading Tree
Cookie's Week	Progressing	10/F	84	Scholastic	Ward, Cindy
Cooking Pot, The	Progressing	10/F	132	Wright Group	Sunshine
Cow in the Garden, The	Progressing	8/E	158	Steck-Vaughn	New Way
Cows in the Garden	Progressing	11/G	163	Rigby	PM Story Books
Crazy Quilt, The	Progressing	11/G	148	Celebration Press	Little Celebrations
Crunchy Munchy	Progressing	12*/G	189	Mondo	Bookshop
Dad's Headache	Progressing	10/F	86	Wright Group	Sunshine
Dark, Dark Tale, A	Progressing	10/F	115	Penguin	Brown, Ruth
Dear Zoo	Progressing	9 /F	115	Macmillan	Campbell, Rod
Dee and Me	Progressing	12/G	189	Modern Curriculum	Ready Readers
Did You Say "Fire"?	Progressing	11/G	158	Pacific Learning	Ready to Read
Dinosaurs Galore	Progressing	4–5/D	34	Seedling	Eaton, A. & Kennedy, J.
Dive In!	Progressing	9/F	133	Modern Curriculum	Ready Readers
Dog at School	Progressing	10/F	94	Richard C. Owen	Books For Young Learners
Don't Panic!	Progressing	8/E	122	Wright Group	Book Bank
Don't You Laugh at Me!	Progressing	7/E	167	Wright Group	Sunshine
Down at the River	Progressing	8/E	51	Pacific Learning	Ready to Read
Dragon Flies	Progressing	11/G	53	Richard C. Owen	Books For Young Learners
Dragon Hunt, The	Progressing	9/F	53	Steck-Vaughn	New Way
Dragon's Lunch	Progressing	9/F	85	Modern Curriculum	Ready Readers
Drawbridge	Progressing	7/E	29	Richard C. Owen	Books For Young Learners
Dream, The	Progressing	9/F	54	Oxford Univ. Press	Oxford Reading Tree
Dreams	Progressing	8 /E	93	Wright Group	Book Bank
Dressed Up Sammy	Progressing	7/E	91	Kaeden	Urmston, K. & Evans, K.
Each Peach Pear Plum	Progressing	11/G	115	Penguin	Ahlberg, A. & J.
Elves and Shoemaker, The	Progressing	10	317	Ladybird	Read It Yourself
Excuses, Excuses	Progressing	8/E	104	Rigby	Tadpoles
Farmer and the Skunk	Progressing	8 /E	127	Peguis	Tiger Cub
Farmer Had a Pig	Progressing	11/G	149	Peguis	Tiger Cub
Fire, Fire	Progressing	8/E	164	Rigby	PM Story Books
Fishing	Progressing	7/D	48	Kaeden	Yukish, J.
Five Little Dinosaurs	Progressing	8/E	113	Modern Curriculum	Ready Readers
Five Little Monkeys	Progressing	8*/F	81	Mondo	Bookshop
Five Little Monkeys Going to the Zoo	Progressing	8–9/E	201	Seedling	Cutteridge's 1st Grade, V.
Five Little Monkeys Jumping On The Bed	Progressing	8/E	200	Clarion	Christelow, Eileen
Flip Flop	Progressing	11/G	70	Richard C. Owen	Books For Young Learners

*Tentatively leveled

Title	Level	RR–GR Level	Words	Publisher	Series/Author
Floating and Sinking	Progressing	11/D	220	Sundance	AlphaKids
Floppy the Hero	Progressing	9/F	74	Oxford Univ. Press	Oxford Reading Tree
Floppy's Bath	Progressing	8/E	55	Oxford Univ. Press	Oxford Reading Tree
Forgetful Fred	Progressing	7/E	78	Rigby	Tadpoles
Four Getters and Arf, The	Progressing	11/G	123	Celebration Press	Little Celebrations
Fox and the Crow, The	Progressing	9/D	201	Sundance	AlphaKids
Free to Fly	Progressing	8–9/E	96	Seedling	Gibson, Kathleen
Friend For Little White Rabbit	Progressing	8/E	113	Rigby	PM Story Books
Friendly Snowman	Progressing	11/F	134	Troll	First Start
Friends	Progressing	12/G	195	Celebration Press	Reading Unlimited
Fun Place to Eat, A	Progressing	7/E	90	Modern Curriculum	Ready Readers
Funny Man, A	Progressing	E	244	Scholastic	Guided Reading Program
Gecko's Story	Progressing	12/F	61	Richard C. Owen	Books for Young Learners
Get Lost, Becka!	Progressing	8/E	102	School Zone	Start to Read
Giant Gingerbread Man, The	Progressing	9/D	243	Sundance	AlphaKids
Gingerbread Boy, The	Progressing	10–11/F	137	Steck-Vaughn	New Way
Good Catch!, A	Progressing	6–7/E	191	Steck-Vaughn	New Way
Grandmother	Progressing	7/E	60	Dominie Press	Joy Readers
Grandpa, Grandpa	Progressing	11/G	122	Wright Group	Read-Togethers
Great Day	Progressing	10/D	162	Sundance	AlphaKids
Greedy Cat	Progressing	11/G	166	Pacific Learning	Ready to Read
Greedy Gray Octopus, The	Progressing	12/G	195	Rigby	Tadpoles
Green	Progressing	12/E	174	Sundance	AlphaKids
Green Eyes	Progressing	10/F	111	Rigby	Literacy 2000
Green Footprints	Progressing	7/E	42	Rigby	Literacy 2000
Growing Tomatoes	Progressing	8/C	92	Sundance	AlphaKids
Grumpy Elephant	Progressing	7/E	100	Wright Group	Story Box
Hairy Bear	Progressing	11/G	109	Wright Group	Read-Togethers
Henry	Progressing	8/E	77	Richard C. Owen	Books For Young Learners
Hermit Crab, The	Progressing	12/G	119	Wright Group	Sunshine
How Far Will I Fly?	Progressing	F	94	Scholastic	Guided Reading Program
How Have I Grown?	Progressing	G	235	Scholastic	Guided Reading Program
How the Chick Tricked the Fox	Progressing	12/G	167	Modern Curriculum	Ready Readers
Hunt For Clues, A	Progressing	12/G	157	Modern Curriculum	Ready Readers
I Got a Goldfish	Progressing	8/E	92	Modern Curriculum	Ready Readers
I Love Camping	Progressing	8/E	83	Dominie Press	Carousel Readers
I Shop With My Daddy	Progressing	G	131	Scholastic	Guided Reading Program
I'm a Big Brother	Progressing		79	Fairfax County	Books for Budding Readers
I'm a Caterpillar	Progressing	G	169	Scholastic	Guided Reading Program
I'm King of the Mountain	Progressing	12/G	285	Pacific Learning	Ready to Read
Is Tomorrow My Birthday?	Progressing	E	87	Scholastic	Guided Reading Program
Itchy, Itchy Chicken Pox	Progressing	F	131	Scholastic	Guided Reading Program
Jan and the Jacket	Progressing	7/E	74	Oxford Univ. Press	Oxford Reading Tree
Jigaree, The	Progressing	7/E	128	Wright Group	Story Box
Jim's Visit to Kim	Progressing	12/G	149	Modern Curriculum	Ready Readers

*Tentatively leveled

Title	Level	RR–GR Level	Words	Publisher	Series/Author
Joe and the BMX Bike	Progressing	8/E	91	Oxford Univ. Press	Oxford Reading Tree
Joe and the Mouse	Progressing	10/F	138	Oxford Univ. Press	Oxford Reading Tree
Just a Seed	Progressing	E	74	Scholastic	Guided Reading Program
Just Like Grandpa	Progressing	8/E	81	Rigby	Literacy Tree
Just Like Me	Progressing	7/E	138	Children's Press	Rookie Reader
Just Like Us	Progressing	7/E	55	Modern Curriculum	Ready Readers
Kate's Skates	Progressing		80	Scholastic	Reading Discovery
Katie Did It	Progressing	7/G	105	Children's Press	Rookie Reader
Katydids	Progressing	7/E	20	Richard C. Owen	Books For Young Learners
Late For Soccer	Progressing	11/F	185	Rigby	PM Story Books
Lion and the Mouse, The	Progressing	10/F	115	Steck-Vaughn	New Way
Lion's Tail, The	Progressing	9/F	147	Celebration Press	Reading Unlimited
Little Bulldozer Helps Again	Progressing	9/F	197	Rigby	PM Extensions
Little Monkey	Progressing	11/D	315	Sundance	AlphaKids
Lost at the Fun Park	Progressing	9/F	192	Rigby	PM Extensions
Lucky Day For Little Dinosaur, A	Progressing	8/F	135	Rigby	PM Extensions
Lucky Duck, The	Progressing	7/E	73	Modern Curriculum	Ready Readers
Lucky Goes to Dog School	Progressing	7/E	127	Rigby	PM Story Books
Lydia and Her Garden	Progressing	11/G	88	Oxford Univ. Press	Oxford Reading Tree
Lydia and Her Kitten	Progressing	12/G	77	Oxford Univ. Press	Oxford Reading Tree
Lydia and the Ducks	Progressing	11/G	87	Oxford Univ. Press	Oxford Reading Tree
Lydia and the Present	Progressing	9/F	77	Oxford Univ. Press	Oxford Reading Tree
Mai-Li's Surprise	Progressing	7/F	61	Richard C. Owen	Books For Young Learners
Making Concrete	Progressing	9/D	134	Sundance	AlphaKids
Meanies	Progressing	8/F	158	Wright Group	Story Box
Meeka Goes Swimming	Progressing		65	Fairfax County	Books for Budding Readers
Meet Mr. Cricket	Progressing	8/E	86	Dominie Press	Carousel Readers
Message on a Rocket	Progressing	12/E	174	Sundance	AlphaKids
Messages	Progressing	F	79	Scholastic	Guided Reading Program
Messy Mark	Progressing	9/F	180	Troll	First Start
Michael in the Hospital	Progressing	8/E	91	Oxford Univ. Press	Oxford Reading Tree
Mike's First Haircut	Progressing	9/G	136	Troll	First Start
Mike's New Bike	Progressing	9/F	183	Troll	First Start
Monkey See, Monkey Do	Progressing	F	89	Scholastic	Guided Reading Program
Monster Math Picnic	Progressing	F	98	Scholastic	Guided Reading Program
Monster Math School Time	Progressing	G	120	Scholastic	Guided Reading Program
Mr. Cricket Finds a Friend	Progressing	11/G	134	Dominie Press	Carousel Readers
Mr. Cricket's New Home	Progressing	10/F	121	Dominie Press	Carousel Readers
Mr. Cricket Takes a Vacation	Progressing	8/E	165	Dominie Press	Carousel Readers
Mr. Wolf Leaves Town	Progressing	10/D	211	Sundance	AlphaKids
Mr. Wolf Tries Again	Progressing	9/D	215	Sundance	AlphaKids
Mrs. Wishy-Washy	Progressing	8/E	102	Wright Group	Story Box
My Bike	Progressing	8/D	108	Pacific Learning	Ready to Read
My Brother Wants to Be Like Me	Progressing	8/D	62	Kaeden	Mader, Jan
My Bug Box	Progressing	7/E	98	Richard C. Owen	Books For Young Learners

*Tentatively leveled

Title	Level	RR–GR Level	Words	Publisher	Series/Author
My Dad's Truck	Progressing	E	57	Scholastic	Guided Reading Program
My Dog's The Best	Progressing	F	175	Scholastic	Guided Reading Program
My Friends	Progressing	G	152	Scholastic	Guided Reading Program
My Grandpa	Progressing	9*/F	75	Mondo	Bookshop
My Lost Top	Progressing	7/E	70	Modern Curriculum	Ready Readers
My New School	Progressing		63	Fairfax County	Books for Budding Readers
My Shadow	Progressing	10/F	116	Modern Curriculum	Ready Readers
My Shadow	Progressing	8/E	116	Pacific Learning	Ready to Read
New York City Buildings	Progressing	12/F	59	Richard C. Owen	Books For Young Learners
Nick's Glasses	Progressing	7/E	51	Pacific Learning	Ready to Read
Nicky Upstairs and Down	Progressing	12/G	179	Penguin	Ziefert, Harriet
Night Walk	Progressing	9/F	51	Richard C. Owen	Books For Young Learners
No Dogs Allowed	Progressing	10/F	73	Richard C. Owen	Books For Young Learners
No Luck	Progressing	10/F	120	Seedling	Stewart, J. & Salem, L.
No Singing Today	Progressing	12–13*/H	419	Mondo	Bookshop
Not Enough Water	Progressing	D	84	Scholastic	Reading Discovery
Notes From Mom	Progressing	10/F	99	Seedling	Salem, L. & Stewart, J.
Notes to Dad	Progressing	9/F	114	Seedling	Stewart, J. & Salem, L.
Nothing In the Mailbox	Progressing	9/F	73	Richard C. Owen	Books For Young Learners
Oh, No, Sherman!	Progressing	7/E	66	Seedling	Erickson, Betty
Old Train, The	Progressing	11/F	68	Richard C. Owen	Books For Young Learners
On Top of Spaghetti	Progressing	11/G	105	Celebration Press	Little Celebrations
One Hot Summer Night	Progressing	10*/I	126	Mondo	Bookshop
One Sock, Two Socks	Progressing	12/H	285	Dominie Press	Reading Corners
Our House Had a Mouse	Progressing	8/E	102	Seedling	Worthington, Denise
Paco's Garden	Progressing	12/G	120	Richard C. Owen	Books For Young Learners
Pancakes!	Progressing	10/F	106	Modern Curriculum	Ready Readers
Papa's Spaghetti	Progressing	12/G	248	Rigby	Literacy 2000
Paper Bag Trail	Progressing	E	67	Scholastic	Guided Reading Program
Pat's New Puppy	Progressing	7/E	88	Celebration Press	Reading Unlimited
Pet For Me, A	Progressing	8/C	145	Sundance	AlphaKids
Pete Little	Progressing	12/G	222	Rigby	PM Story Books
Pip and the Little Monkey	Progressing	10/F	111	Oxford Univ. Press	Oxford Reading Tree
Pip at the Zoo	Progressing	9/F	69	Oxford Univ. Press	Oxford Reading Tree
Play Ball, Sherman	Progressing	8–9/F	88	Seedling	Erickson, Betty
Polly's Shop	Progressing	7/E	130	Modern Curriculum	Ready Readers
Praying Mantis, The	Progressing	8/D	46	Pacific Learning	Ready to Read
Quack!	Progressing	7/E	54	Modern Curriculum	Ready Readers
Rainforest Plants	Progressing	10/D	145	Sundance	AlphaKids
Red and I Visit the Vet	Progressing	10/F	196	Modern Curriculum	Ready Readers
Red Rose, The	Progressing	7/E	127	Wright Group	Story Box
Red Socks and Yellow Socks	Progressing	12/G	155	Wright Group	Sunshine
Roads and Bridges	Progressing	11/D	253	Sundance	AlphaKids
Rope Swing, The	Progressing	7/E	77	Oxford Univ. Press	Oxford Reading Tree
Rosie's Walk	Progressing	9/F	32	Scholastic	Hutchins, Pat

*Tentatively leveled

Title	Level	RR–GR Level	Words	Publisher	Series/Author
Roy and the Parakeet	Progressing	8/E	74	Oxford Univ. Press	Oxford Reading Tree
Roy at the Fun Park	Progressing	11/G	111	Oxford Univ. Press	Oxford Reading Tree
Rummage Sale, The	Progressing	8/E	81	Oxford Univ. Press	Oxford Reading Tree
Rush, Rush, Rush	Progressing	8/E	52	Modern Curriculum	Ready Readers
Sally and the Sparrows	Progressing	7/E	151	Rigby	PM Extensions
Sally's Space Ship	Progressing	7/E	87	Modern Curriculum	Ready Readers
Sam's Mask	Progressing	7/E	36	Pacific Learning	Ready to Read
Sammy Gets a Ride	Progressing	10/F	91	Kaeden	Evans, K. & Urmston, K.
Sarah and Will	Progressing	10/D	258	Sundance	AlphaKids
Say It, Sign It	Progressing	G	169	Scholastic	Guided Reading Program
Scare and Dare	Progressing	9/D	281	Sundance	AlphaKids
School Bus Ride, The	Progressing	10/11*	160	Sundance	Little Red Readers
Sea Star, A	Progressing	7/E	82	Modern Curriculum	Ready Readers
Sebastian	Progressing	9/D	158	Sundance	AlphaKids
Sebastian Gets the Hiccups	Progressing	12/E	320	Sundance	AlphaKids
Secret Soup	Progressing	8/E	51	Rigby	Literacy Tree
Shadow Puppets	Progressing	7/C	162	Sundance	AlphaKids
Shell Shopping	Progressing	9/F	145	Modern Curriculum	Ready Readers
Shoes	Progressing	8/D	79	Wright Group	Book Bank
Shoveling Snow	Progressing	F	109	Scholastic	Guided Reading Program
Show and Tell	Progressing	8/C	213	Sundance	AlphaKids
Sick in Bed	Progressing	9/F	109	Sundance	Little Red Readers
Sing a Song	Progressing	7/E	154	Wright Group	Story Box
Skipper's Birthday	Progressing	8/E	64	Oxford Univ. Press	Oxford Reading Tree
Skipper's Idea	Progressing	10/F	81	Oxford Univ. Press	Oxford Reading Tree
Skipper's Laces	Progressing	9/F	66	Oxford Univ. Press	Oxford Reading Tree
Small Baby Raccoon, A	Progressing	11/G	104	Modern Curriculum	Ready Readers
Snake's Dinner	Progressing	7/C	156	Sundance	AlphaKids
Snowman, The	Progressing	8/E	76	Oxford Univ. Press	Oxford Reading Tree
Snowy Gets a Wash	Progressing	8/F	181	Rigby	PM Extensions
Soccer at the Park	Progressing	8/F	131	Rigby	PM Extensions
Socks Off!	Progressing	10/D	178	Sundance	AlphaKids
Sooty	Progressing	12/E	218	Sundance	AlphaKids
Sparrows, The	Progressing	11/F	60	Richard C. Owen	Books For Young Learners
Spots!	Progressing	8/E	53	Oxford Univ. Press	Oxford Reading Tree
Staying With Grandma Norma	Progressing	10/F	168	Seedling	Salem, L. & Stewart, J.
Steve's Room	Progressing	12/G	171	Modern Curriculum	Ready Readers
Stew For Igor's Mom, A	Progressing	12/G	162	Modern Curriculum	Ready Readers
Stop That Rabbit	Progressing	12/G	168	Troll	First Start
Storm, The	Progressing	11/G	75	Richard C. Owen	Books For Young Learners
Strawberry Jam	Progressing	8/E	77	Oxford Univ. Press	Oxford Reading Tree
Strongest Animal, The	Progressing	7/F	58	Richard C. Owen	Books For Young Learners
Stubborn Goat, The	Progressing	11/D	222	Sundance	AlphaKids
Summer at Cove Lake	Progressing	11/G	288	Modern Curriculum	Ready Readers
Super Pig's Adventure	Progressing	8–9/E	133	Steck-Vaughn	New Way

*Tentatively leveled

Title	Level	RR–GR Level	Words	Publisher	Series/Author
Susie Goes Shopping	Progressing	10/F	194	Troll	First Start
T-Shirts	Progressing	9/F	112	Pacific Learning	Ready to Read
Taking Care of Rosie	Progressing	7/E	61	Seedling	Salem, L. & Stewart, J.
Tarantula	Progressing	11/D	140	Sundance	AlphaKids
Tarantulas Are Spiders	Progressing	9*/F	39	Mondo	Bookshop
Teasing Dad	Progressing	9/F	158	Rigby	PM Extensions
Thank You, Nicky!	Progressing	10/F	119	Penguin	Ziefert, Harriet
That Cat!	Progressing	12/G	146	Modern Curriculum	Ready Readers
That Pig Can't Do a Thing	Progressing	10/F	83	Modern Curriculum	Ready Readers
Thomas Had a Temper	Progressing	8/C	137	Sundance	AlphaKids
Three Billy Goats Gruff, The	Progressing	8/E	123	Modern Curriculum	Ready Readers
Three Billy Goats Gruff, The	Progressing	11	387	Scholastic	Blair, Susan
Three Little Pigs, The	Progressing	8/C	272	Sundance	AlphaKids
Three Little Pigs, The	Progressing		159	Fairfax County	Books for Budding Readers
Three Little Witches	Progressing	12/G	189	Troll	First Start
Tiger Dave	Progressing	12/G	33	Richard C. Owen	Books For Young Learners
Tiny and the Big Wave	Progressing	8/F	163	Rigby	PM Extensions
Titch	Progressing	12/G	121	Penguin	Hutchins, Pat
Too Many Animals	Progressing	7/C	111	Sundance	AlphaKids
Too Many Bones	Progressing	12/G	125	Steck-Vaughn	New Way
Tortillas	Progressing	E	71	Scholastic	Guided Reading Program
Tree Can Be…, A	Progressing	E	74	Scholastic	Guided Reading Program
Tricking Tracy	Progressing	9/F	125	Rigby	Tadpoles
Trip, The	Progressing	7/E	108	Modern Curriculum	Ready Readers
Two Little Dogs	Progressing	7/E	74	Wright Group	Story Box
Two Ogres, The	Progressing	9/F	116	Dominie Press	Joy Readers
Under My Sombrero	Progressing	9/F	79	Richard C. Owen	Books For Young Learners
Until We Got Princess	Progressing	10*/E	94	Mondo	Bookshop
Very Strong Baby, The	Progressing	8/E	74	Dominie Press	Joy Readers
Victor and the Kite	Progressing	10/F	84	Oxford Univ. Press	Oxford Reading Tree
Victor and the Sail-cart	Progressing	12/H	91	Oxford Univ. Press	Oxford Reading Tree
Victor the Champion	Progressing	12/G	102	Oxford Univ. Press	Oxford Reading Tree
Video Game	Progressing	7/C	115	Sundance	AlphaKids
Wake Me in Spring	Progressing	E	250+	Scholastic	Guided Reading Program
Washing Our Dog	Progressing	7/C	120	Sundance	AlphaKids
Waterfight, The	Progressing	8/E	64	Oxford Univ. Press	Oxford Reading Tree
What a Dog!	Progressing	9/F	134	Troll	First Start
What a Mess!	Progressing	11/G	124	Steck-Vaughn	New Way
What a School	Progressing	10/F	100	Seedling	Salem, L. & Stewart, J.
What I'd Like to Be	Progressing	9/10*/F	112	Sundance	Little Red Readers
What is That? said the Cat	Progressing	F	118	Scholastic	Guided Reading Program
What's For Dinner?	Progressing	7/E	115	Seedling	Salem, L. & Stewart, J.
When I Grow Up	Progressing	12/E	227	Sundance	AlphaKids
When We Are Big	Progressing	7/E	123	Modern Curriculum	Ready Readers
Where's My Pencil?	Progressing		86	Fairfax County	Books for Budding Readers

*Tentatively leveled

Title	Level	RR–GR Level	Words	Publisher	Series/Author
Which Hat Today?	Progressing	E	94	Scholastic	Guided Reading Program
Who is the Tallest?	Progressing	7/C	89	Sundance	AlphaKids
Who Stole the Cookies From the Cookie Jar?	Progressing	G	153	Scholastic	Guided Reading Program
Who Will Be My Mother?	Progressing	8/E	156	Wright Group	Story Box
Willie the Slowpoke	Progressing	11/G	125	Troll	First Start
Willy's Hats	Progressing	7–8/E	65	Seedling	Salem, L. & Stewart, J.
Witch's Haircut, The	Progressing	12/G	135	Wright Group	Windmill
Wobbly Tooth, The	Progressing	10/E	74	Oxford Univ. Press	Oxford Reading Tree
Worm Rap	Progressing	10/D	249	Sundance	AlphaKids
Zoo in Willy's Bed, The	Progressing	8/E	81	Seedling	Sturnman Gorman, Kate
Zoo Looking	Progressing	7*/G	149	Mondo	Bookshop
Abracadabra	Transitional	18/L	372	Celebration Press	Reading Unlimited
All About	Transitional	17/J	259	Modern Curriculum	Ready Readers
All About You	Transitional	G	250+	Scholastic	Anholt, Catherine L.
Amalia and the Grasshopper	Transitional	I	250+	Scholastic	Guided Reading Program
Andi's Wool	Transitional	14/H	107	Richard C. Owen	Books For Young Learners
Animal Builders	Transitional	17/F	217	Sundance	AlphaKids
Animal Diggers	Transitional	16/F	262	Sundance	AlphaKids
Animal Feet	Transitional		164	Scholastic	Reading Discovery
Ant and the Dove, The	Transitional	14–16/I	173	Steck-Vaughn	New Way
Ant and the Grasshopper, The	Transitional	15*/I	231	Dominie Press	Aesop's Fables
Apples and Pumpkins	Transitional	I	185	Scholastic	Guided Reading Program
Art Lesson, The	Transitional	20/M	246	Putnam	dePaola, Tommi
Arthur's Reading Race	Transitional		250+	Random House	Brown, Marc
Away Went the Hat	Transitional	15,15,18/I	260	Steck-Vaughn	New Way
Bakery, The	Transitional	13/E	196	Sundance	AlphaKids
Bath Day For Brutus	Transitional	18/K	348	Sundance	Little Red Readers
Bats	Transitional			Scholastic	Reading Discovery
Bear Shadow	Transitional	18/J	489	Simon & Schuster	Asch, Frank
Bear's Bargain	Transitional	J	250+	Scholastic	Asch, Frank
Big Bed, The	Transitional	16/I	346	Pacific Learning	Ready to Read
Big Block of Chocolate	Transitional		250+	Scholastic	Redhead, Janice S.
Big Dog, The	Transitional	14/E	324	Sundance	AlphaKids
Biggest Fish, The	Transitional	I	254	Rigby	PM Story Books
Billy Goats Gruff	Transitional	18*		Dominie Press	Traditional Tales
Bird's Eye View	Transitional	K	393	Rigby	PM Story Books
Birds	Transitional		156	Scholastic	Reading Discovery
Boy Who Cried Wolf, The	Transitional	18*/K	460	Dominie Press	Aesop's Fables
Brave Little Tailor	Transitional	18/K	250+	Rigby	PM Traditional Tales & Plays
Busy Beavers, The	Transitional	I	362	Rigby	PM Story Books
Butterfly, the Bird, the Beetle, and Me, The	Transitional	15/F	200	Sundance	AlphaKids
Cabin in the Hills	Transitional	J	349	Rigby	PM Story Books
Caps For Sale	Transitional	20/K	675	Harper & Row	Slobodkina, Esphyr
Careful Crocodile, The	Transitional	I	271	Rigby	PM Story Books
Cat Concert	Transitional	J	250+	Rigby	Literacy Tree

*Tentatively leveled

Title	Level	RR–GR Level	Words	Publisher	Series/Author
Cat With No Tail, The	Transitional	15/I	137	Richard C. Owen	Books For Young Learners
Caterpillars	Transitional	19–20*/M	114	Mondo	Bookshop
Changing Land, The	Transitional	16/I	64	Pacific Learning	Ready to Read
Chicken in the Middle of the Road	Transitional	16–18*/J	478	Mondo	Bookshop
Chicken Little	Transitional	20 /L	250+	Rigby	Traditional Tales
Chicken Soup With Rice	Transitional	20/M	250+	Scholastic	Sendak, Maurice
Children of Sierra Leone, The	Transitional	16/J	142	Richard C. Owen	Books for Young Learners
Cinderella	Transitional	18*/ I	580	Dominie Press	Traditional Tales
Clean House For Mole and Mouse, A	Transitional	H	201	Scholastic	Guided Reading Program
Clifford the Big Red Dog	Transitional	18/K	241	Scholastic	Bridwell, Norman
Clifford the Small Red Puppy	Transitional	18/K	499	Scholastic	Bridwell, Norman
Cloudy With a Chance of Meatballs	Transitional	M	250+	Atheneum	Barrett, Judi
Cow Up a Tree	Transitional	13/H	215	Rigby	Read Along
Coyote Plants a Peach Tree	Transitional	16/I	233	Richard C. Owen	Books For Young Learners
Crabbing Time	Transitional	15/I	76	Richard C. Owen	Books For Young Learners
Crosby Crocodile's Disguise	Transitional	K	250+	Rigby	Literacy Tree
Cross Country Race, The	Transitional	14/H	246	Rigby	PM Story Books
Crow and the Pitcher, The	Transitional	15*/I	265	Dominie Press	Aesop's Fables
Debra's Dog	Transitional	14/H	157	Rigby	Tadpoles
Digging To China	Transitional	13/H	108	Richard C. Owen	Books For Young Learners
Dinosaur Chase, The	Transitional	I	240	Rigby	PM Story Books
Dinosaur Who Lived in My Backyard, The	Transitional	H	325	Scholastic	Guided Reading Program
Doctor Has the Flu, The	Transitional	13/H	106	Modern Curriculum	Ready Readers
Dogstar	Transitional	J	250+	Rigby	Literacy 2000
Don't Forget the Bacon	Transitional	20/M	174	Puffin Books	Hutchins, Pat
Doorbell Rang, The	Transitional	17/J	283	Scholastic	Hutchins, Pat
Dragon Feet	Transitional	15/K	153	Richard C. Owen	Books For Young Learners
Dragon, The	Transitional	15/F	374	Sundance	AlphaKids
Duckling, The	Transitional	14/E	405	Sundance	AlphaKids
Early One Morning	Transitional	13/E	240	Sundance	AlphaKids
Edgar Badger's Balloon Day	Transitional	18–20/I–J	864	Mondo	Bookshop
Elves and Shoemaker, The	Transitional	18/K	622	Steck-Vaughn	New Way
Elves and the Shoemaker, The	Transitional	14/E	251	Sundance	AlphaKids
Elves and the Shoemaker, The	Transitional	18/K	300	Rigby	PM Traditional Tales & Plays
Emma's Problem	Transitional	13/H	190	Rigby	Literacy 2000
Enjoy! Enjoy!	Transitional	17/F	268	Sundance	AlphaKids
Enormous Turnip, The	Transitional	14/H	431	Ladybird	Read It Yourself
Enormous Watermelon, The	Transitional	14/H	304	Rigby	Traditional Tales
Farmer and His Two Lazy Sons, The	Transitional	17*/J	250	Dominie Press	Aesop's Fables
Farmer Joe's Hat Day	Transitional	17/J	406	Scholastic	Richards/Zimmerman
Father Bear Comes Home	Transitional	19/ I	331	HarperCollins	Minarik, E. H.
Father Who Walked on Hands	Transitional	18/K	344	Rigby	Literacy 2000
Fern and Bert	Transitional	14/H	375	Modern Curriculum	Ready Readers
Flip's Trick	Transitional	14/H	134	Modern Curriculum	Ready Readers
Flying Fish, The	Transitional	14/H	215	Rigby	PM Extensions

*Tentatively leveled

Title	Level	RR–GR Level	Words	Publisher	Series/Author
Fox and , The	Transitional	19/L	400	Rigby	PM Traditional Tales & Plays
Fox and His Friends	Transitional	18/J	417	Scholastic	Marshall, E. & Marshall, J.
Fox and the Crow, The	Transitional	17*	250+	Dominie Press	Aesop's Fables
Frog and Toad Are Friends	Transitional	19/K	250+	HarperCollins	Lobel, Arnold
Frog and Toad Together	Transitional	19/K	250+	HarperCollins	Lobel, Arnold
Frog Prince, The	Transitional	20/ H	908	Wright Group	Sunshine
Frog Princess, The	Transitional	18/K	206	Rigby	Literacy Tree
Frogs	Transitional		190	Scholastic	Reading Discovery
Fun at Camp	Transitional	13/H	178	Troll	First Start
Funny Old Man and the Funny Old Woman, The	Transitional	16–18*/M	562	Mondo	Bookshop
George Shrinks	Transitional	H	114	Scholastic	Guided Reading Program
Giant's Job, The	Transitional	13–14/H	180	Seedling	Stewart, J. & Salem, L.
Gifts For Dad	Transitional	14/H	178	Kaeden	Urmston, K. & Evans, K.
Gingerbread Man, The	Transitional	15/J	535	Rigby	PM Traditional Tales & Plays
Gingerbread Man, The	Transitional	I	250+	Scholastic	Guided Reading Program
Gingerbread Man, The	Transitional	15*/ I	534	Dominie Press	Traditional Tales
Goha and His Donkey	Transitional	15/I	114	Richard C. Owen	Books For Young Learners
Goldilocks and the Three Bears	Transitional	17/H	250+	Rigby	PM Traditional Tales & Plays
Good-bye Summer, Hello Fall	Transitional	14/H	169	Modern Curriculum	Ready Readers
Grandpa Comes to Stay	Transitional	18–20*/K	1083	Mondo	Bookshop
Grandpa, Grandma and the Tractor	Transitional	14/H	220	Modern Curriculum	Ready Readers
Greedy Goat, The	Transitional	19/L	451	Mondo	Bookshop
Green Dragons	Transitional	K	250+	Rigby	PM Story Books
Heather's Book	Transitional	18/K	469	Modern Curriculum	Ready Readers
Henny Penny	Transitional	I	582	Scholastic	Guided Reading Program
Hoketichee and the Manatee	Transitional	15/I	113	Richard C. Owen	Books For Young Learners
House That Stood on Booker Hill, The	Transitional	17/J	324	Modern Curriculum	Ready Readers
How Fire Came to Earth	Transitional	19/K	250+	Rigby	Literacy 2000
How The Mouse Got Brown Teeth	Transitional	16*/I	460	Mondo	Bookshop
How to Draw a Dinosaur	Transitional	16/F	229	Sundance	AlphaKids
How Turtle Raced Beaver	Transitional	17/J	182	Rigby	Literacy 2000
Hungry Sea Star, The	Transitional	14/I	69	Richard C. Owen	Books For Young Learners
I Can Do It	Transitional	13*/I	200	Mondo	Bookshop
I Was Walking Down the Road	Transitional	H	299	Scholastic	Guided Reading Program
I'm a Good Reader	Transitional	13/H	188	Dominie Press	Carousel Readers
I'm On the Phone	Transitional	13/E	241	Sundance	AlphaKids
Insects	Transitional	14/E	256	Sundance	AlphaKids
Insects	Transitional	J	171	Scholastic	Maclulich, Carolyn
Jack & Chug	Transitional	I	337	Rigby	PM Story Books
Jessica in the Dark	Transitional	I	362	Rigby	PM Story Books
Jonathan Buys a Present	Transitional	J	353	Rigby	PM Story Books
Jump the Broom	Transitional	15/L	119	Richard C. Owen	Books For Young Learners
Just One Guinea Pig	Transitional	I	339	Rigby	PM Story Books
Kangaroos	Transitional		155	Scholastic	Reading Discovery
Lad Who Went To The North Wind, The	Transitional	20*/J	796	Mondo	Bookshop

*Tentatively leveled

Title	Level	RR–GR Level	Words	Publisher	Series/Author
Last One Picked	Transitional	13/E	329	Sundance	AlphaKids
Lines	Transitional	13/E	262	Sundance	AlphaKids
Lionel and Amelia	Transitional	20*/L	702	Mondo	Bookshop
Little Girl and Her Beetle, The	Transitional	15/I	250+	Rigby	Literacy 2000
Little Mouse's Trail Tale	Transitional	13*/I	349	Mondo	Bookshop
Little Red Hen, The	Transitional	13*/H	375	Dominie Press	Traditional Tales
Little Red Hen, The	Transitional	16/I	416	Rigby	PM Traditional Tales & Plays
Little Red Hen, The	Transitional	15	250+	Scholastic	Easy to Read
Little Red Riding Hood	Transitional	17/J	250+	Rigby	PM Traditional Tales & Plays
Lonely Giant, The	Transitional	18/K	449	Rigby	Literacy 2000
Lonely Troll, The	Transitional	17/F	518	Sundance	AlphaKids
Look-Alike Animals	Transitional	I	132	Scholastic	Guided Reading Program
Looking After Chicks	Transitional	15/F	327	Sundance	AlphaKids
Loose Laces	Transitional	17/L	209	Celebration Press	Reading Unlimited
Lots of Caps	Transitional	15/I	205	Steck-Vaughn	New Way
Lottie Goat and Donny Goat	Transitional	13/H	145	Modern Curriculum	Ready Readers
Loudest Sneeze, The	Transitional	16/F	255	Sundance	AlphaKids
Magic Fish, The	Transitional	J	250+	Scholastic	Guided Reading Program
Miss Nelson Is Missing	Transitional	20/L	598	Scholastic	Allard, Harry
Missing Necklace, The	Transitional	14/H	231	Celebration Press	Reading Unlimited
Mitch to the Rescue	Transitional	I	302	Rigby	PM Story Books
Mom's Haircut	Transitional	13/H	99	Rigby	Literacy 2000
Mom's Secret	Transitional	H	141	Scholastic	Guided Reading Program
Monkey and Fire	Transitional	18 /J	372	Rigby	Literacy Tree
Monster Bus	Transitional	13/H	103	Dominie Press	Monster Bus Series
Monster Bus Goes on a Hot Air Balloon Trip	Transitional	16/I	254	Dominie Press	Monster Bus Series
Monster Bus Goes to the Races	Transitional	13/H	158	Dominie Press	Monster Bus Series
Monster Bus Goes to Yellowstone Park	Transitional	15/I	259	Dominie Press	Monster Bus Series
More Spaghetti, I Say!	Transitional	H	250+	Scholastic	Guided Reading Program
Mouse Soup	Transitional	J	1350	Scholastic	Guided Reading Program
Mr. Grindy's Shoes	Transitional	15	211	Wright Group	Sunshine
Mr. McCready's Cleaning Day	Transitional	H	119	Scholastic	Guided Reading Program
Mr. Pepperpot's Pet	Transitional	K	250+	Rigby	Literacy 2000
Mrs. Murphy's Crows	Transitional	14/H	122	Richard C. Owen	Books For Young Learners
My Father	Transitional	I	194	Scholastic	Guided Reading Program
My Shells	Transitional	16/F	276	Sundance	AlphaKids
My Sloppy Tiger	Transitional	16/I	217	Wright Group	Sunshine
My Street	Transitional	16/F	284	Sundance	AlphaKids
Nelson the Baby Elephant	Transitional	J	350	Rigby	PM Story Books
Nesting Place	Transitional	K	356	Rigby	PM Story Books
New Baby Calf, The	Transitional	H	240	Scholastic	Guided Reading Program
Noisy Nora	Transitional	I	204	Scholastic	Guided Reading Program
Old Man's Mitten, The	Transitional	19*/I	378	Mondo	Bookshop
Old Woman Who Lived in a Vinegar Bottle, The	Transitional	18*/M	1161	Mondo	Bookshop
Our Polliwogs	Transitional	15/I	91	Richard C. Owen	Books For Young Learners

*Tentatively leveled

Title	Level	RR–GR Level	Words	Publisher	Series/Author
Paint My Room!	Transitional	14/E	317	Sundance	AlphaKids
Pheasant and Kingfisher	Transitional	18–20*/L	910	Mondo	Bookshop
Pig William's Midnight Walk	Transitional	14/H	354	Wright Group	Book Bank
Pot of Gold, The	Transitional	16/I	266	Celebration Press	Reading Unlimited
Predators	Transitional	16/F	283	Sundance	AlphaKids
Princess and the Pea	Transitional	17*/I	304	Dominie Press	Traditional Tales
Princess and the Wise Woman, The	Transitional	18/K	320	Modern Curriculum	Ready Readers
Pterosaur's Long Flight	Transitional	I	301	Rigby	PM Story Books
Pumpkin House, The	Transitional	J	250+	Rigby	Literacy 2000
Race to Green End, The	Transitional	K	506	Rigby	PM Story Books
Raven's Gift	Transitional	20/L	160	Richard C. Owen	Books For Young Learners
Red Tailed Hawk, The	Transitional	19/L	199	Richard C. Owen	Books For Young Learners
Rescuing Nelson	Transitional	J	369	Rigby	PM Story Books
Riding to Craggy Rock	Transitional	K	386	Rigby	PM Story Books
Robert and the Rocket	Transitional	H		Scholastic	Guided Reading Program
Rosa at the Zoo	Transitional	13/H	135	Pacific Learning	Ready to Read
Royal Drum, The	Transitional	20*/L	526	Mondo	Bookshop
Sammy's Supper	Transitional	16/I	293	Celebration Press	Reading Unlimited
Sarah and the Barking Dog	Transitional	I	328	Rigby	PM Story Books
Sea Animals	Transitional	15/16*	326	Sundance	Little Red Readers
Seat Belt Song, The	Transitional	K	505	Rigby	PM Story Books
Sebastian's Special Present	Transitional	15/F	300	Sundance	AlphaKids
Sharks	Transitional	13/H	155	Modern Curriculum	Ready Readers
Sharks	Transitional		228	Scholastic	Reading Discovery
Shintaro's Umbrella	Transitional	16/I	101	Richard C. Owen	Books For Young Learners
Skates for Luke	Transitional	I	346	Rigby	PM Story Books
Snakes	Transitional		227	Scholastic	Reading Discovery
Snowy Day, The	Transitional	18/J	319	Scholastic	Keats, Ezra Jack
Space Travel	Transitional	15/F	225	Sundance	AlphaKids
Starfish	Transitional	17/F	241	Sundance	AlphaKids
Staying Alive	Transitional	17/F	296	Sundance	AlphaKids
Stone Soup	Transitional	17/J	250+	Rigby	PM Traditional Tales & Plays
Stone Soup	Transitional	J	932	Scholastic	Guided Reading Program
Suki and the Case of the Lost Bunnies	Transitional	18/K	529	Modern Curriculum	Ready Readers
T-Shirt Triplets, The	Transitional	19/L	344	Rigby	Literacy 2000
Tale of the Turnip, The	Transitional	16/I	250+	Rigby	PM Traditional Tales & Plays
This is the Place For Me	Transitional	I	250+	Scholastic	Guided Reading Program
Three Bears	Transitional	17/K	873	Scholastic	Galdone, Paul
Three Billy Goats Gruff, The	Transitional	16/I	450	Rigby	PM Traditional Tales & Plays
Three Little Pigs, The	Transitional	13/H	392	Steck-Vaughn	New Way
Three Little Pigs, The	Transitional	13/H	276	Celebration Press	Reading Unlimited
Three Little Pigs, The	Transitional	16/I	523	Rigby	PM Traditional Tales & Plays
Three Little Pigs, The	Transitional	13/H	346	Dominie Press	Reading Corners
Three Wishes, The	Transitional	18–20/L	717	Mondo	Bookshop
Toby and B. J.	Transitional	I	307	Rigby	PM Story Books

*Tentatively leveled

Title	Level	RR–GR Level	Words	Publisher	Series/Author
Toby and the Accident	Transitional	J	329	Rigby	PM Story Books
Toby and the Big Red Van	Transitional	I	291	Rigby	PM Story Books
Toby and the Big Tree	Transitional	I	298	Rigby	PM Story Books
Too Many Puppies	Transitional	I		Scholastic	Guided Reading Program
Toy Farm, The	Transitional	I	311	Rigby	PM Story Books
Trash or Treasure	Transitional	14/E	298	Sundance	AlphaKids
Trouble With Herbert, The	Transitional	18–20*/L	1830	Mondo	Bookshop
Turtle Nest	Transitional	13/H	84	Richard C. Owen	Books For Young Learners
Ugly Duckling, The	Transitional	18/K	452	Rigby	PM Traditional Tales & Plays
Very Greedy Dog, The	Transitional	14*/H	228	Dominie Press	Aesop's Fables
Very Hungry Caterpillar	Transitional	18/H	237	Scholastic	Carle, Eric
Victor and the Martian	Transitional	14/H	109	Oxford Univ. Press	Oxford Reading Tree
Victor the Hero	Transitional	13/H	103	Oxford Univ. Press	Oxford Reading Tree
Weather Watching	Transitional	15/F	196	Sundance	AlphaKids
Wet Grass	Transitional	14/H	188	Wright Group	Storybox
What Are Purple Elephants Good For?	Transitional	13/H	136	Dominie Press	Reading Corners
What People Do	Transitional	14/H	148	Sundance	Little Red Readers
Where Are We Going?	Transitional	13/E	255	Sundance	AlphaKids
Where Jeans Come From	Transitional	18/K	351	Modern Curriculum	Ready Readers
Who's in the Shed?	Transitional	16/ I	202	Rigby	Traditional Tales
Whose Mouse Are You?	Transitional	13/H	98	Scholastic	Guided Reading Program
Yes, Ma'am	Transitional	14/H	125	Wright Group	Read-Togethers
You'll Soon Grow Into Them, Titch	Transitional	14*/H	191	Rigby	Hutchins, Pat
Abiyoyo	Fluent		250+	Scholastic	Seeger, Pete
Adventures of Ali Baba Bernstein	Fluent	O	250+	Scholastic	Hurwitz, Joanna
Afternoon on the Amazon	Fluent	L	250+	Random House	Pope Osborne, Mary
Aladdin and the Magic Lamp	Fluent	22*/J	250+	Dominie Press	Traditional Tales
Aldo Ice Cream	Fluent	O	250+	Penguin	Hurwitz, Joanna
Alexander and the Wind-up Mouse	Fluent	L	250+	Scholastic	Guided Reading Program
Alfie's Gift	Fluent	L	250+	Rigby	Literacy 2000
Alison Wendlebury	Fluent	J	250+	Rigby	Literacy Tree
Alison's Puppy	Fluent	K	250+	Hyperion	Bauer, Marion
Amazing Rescues	Fluent		250+	Random House	Shea, George
Amber Brown Goes Fourth	Fluent	N	250+	Scholastic	Danziger, Paula
Amber Brown Is Not a Crayon	Fluent	N	250+	Scholastic	Danziger, Paula
Amber Brown Sees Red	Fluent	N	250+	Scholastic	Danziger, Paula
Amber Brown Wants Extra Credit	Fluent	N	250+	Scholastic	Danziger, Paula
Amelia Bedelia	Fluent	L	250+	Harper & Row	Parish, Peggy
Amelia Bedelia Helps Out	Fluent	L	250+	Avon Camelot	Parish, Peggy
Amelia Bedelia and the Surprise Shower	Fluent	L	250+	HarperTrophy	Parish, Peggy
Amelia Bedelia Goes Camping	Fluent	L	250+	Avon Camelot	Parish, Peggy
Animal Champions	Fluent		250+	Modern Curriculum	First Chapters
Animal Tracks	Fluent	L		Scholastic	Dorros, Arthur
Animals of the Ice & Snow	Fluent	R	250+	Rigby	Literacy 2000
Armies of Ants	Fluent	O	250+	Scholastic	Retan, Walter

*Tentatively leveled

Title	Level	RR–GR Level	Words	Publisher	Series/Author
Arthur Writes a Story	Fluent		250+	Little, Brown	Brown, Marc
Arthur's First Sleepover	Fluent		250+	Little, Brown	Brown, Marc
Baby Sister For Frances, A	Fluent	K	250+	Scholastic	Hoban, Russell
Bad Luck of King Fred	Fluent	N	250+	Rigby	Literacy Tree
Barry the Bravest Saint Bernard	Fluent		250+	Random House	Hall, Lynn
Bathwater Gang	Fluent		250+	Little, Brown	Spinnelli, Jerry
Bats	Fluent	M	250+	Rigby	Literacy 2000
Bears on Hemlock Mountain, The	Fluent	M	250+	Aladdin	Dalgliesh, Alice
Beauregard the Cat	Fluent	20–22*/M	876	Mondo	Bookshop
Bedtime For Frances	Fluent	K	250+	Scholastic	Guided Reading Program
Beekeeper, The	Fluent	M	250+	Rigby	Literacy 2000
Best Clown in Town	Fluent		250+	Dominie Press	Chapter Books
Best Way to Play, The	Fluent	K	250+	Scholastic	Cosby, Bill
Big Al	Fluent	L	250+	Scholastic	Guided Reading Program
Biggest Bear, The	Fluent		250+	Houghton Mifflin	Ward, Lynd
Blind Man and the Elephant, The	Fluent	K	250+	Scholastic	Backstein, Karen
Blueberries For Sal	Fluent	M	250+	Scholastic	McCloskey, Robert
Box Car Children Mystery Bookstore	Fluent	O	250+	Albert Whitman	Warner, Gertrude Chandler
Box Car Children Mystery of the Missing Cat	Fluent	O	250+	Albert Whitman	Warner, Gertrude Chandler
Box Car Children Schoolhouse Mystery	Fluent	O	250+	Albert Whitman	Warner, Gertrude Chandler
Box Car Children Snowbound Mystery	Fluent	O	250+	Albert Whitman	Warner, Gertrude Chandler
Box Car Children, The	Fluent	O	250+	Albert Whitman	Warner, Gertrude Chandler
Boy Who Cried Wolf, The	Fluent	L	250+	Rigby	Literacy 2000
Bravest Dog Ever, The True Story of Balto	Fluent	L	250+	Random House	Standiford, Natalie
Bringing the Rain to Kapiti Plain	Fluent		250+	Dial	Aardema, Verna
Brith the Terrible	Fluent	M	250+	Rigby	Literacy 2000
Bully Brothers Making the Grade	Fluent		250+	Scholastic	Thaler, Mike
Bush Bunyip, The	Fluent	J	396	Mondo	Bookshop
Cabbage Princess, The	Fluent	K	250+	Rigby	Literacy 2000
Cam Jansen and Mystery of UFO	Fluent	L	250+	Puffin Books	Adler, David A.
Cam Jansen and Mystery of Monster Movie	Fluent	L	250+	Puffin Books	Adler, David A.
Cam Jansen and Mystery of the Dinosaur Bones	Fluent	L	250+	Puffin Books	Adler, David A.
Camp Knock Knock	Fluent	K	250+	Dell	Duffey, Betsy
Camping With Claudine	Fluent	K	250+	Rigby	Literacy 2000
Can Do, Jenny Archer	Fluent	M	250+	Little, Brown	Conford, Ellen
Can I have a Dinosaur?	Fluent	L	250+	Rigby	Literacy 2000
Canoe Diary	Fluent		250+	Pacific Learning	Orbit Chapter Books
Case for Jenny Archer, A	Fluent	M	250+	Little, Brown	Conford, Ellen
Cass Becomes a Star	Fluent	L	250+	Rigby	Literacy 2000
Cat Talk	Fluent		250+	Pacific Learning	Orbit Chapter Books
Chair For My Mother, A	Fluent	M	250+	Scholastic	Williams, Vera
Chasing Tornadoes	Fluent		250+	Modern Curriculum	First Chapters
Chicken Little	Fluent		250+	William Morrow	Kellogg, Steven
Chocolate Touch	Fluent		250+	Dell	Catling, Patrick Skene
Cinderella	Fluent		250+	Scholastic	Wegman, William

*Tentatively leveled

Title	Level	RR–GR Level	Words	Publisher	Series/Author
City Mouse-Country Mouse	Fluent	J	250+	Scholastic	Guided Reading Program
Claudine's Concert	Fluent	L	250+	Rigby	Literacy 2000
Coaching Ms. Parker	Fluent		250+	Aladdin	Heymsfeld, Carla
Commander Toad In Space	Fluent		250+	Scholastic	Yolen, Jane
Curious George and the Ice Cream	Fluent	J	250	Scholastic	Rey, M.
Desert Run	Fluent		250+	Pacific Learning	Orbit Chapter Books
Digging Dinosaurs	Fluent		250+	Modern Curriculum	First Chapters
Dinosaur Girl	Fluent	N	250+	Rigby	Literacy Tree
Doctor DeSoto Goes to Africa	Fluent		250+	HarperCollins	Steig, William
Donkey	Fluent	M	250+	Rigby	Literacy 2000
Double Trouble	Fluent	M	250+	Rigby	Literacy 2000
Down on the Ice	Fluent		250+	Pacific Learning	Orbit Chapter Books
Dragon's Birthday, The	Fluent	L	250+	Rigby	Literacy 2000
Drought Maker, The	Fluent	M	250+	Rigby	Literacy 2000
Duck in the Gun, The	Fluent	M	250+	Rigby	Literacy 2000
Egyptians	Fluent		250+	Gareth Stevens	Allard, Denise
Enormous Crocodile, The	Fluent	N	250+	Puffin Books	Dahl, Roald
Exploring the Titanic	Fluent		250+	Scholastic/Madison	Ballard, Robert D.
Fiddle and the Gun, The	Fluent	M	250+	Rigby	Literacy 2000
Fireflies	Fluent		250	Atheneum	Brinckloe, Julie
Five True Dog Stories	Fluent	M	250+	Scholastic	Davidson, Margaret
Five True Horse Stories	Fluent	M	250+	Scholastic	Davidson, Margaret
Flatfoot Fox	Fluent		250+	Scholastic	Clifford, Eth
Flossie and the Fox	Fluent	O	250+	Scholastic	McKissack, Patricia
Franklin and the Tooth Fairy	Fluent		250+	Scholastic	Bourgeois, P. & Clark, B.
Franklin Goes to School	Fluent	K	250+	Scholastic	Bourgeois, P. & Clark, B.
Franklin Has a Sleepover	Fluent		250+	Scholastic	Bourgeois, P. & Clark, B.
Franklin Plays the Game	Fluent	J	250+	Scholastic	Bourgeois, P. & Clark, B.
Frog Prince, The	Fluent	21*	572	Dominie Press	Traditional Tales
Frogs	Fluent	N	1440	Mondo	Bookshop
Gail and Me	Fluent	L	250+	Rigby	Literacy 2000
George and Martha	Fluent	L	250+	Houghton Mifflin	Marshall, James
Golden Goose, The	Fluent	M	250+	Rigby	Literacy 2000
Gooey Chewy Contest, The	Fluent	22*/N	1512	Mondo	Bookshop
Great Black Heroes: Five Brave Explorers	Fluent	P	250+	Scholastic	Hudson, Wade
Greedy Cat and the Birthday Cake	Fluent		250	Pacific Learning	Orbit Chapter Books
Gregory, The Terrible Eater	Fluent	L	250+	Scholastic	Weinman, Sharmat
Happy Birthday, Martin Luther King	Fluent	L	250+	Scholastic	Marzollo, Jean
Hare and the Tortoise, The	Fluent	K	250+	Rigby	Literacy 2000
Helen Keller	Fluent	P	250+	Dell	Graff, S. & P.
Hello Creatures!	Fluent	K	250+	Rigby	Literacy 2000
Henry and Beezus	Fluent	O	250+	Avon Books	Cleary, Beverly
Henry and Mudge and the Forever Sea	Fluent	J	250+	Aladdin	Rylant, Cynthia
Henry and Mudge in Puddle Trouble	Fluent	J	250+	Aladdin	Rylant, Cynthia
Henry and Mudge in the Green Time	Fluent	J	250+	Aladdin	Rylant, Cynthia

*Tentatively leveled

Title	Level	RR–GR Level	Words	Publisher	Series/Author
Henry and Mudge, The First Book	Fluent	J	250+	Aladdin	Rylant, Cynthia
Henry and Ribsy	Fluent	O	250+	Avon Books	Cleary, Beverly
Henry Huggins	Fluent	O	250+	Avon Books	Cleary, Beverly
Hill of Fire	Fluent	20/L	1099	HarperCollins	Lewis, T. P.
Hooray For the Golly Sisters	Fluent	K	250+	HarperTrophy	Byers, Betsy
How Much Is That Guinea Pig in the Window?	Fluent	L	250+	Scholastic	Guided Reading Program
Huberta the Hiking Hippo	Fluent	L	250+	Rigby	Literacy 2000
Humphrey	Fluent	O	250+	Rigby	Literacy Tree
Hungry, Hungry Sharks	Fluent	L	250+	Random House	Cole, Joanna
I Love the Beach	Fluent	M	250+	Rigby	Literacy 2000
I'm So Hungry and Other Plays	Fluent		250+	Pacific Learning	Orbit Chapter Books
In the Clouds	Fluent	M	250+	Rigby	Literacy 2000
It Came Through the Wall	Fluent	20–22*/O	1182	Mondo	Bookshop
Johnny Appleseed	Fluent		250+	Scholastic	Kellogg, Steven
Josephina Story Quilt	Fluent	L	250+	HarperTrophy	Coerr, Eleanor
Julian's Glorious Summer	Fluent	N	250+	Random House	Cameron, Ann
Junie B. Jones and the Stupid Smelly Bus	Fluent	M	250+	Random House	Park, Barbara
Junie B. Jones and the Yucky Blucky Fruit Cake	Fluent	M	250+	Random House	Park, Barbara
Katy and the Big Snow	Fluent	L	250+	Scholastic	Guided Reading Program
Keep the Lights Burning, Abbie	Fluent	K	250+	Scholastic	Guided Reading Program
Kenny and the Little Kickers	Fluent	J	250+	Scholastic	Mareollo, Claudio
King Beast's Birthday	Fluent	L	250+	Rigby	Literacy 2000
King Kong and the Flower Fairy	Fluent		250+	Rigby	Literacy Tree
King Midas and the Golden Touch	Fluent	22*/J	562	Dominie Press	Traditional Tales
Let's Get Moving	Fluent	M	250+	Rigby	Literacy 2000
Little Bear	Fluent	J	1664	HarperCollins	Minarik, E. H.
Little Bear's Friend	Fluent	J	250+	HarperTrophy	Minarik, E. H.
Little Bear's Visit	Fluent	J	250+	HarperTrophy	Minarik, E. H.
Little Dinosaur Escapes	Fluent	J	389	Rigby	PM Story Books
Little Spider, The	Fluent	L	250+	Rigby	Literacy 2000
Lucky Baseball Bat, The	Fluent	M	250+	Little, Brown	Christopher, Matt
Lucky Feather, The	Fluent	L	250+	Rigby	Literacy 2000
Mailman Mario and His Boris-Busters	Fluent		250+	Dominie Press	Chapter Books
Make a Wish, Molly	Fluent	O	250+	Dell	Cohen, Barbara
Marcella	Fluent	L	250+	Rigby	Literacy 2000
Mario's Mayan Journey	Fluent	22–24*/P	1021	Mondo	Bookshop
Marvin Redpost: Why Pick on Me?	Fluent	L	250+	Random House	Sachar, Louis
Midnight Pig	Fluent	P	250+	Rigby	Literacy Tree
Midnight Rescue	Fluent	N	250+	Rigby	Literacy Tree
Miss Geneva's Lantern	Fluent	22–24*/P	1691	Mondo	Bookshop
Miss Rumphius	Fluent		250+	Puffin Books	Cooney, Barbara
Misty of Chincoteague	Fluent		250+	Scholastic	Henry, Marguerite
Mitten, The	Fluent	M	250+	Scholastic	Brett, Jan
Molly's Pilgrim	Fluent	M	250+	Dell	Cohen, Barbara
More Stories Julian Tells	Fluent	N	250+	Random House	Cameron, Ann

*Tentatively leveled

Title	Level	RR–GR Level	Words	Publisher	Series/Author
Mountain Gorillas	Fluent	P	330	Wright Group	Wonder World
Mr. Putter and Tabby Bake The Cake	Fluent	J	250+	Harcourt Brace	Rylant, Cynthia
Mr. Putter and Tabby Pick The Pears	Fluent	J	250+	Harcourt Brace	Rylant, Cynthia
Mr. Putter and Tabby Pour The Tea	Fluent	J	250+	Harcourt Brace	Rylant, Cynthia
Mr. Putter and Tabby Walk The Dog	Fluent	J	250+	Harcourt Brace	Rylant, Cynthia
Much Ado About Aldo	Fluent	O	250+	Puffin Books	Hurwitz, Joanna
Muggie Maggie	Fluent	O	250+	Avon Camelot	Cleary, Beverly
Nate the Great	Fluent	K	250+	Dell	Sharmat, Marjorie Weinman
Nate the Great and the Sticky Case	Fluent	K	250+	Dell	Sharmat, Marjorie Weinman
Nathan and Nicholas Alexander	Fluent	K	250+	Scholastic	Guided Reading Program
No One Is Going To Nashville	Fluent	O	250+	Bullseye Books	Jukes, Mavis
No Trouble At All	Fluent	O	250+	Rigby	Literacy Tree
No Way, Winky Blue!	Fluent	24*/P	4053	Mondo	Bookshop
Not-So-Jolly Roger	Fluent		250+	Penguin	Scieszka, Jon
Octopuses and Squids	Fluent	N	328	Wright Group	Wonder World
Off to Squintum's/The Four Musicians	Fluent	20–22*/N	1268	Mondo	Bookshop
Oh, What a Daughter!	Fluent	L	250+	Rigby	Literacy 2000
Once When I Was Ship Wrecked	Fluent	L	250	Rigby	Literacy 2000
Patchwork Quilt	Fluent		250+	Scholastic	Flournoy, Valerie
Paul Bunyan	Fluent		250+	William Morrow	Kellogg, Steven
Pecos Bill	Fluent		250+	William Morrow	Kellogg, Steven
Pee Wee Scouts: Cookies and Crutches	Fluent	L	250+	Dell	Delton, Judy
Peter the Pumpkin Eater	Fluent		250+	Rigby	Literacy Tree
Pie, Pie, Beautiful Pie	Fluent		250+	Rigby	Literacy Tree
Pioneer Cat	Fluent	N	250+	Random House	Hooks, William H.
Pocket Full of Acorns, A	Fluent		250+	Dominie Press	Chapter Books
Pony Named Shawnee, A	Fluent	24*/P	3075	Mondo	Bookshop
Present From Aunt Skidoo, The	Fluent	M	250+	Rigby	Literacy 2000
Prize For Purry	Fluent	K	250+	Rigby	Literacy 2000
PS I Love You, Gramps	Fluent		250+	Rigby	Literacy Tree
Puppets	Fluent	K	250+	Rigby	Literacy Tree
Puppy Who Wanted a Boy, The	Fluent	L	250+	Scholastic	Guided Reading Program
Quackers, the Troublesome Duck	Fluent		250+	Modern Curriculum	First Chapters
Rabbit Stew	Fluent	L	250+	Rigby	Literacy 2000
Rabbits	Fluent	M	250+	Rigby	Literacy Tree
Ralph S. Mouse	Fluent	O	250+	Avon Books	Cleary, Beverly
Ramona and Her Father	Fluent	O	250+	Avon Books	Cleary, Beverly
Ramona Quimby, Age 8	Fluent	O	250+	Avon Books	Cleary, Beverly
Ramona the Brave	Fluent	O	250+	Avon Books	Cleary, Beverly
Ramona the Pest	Fluent	O	250+	Avon Books	Cleary, Beverly
Rapunzel	Fluent	L	250+	Rigby	Literacy 2000
River Runners	Fluent	N	250+	Rigby	Literacy Tree
Rosie's House	Fluent	K	250+	Rigby	Literacy 2000
Rough Face Girl, The	Fluent		250+	Scholastic	Martin, Rafe
Rumpelstiltskin	Fluent	23*/J	940	Dominie Press	Traditional Tales

*Tentatively leveled

Title	Level	RR–GR Level	Words	Publisher	Series/Author
Sam's Glasses	Fluent	M	250+	Rigby	Literacy 2000
Saving the Yellow Eye	Fluent		250+	Pacific Learning	Orbit Chapter Books
Schoolyard Mystery	Fluent	L	250+	Scholastic	Guided Reading Program
Selfish Giant, The	Fluent	L	250+	Rigby	Literacy 2000
Shark Lady: The Adventures of Eugenia Clark	Fluent	N	250+	Scholastic	McGovern, Ann
Sheeba	Fluent		250+	Dominie Press	Chapter Books
Shorty	Fluent	M	250+	Rigby	Literacy 2000
SkyFire	Fluent	J	250+	Scholastic	Asch, Frank
Slugs and Snails	Fluent	J	426	Mondo	Bookshop
Smokey the Dragon	Fluent		250+	Dominie Press	Chapter Books
Snow Goes To Town	Fluent	L	250+	Rigby	Literacy 2000
Sock Gobbler, The	Fluent		250+	Pacific Learning	Orbit Chapter Books
Spider and the King, The	Fluent	L	250+	Rigby	Literacy 2000
Spider Man	Fluent	M	250+	Rigby	Literacy 2000
Spiders	Fluent	M	447	Mondo	Bookshop
Spirit of Hope	Fluent	22*/N	878	Mondo	Bookshop
Squanto and the First Thanksgiving	Fluent	L	250+	Steck-Vaughn	Celso, Teresa
Storm Chasers: Tracking Twisters	Fluent		250+	Grossett & Dunlap	Herman, Gayle
Story of Hungbu and Nolbu, The	Fluent	K	802	Mondo	Bookshop
Story of the White House	Fluent		250+	Scholastic	Waters, Kate
Strange Creatures	Fluent		250+	Pacific Learning	Orbit Chapter Books
Sugar Cakes Cyril	Fluent	22*/N	4022	Mondo	Bookshop
Sunday Horse	Fluent	O	250+	Rigby	Literacy Tree
Tale of Veruschka Babuschka, The	Fluent	M	250+	Rigby	Literacy 2000
Tar Beach	Fluent		250+	Scholastic	Ringgold, Faith
Teach Us, Amelia Bedelia	Fluent	L	250+	Scholastic	Guided Reading Program
Teeny Tiny Woman, The	Fluent	J	369	Scholastic	Seuling, Barbara
That's a Laugh! Four Funny Fables	Fluent	M	250+	Rigby	Literacy 2000
Three Sillies, The	Fluent	L	250+	Rigby	Literacy 2000
Treasure Hunting	Fluent	M	250+	Rigby	Literacy 2000
Trees Belong to Everyone	Fluent	L	250+	Rigby	Literacy 2000
Tubes In My Ears: My Trip to the Hospital	Fluent	K	658	Mondo	Bookshop
Two Foolish Cats	Fluent	K	250+	Rigby	Literacy Tree
Uncle Tease	Fluent		250+	Rigby	Literacy Tree
Very Thin Cat of Alloway Road, The	Fluent	L	250+	Rigby	Literacy 2000
Whales	Fluent	N	1617	Mondo	Bookshop
When the King Rides By	Fluent	17/J	247	Mondo	Bookshop
When the Truck Got Stuck	Fluent		250+	Pacific Learning	Orbit Chapter Books
Which Way Jack?	Fluent		250+	Rigby	Literacy Tree
Whipping Boy, The	Fluent	O	250+	Troll	Fleischman, Sid
Who's Afraid of the Big Bad Bully?	Fluent	K	250+	Scholastic	Slater, Teddy
Wish Fish	Fluent		250+	Rigby	Literacy Tree
Wonder Women of Sports	Fluent		250+	Grosset & Dunlap	Kramer, S. A.
You Can't Eat Your Chicken Pox, Amber Brown	Fluent	N	250+	Scholastic	Danziger, Paula
Zoe at the Fancy Dress Ball	Fluent	J	250+	Rigby	Literacy 2000

*Tentatively leveled

Sources of Information/Teacher Prompts Bookmarks

Reproduce on cardstock. Laminate. Cut apart for two bookmarks.

SOURCES OF INFORMATION

Meaning (M)

What we read needs to make sense with our experiences, what we know about the world, and what is happening in the story.

- *Did that make sense?*
- *What do you think it could be?*
- *Let's read it again to make sense.*

Knowledge of Language Structure (S)

We use our knowledge of the way we talk to read. Our reading sounds like the language patterns we speak and the language of the books we read.

- *Can we say it that way?*
- *Is that like the way we talk?*
- *Does that sound right?*

Visual/Grapho-phonic (V)

The words we read must match the letters/sounds we see. We look at the first, middle, or last letter of a word, or a familiar part of a word.

- *Does it look right?*
- *What letter would you expect to see at the beginning? At the end?*
- *You saw the little work be at the beginning of beside.*
- *Read it again. Get your mouth ready for the first sound.*
- *Say it slowly.*

SOURCES OF INFORMATION

Meaning (M)

What we read needs to make sense with our experiences, what we know about the world, and what is happening in the story.

- *Did that make sense?*
- *What do you think it could be?*
- *Let's read it again to make sense.*

Knowledge of Language Structure (S)

We use our knowledge of the way we talk to read. Our reading sounds like the language patterns we speak and the language of the books we read.

- *Can we say it that way?*
- *Is that like the way we talk?*
- *Does that sound right?*

Visual/Grapho-phonic (V)

The words we read must match the letters/sounds we see. We look at the first, middle, or last letter of a word, or a familiar part of a word.

- *Does it look right?*
- *What letter would you expect to see at the beginning? At the end?*
- *You saw the little work be at the beginning of beside.*
- *Read it again. Get your mouth ready for the first sound.*
- *Say it slowly.*

Sources of Information/Teacher Prompts Chart

Reproduce on cardstock. Laminate.

Sources of Information

Teacher Prompts

Meaning (M)

What we read needs to make sense with our experiences, what we know about the world, and what is happening in the story.

- Did that make sense?
- What do you think it could be?
- Let's read it again to make sense.

Knowledge of Language Structure (S)

We use our knowledge of the way we talk to read. Our reading sounds like the language patterns we speak and the language of the books we read.

- Can we say it that way?
- Is that like the way we talk?
- Does that sound right?

Visual/Grapho-phonic (V)

The words we read must match the letters/sounds we see. We look at the first, middle, or last letter of a word, or a familiar part of a word.

- Does it look right?
- What letter would you expect to see at the beginning? At the end?
- You saw the little work *be* at the beginning of beside.
- Read it again. Get your mouth ready for the first sound.
- Say it slowly.

Reading Strategy/Teacher Prompts Bookmark

Reproduce on cardstock. Fold on the solid line. Laminate.

Monitor

The student notices that something is not right with the reading and may attempt to check and/or correct errors.

- *Did it match?*
- *What did you notice?*
- *I like the way you noticed something wasn't right.*
- *Something's not right. Why did you stop?*
- *Were you right? How did you know?*
- *How do you know it was _____ ?*
- *Show me where it wasn't correct.*

Search

When the reader notices something is not right in her reading, she searches for more information to correct it.

- *You said _____ . Does that make sense? (M)*
  Does it sound right? (S)
  Does it look right? (V)
- *If it was _____ , what letter would you expect to see first? Last?*
- *Something's not right on that page. Can you find what's wrong?*
- *What do you know that might help?*

Predict

The student anticipates as he reads to predict a word or event in the story. He uses prior knowledge, his knowledge of language, what makes sense, and what would look right.

- *Think about what has happened in the story so far. What would make sense?*
- *Look at the picture. What do you know?*
- *What would you expect to see? (letter[s], word[s])*
- *What do you think will happen next?*

Check

The reader checks that what is read makes sense, looks right, and sounds right. This may occur after an error, or when she comes to an unknown word.

- *It could be _____ , but does it…*
  Make sense? (M)
  Sound right? (S)
  Look right? (V)
- *What did you notice?*
- *What did you expect to see?*
- *Check to see if what you read…*
  Makes sense. (M)
  Sounds right. (S)
  Looks right. (V)
- *I like how you tried more than one way to work that out.*

Confirm

The student uses one or more sources of information to make certain that what he expected to read is what he actually read.

- *Are you right?*
- *Did you check to make sure you're right?*
- *Did you reread to see if you're right?*

Self-correct

The student notices on her own that something is not right in the reading. She searches and checks for more information to self-correct or make it right.

- *I like the way you corrected that all by yourself.*
- *Were you right? How did you know?*
- *Something's not right on that page…in that sentence. Can you find it?*

Guided Reading: Making It Work • Scholastic Professional Books

Reading Strategy/Teacher Prompts Chart

Reproduce on cardstock. Laminate.

Reading Strategy	Teacher Prompts
Monitor The student notices that something is not right with the reading and may attempt to check and/or correct errors.	*Did it match?* *What did you notice?* *I like the way you noticed something wasn't right.* *Something's not right. Why did you stop?* *Were you right? How did you know?* *How do you know it was _____ ?* *Show me where it wasn't correct.*
Search When the reader notices something is not right in her reading, she searches for more information to correct it.	*You said _____ . Does that make sense? (M) Does it sound right? (S) Does it look right? (V)* *If it was ___ , what letter would you expect to see first? Last?* *Something's not right on that page. Can you find what's wrong?* *What do you know that might help?*
Predict The student anticipates as he reads to predict a word or event in the story. He uses prior knowledge, his knowledge of language, what makes sense, and what would look right.	*Think about what has happened in the story so far. What would make sense?* *Look at the picture. What do you know?* *What would you expect to see? (letter[s], word[s])* *What do you think will happen next?*
Check The reader checks that what is read makes sense, looks right, and sounds right. This may occur after an error, or when she comes to an unknown word.	*It could be ___ , but does it make sense? (M) Sound right? (S) Look right? (V)* *What did you notice?* *What did you expect to see?* *Check to see if what you read makes sense. (M) Sounds right. (S) Looks right. (V)* *I like how you tried more than one way to work that out.*
Confirm The student uses one or more sources of information to make certain that what he expected to read is what he actually read.	*Are you right?* *Did you check to make sure you're right?* *Did you reread to see if you're right?*
Self-correct The student notices on her own that something is not right in the reading. She searches and checks for more information to self-correct or make it right.	*I like the way you corrected that all by yourself.* *Were you right? How did you know?* *Something's not right on that page…in that sentence. Can you find it?*

Emergent, Progressing, Transitional, and Fluent Literacy Stages

Grades K to 3

Emergent Readers:

- learn print carries a message
- display directional movement:
  - *left to right*
  - *top to bottom*
  - *return sweep*
- match voice to print with one-to-one word matching
- locate some known words and unknown words
- use picture clues
- recognize the difference between *a letter* and *a word*
- may invent text
- begin to use pattern and repetition of text to read
- use oral language/story structure to make a connection to print
- use some letter sounds (beginning/ending)
- begin to use known, high-frequency words to monitor reading

Book Characteristics— Emergent Readers

Early

- consistent placement of print on each page
- illustrations provide high support
- natural language structure
- familiar experiences
- some known, high-frequency words
- one/two lines of print (L to R with return sweep)
- predictable, repetitive sentence pattern with one/two word changes

Later

- some punctuation conventions
- illustrations provide high support
- repeated sentence pattern every few pages
- print in various positions on page
- varied sentence patterns
- multiple lines of print
- familiar objects and experiences
- simple story line

Some Titles of Emergent Level Books

A Bear Lived in a Cave, Little Red Readers, Sundance

Cat on the Mat, Brian Wildsmith

The Cat Who Loved Red, Lynn Salem and J. Stewart

The Chick and the Duckling, Mirra Ginsburg

Dad's Shirt, Joy Readers, Dominie

Father Bear Goes Fishing, PM Story Books, Rigby

Freddie the Frog, First Start, Rigby

The Ghost, Story Box, Wright Group

Have You Seen My Duckling?, Nancy Tafuri

I Like, Literacy 2000, Rigby

I Went Walking, Sue Williams

James is Hiding, Windmill, Rigby

Jolly Roger, the Pirate, PM Extensions, Rigby

Lazy Mary, Read-Togethers, Wright Group

Little Pig, Windmill, Wright Group

Little Red Hen, Windmill, Wright Group

Lunch at the Zoo, Wendy Blaxland and C. Bimage

Making a Memory, Margaret Ballinger

Not Enough Water, Shane Armstrong and S. Hartley

What Has Stripes?, Margaret Ballinger

Emergent, **Progressing**, Transitional, and Fluent Literacy Stages
Grades K to 3

Progressing Readers:

- have good control of early reading strategies (directionality, one-to-one word matching, locate known and unknown words)
- rely less on pictures and use more information from print
- search the print, check, and self-correct more frequently (both with and without teacher prompting)
- often cross-check one source of information (meaning, language structure, visual/grapho-phonic) with another source
- check and confirm, sometimes using *beginning, middle, and ending* letters/sounds
- read familiar text with some phrasing and fluency
- begin to attend to punctuation while reading
- begin to build a core of high-frequency words known automatically
- begin to engage in discussions about what is read

Book Characteristics— Progressing Readers

Early
- varied placement of print on page
- natural language structures
- variety of simple sentences
- multiple lines of print
- more punctuation conventions
- some repetitive sentence patterns
- illustrations provide moderate to high support

Later
- variety of sentence patterns and lengths
- variety of punctuation and fonts
- use of direct speech
- longer story (beginning-middle-end)
- illustrations provide moderate support

Some Titles of Progressing Level Books

The Biggest Cake in the World, Ready to Read, Pacific Learning

Billy Goats Gruff, Read It Yourself, Ladybird

Buzzzzz Said the Bee, Hello Reader, Scholastic

Carla's Breakfast, Leslie Harper

Catch That Frog, Reading Unlimited, Scott Foresman

Cookie's Week, Cindy Ward

Dressed Up Sammy, K. Urmston and K. Evans

Five Little Monkeys Jumping on the Bed, Eileen Christelow

I Love Camping, Carousel Readers, Dominie Press

The Lion's Tail, Reading Unlimited, Scott Foresman

Messy Mark, First Start, Troll

My Friends, Little Celebrations, Scott Foresman

Notes From Mom, L. Salem and J. Stewart

Notes To Dad, J. Stewart and L. Salem

Papa's Spaghetti, Literacy 2000, Rigby

Rosie's Walk, Pat Hutchins

T-Shirts, Ready to Read, Pacific Learning

Two Little Dogs, Story Box, Wright Group

Who Will Be My Mother?, Read-Together, Wright Group

Witch's Haircut, Windmill—Look and Listen, Wright Group

Emergent, Progressing, **Transitional**, and Fluent Literacy Stages
Grades K to 3

Transitional Readers:

- use multiple sources of information (meaning, language structure, visual/grapho-phonic) and a variety of strategies to problem-solve while reading
- make predictions and confirm or revise them while reading
- recognize the importance of monitoring reading for understanding
- use familiar parts of words (beginning, middle, or end) to problem-solve unknown words
- know a large core of high-frequency words automatically
- read many punctuation marks appropriately
- read most texts with phrasing and fluency
- begin to read a greater variety of longer and more complex texts (fiction and informational)
- attend more to story structure and literary language
- engage in discussions about what is read

Book Characteristics—Transitional Readers

Early

- conventional story
- varied sentence patterns
- more print on page
- some literary language
- variety of literature selections
- illustrations provide some support
- more varied punctuation and fonts

Later

- illustrations provide low support
- some challenging vocabulary
- longer selections
- variety of text layout
- more print on page
- developed story line
- font varies in size and type
- literary language

Some Titles of Transitional Level Books

Caterpillars, Bookshop, Mondo

Clifford the Big Red Dog, Norman Bridwell

The Elves and the Shoemaker, New Way, Steck-Vaughn

The Enormous Watermelon, Traditional Tales, Rigby

Father Bear Comes Home, E. H. Minarik

Fox and His Friends, Edward and James Marshall

Frog and Toad Are Friends, Arnold Lobel

Gifts For Dad, K. Urmston and K. Evans

The Greedy Goat, Bookshop, Mondo

How Fire Came to Earth, Literacy 2000, Rigby

How Turtle Raced Beaver, Literacy 2000, Rigby

Insects, Reading Discovery, Scholastic

The Missing Necklace, Reading Unlimited, Scott Foresman

Mom's Haircut, Literacy 2000, Rigby

Old Woman Who Lived in a Vinegar Bottle, Bookshop, Mondo

Rosa at the Zoo, Ready to Read, Pacific Learning

The Snowy Day, Ezra Jack Kerts

The Three Little Pigs, Reading Corners, Dominie Press

Very Hungry Caterpillar, Eric Carle

Whose Mouse Are You?, Robert Kraus

Emergent, Progressing, Transitional, and **Fluent** Literacy Stages
Grades K to 3

Fluent Readers:

- use all sources of information (meaning, language structure, visual/grapho-phonic) quickly and flexibly to problem-solve independently

- detect and correct errors, often silently

- use knowledge of how words work (letters/sounds, word parts, and analogies) to efficiently problem-solve unfamiliar words

- read and understand more challenging vocabulary using context and knowledge of how words work

- consistently monitor reading for understanding

- read with phrasing and fluency

- adjust reading pace to accommodate the purposes for reading and the difficulty of the text

- exhibit an ability to infer the author's subtleties in the text

- revisit text to support ideas and understandings during literary discussions

- read a variety of genres for information and pleasure

- synthesize and interpret what is read

Book Characteristics— Fluent Readers

Early

- some challenging vocabulary
- literary terms and language
- extended story line
- variety of simple and complex sentences
- longer literature selections (e.g., beginning chapter books)
- fewer illustrations
- more print on a page

Later

- more challenging vocabulary
- more complex literary genres
- more complicated text features
- variety of fonts and print layouts
- print provides primary source of information
- more complex sentence structures
- more complex story line and concepts
- few to no illustrations

Some Titles of Fluent Level Books

Amber Brown is Not a Crayon, Paula Danzinger

Amelia Bedelia and the Surprise Shower, Peggy Parish

Best Clown in Town, Tom Bradley

Box Car Children Mystery of the Missing Cat, Gertrude C. Warner

Bravest Dog Ever: The True Story of Balto, Natalie Standiford

Bringing the Rain to Kapiti Plain, Verna Aardema

Cam Jansen and the Mystery of the Monster Movie, David Adler

Canoe Diary, Nic Bishop

Chair For My Mother, Vera B. Williams

Commander Toad in Space, Jane Yolen

Duck in the Gun, Joy Cowley

Exploring the Titanic, Robert D. Ballard

Five True Dog Stories, Margaret Davidson

Gregory, the Terrible Eater, M. Weinman Sharmat

Henry and Mudge in Puddle Trouble, Cynthia Rylant

Nate the Great, M. Weinman Sharmat

Shark Lady, Ann McGovern

Skyfire, Frank Asch

Spiders, Bookshop, Mondo

Story of the White House, Kate Waters

Book Selection: Text Features Checklist

Concepts in Book

- *Can students relate to the concepts or experiences in the text?*
- *What background knowledge is necessary to understand in the text?*
- *Do events in the story follow a sequential and/or predictable pattern?*
- *Are students able to understand this type of literary genre?*

Illustrations

- *Do they provide high, moderate, or low support?*
- *Where are they located on the page?*
- *Are they clear or do they need interpretation?*

Language/Structure

- *Is the text repetitive, familiar, or natural to spoken language?*
- *Are there high-frequency words that can serve as anchors for emergent readers?*
- *Is there difficult or technical vocabulary that might present a problem?*

Text Features/Layouts

- *How many lines of print on a page?*
- *Is there clear spacing between words?*
- *Are the size and placement of the print supportive to the reader?*
- *Are there unusual print fonts that are distracting or confusing?*
- *Is the text length appropriate for the reader?*
- *Are there any unusual text formats—such as diagrams, charts, or maps—that require explanation?*

Guided Reading: Making It Work Scholastic Professional Books

Masking Cards

Reproduce on cardstock. Laminate. Cut out.

Cut Out

Cut Out

Cut Out

Cut Out

Weekly Language Arts Record Sheet

Name: _____

Date: _____

Date: _____

Date: _____

Date: _____

Date: _____

Use to create a literacy center record sheet. Place icons above names of centers. (See page 66 for a completed sample.)

Guided Reading: Making It Work   Scholastic Professional Books

240

Take-Home Reading Bookmarks

Reproduce on cardstock. Laminate. Cut out.

Read with your child

- You may want to read the book to your child first, or read along with him or her.

- Talk about the story.

- Share your favorite parts.

Read by your child

- You may need to read the book to your child first, or read along with him or her.

- Ask the questions:
  "Does it make sense?"
  "Does it sound right?"
  "Does the beginning sound of the word match the word you think it is?"

- It's all right to tell your child a word when he or she is "stuck" and unable to proceed.

Read to your child

- Read the book to your child.

- Ask your child to predict what the story might be about based on the title and/or picture on the cover of the book.

- Talk about the story as you read to your child.

- Share your favorite parts.

Reading Buddy Record

Partners' Names _____

Teacher's Name _____

Date	Title	Comments

Guided Reading: Making It Work   Scholastic Professional Books

Nonfiction Quick-Book-Look

Name: _____

Title: _____

Things you found:

Reproducible Word Cards

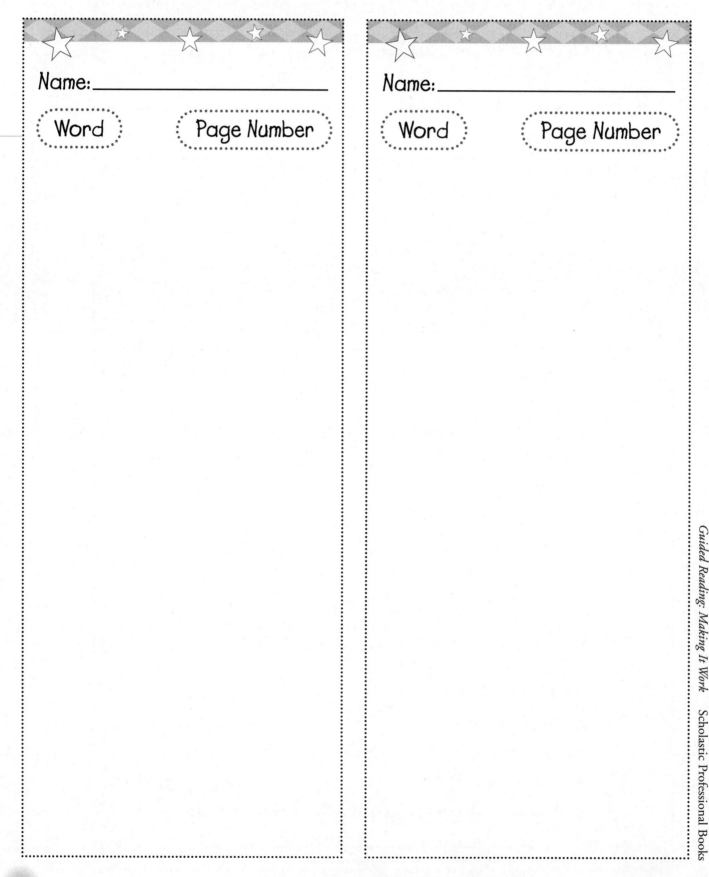

Name: _____

Word	Page Number

Name: _____

Word	Page Number

Guided Reading: Making It Work   Scholastic Professional Books

Some Principles for Letter and Word Study

(This list is not inclusive or in order of instruction)

- **a group of letters make a word**

    Stephen   mom   go

- **letters in words are read left to right**

- **words can vary in length (long or short)**

    I   Alexandra   like

- **letters have an alphabetic sequence**

    a, b, c, …x, y, z

- **letters in words represent sounds**

    /n/ as in *nut*

- **sounds of the letters can be heard in words**

    c-a-t   n-e-s-t   s-t-a-n-d

- **words are the same in writing and reading**

    (I use the same letters to write the word *dog* that I see when I read the word *dog*.)

- **initial letters can be upper or lowercase**

    i̱t   I̱t   the   The

- **initial letters can be changed**

    like   ḇike   ḏay   p̱lay

- **final letters can be changed**

    is̱   iṯ   cat   caṉ

- **letters can be added to the ends of words**

    play   plays̱   playiṉg̱   playe̱ḏ   playe̱r
    see   sees̱   seeiṉg̱   seeṉ

- **words can be abbreviated or shortened**

    isn't   is not   VA   Virginia

- **words can be put together to make a new word**

    to day   today̱   can not   cannoṯ

- **letter clusters at the beginning of words can be changed**

    p̱lay   s̱tay   s̱top   s̱hop

(Continued)

Some Principles for Letter and Word Study
(Continued)

🍀 **letter clusters at the end of words can be changed**

tra<u>ck</u>   tra<u>sh</u>   pa<u>st</u>   pa<u>th</u>

🍀 **letters can be added to the first part of words or word segments**

it   <u>s</u>it   an   <u>r</u>an

🍀 **letters can be added to the beginning and end of words**

and   <u>st</u>and   <u>st</u>and<u>ing</u>
mind   <u>re</u>mind   <u>re</u>mind<u>er</u>

🍀 **middle letters can be changed**

c<u>a</u>t   c<u>u</u>t   b<u>i</u>g   b<u>u</u>g

🍀 **words can be learned through analogy**

<u>n</u>o   <u>g</u>o
<u>w</u>ent   <u>s</u>ent
<u>st</u>op   d<u>ay</u>   st<u>ay</u>

🍀 **letter clusters in the middle of words can be changed**

f<u>ar</u>m   f<u>or</u>m   gr<u>ee</u>n   gr<u>ai</u>n

🍀 **some words sound the same but are spelled differently and have different meanings**

see   sea
blue   blew
to   too   two

🍀 **some words are spelled the same but sound differently and may have different meanings**

read   read   bow   bow

🍀 **some words look differently than they sound**

eight   buy   eyes

🍀 **some words have silent letters**

knit   right   lamb

🍀 **some words can be broken into parts or syllables**

dinosaur   understand   wonderful

Guided Reading: Making It Work   Scholastic Professional Books

The Alphabet

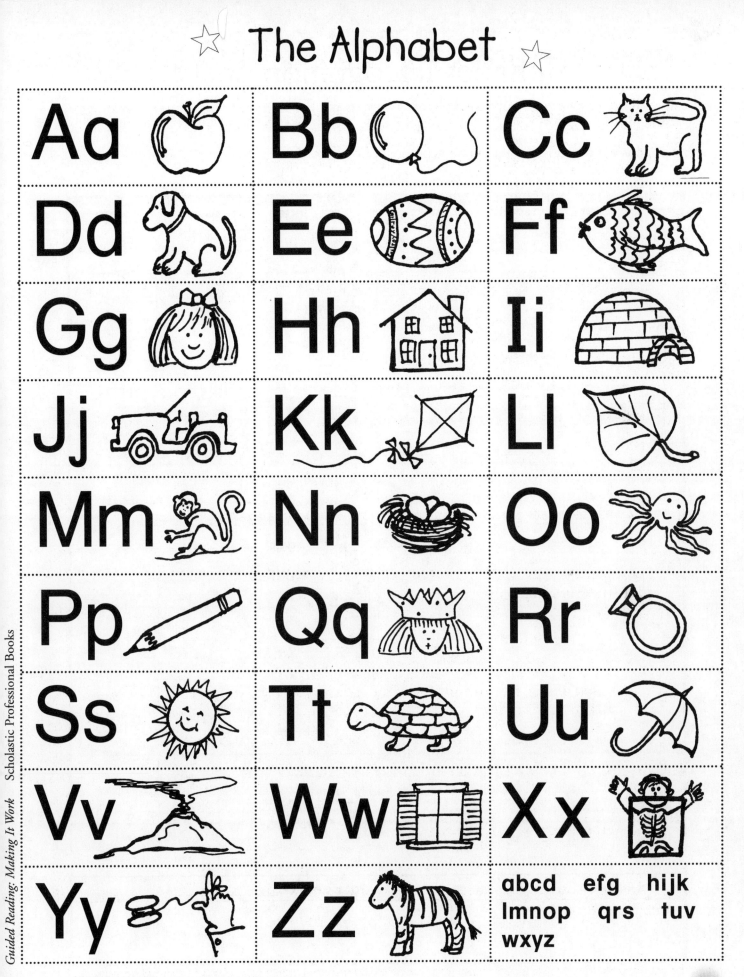

Aa	Bb	Cc
Dd	Ee	Ff
Gg	Hh	Ii
Jj	Kk	Ll
Mm	Nn	Oo
Pp	Qq	Rr
Ss	Tt	Uu
Vv	Ww	Xx
Yy	Zz	abcd efg hijk lmnop qrs tuv wxyz

Guided Reading: Making It Work Scholastic Professional Books

Alphabet Recognition Sheet

Name_____ Date_____

✔ = correct response for letter name, letter sound or word
● = incorrect response

	letter	sound	word		letter	sound	word
A				a			
E				e			
X				x			
M				m			
Q				q			
U				u			
G				g			
B				b			
F				f			
J				j			
T				t			
R				r			
V				v			
N				n			
C				c			
Y				y			
K				k			
O				o			
I				i			
W				w			
D				d			
L				l			
S				s			
P				p			
Z				z			
H				h			
				a			
				g			

Total Correct: _____   Total Correct: _____

Comments:

Guided Reading: Making It Work   Scholastic Professional Books

Adapted from *An Observation Survey* by Marie Clay

Student Alphabet Chart

A E X M Q U G

B F J T R V N

C Y K O I W D

L S P Z H

a e x m q u g

b f j t r v n

c y k o i w d

l s p z h a g

Summary of Running Record Conventions Chart

Reading Behavior	Recording Convention	Scoring
Accurate reading	$\dfrac{\text{CHILD}}{\text{TEXT}}$ ✓	Correct/no error
Substitution	$\dfrac{\text{CHILD}}{\text{TEXT}}$ $\dfrac{\text{looks}}{\text{looked}}$	One error
Omission	$\dfrac{\text{CHILD}}{\text{TEXT}}$ $\dfrac{\text{———}}{\text{and}}$	One error
Insertion	$\dfrac{\text{CHILD}}{\text{TEXT}}$ $\dfrac{\text{big}}{\text{———}}$	One error
Repetition or reread Repeated rereads	↓ ✓ ✓ ✓ ✓ ⎯ R ↓ ✓ ✓ ✓ ✓ ⎯ R 2 , 3 , 4 , etc.	No error
Self-correction	$\dfrac{\text{CHILD}}{\text{TEXT}}$ looks | SC looked |	No error
Intervention	[ ] teacher assistance **TTA** "Try that again." **A** Appeal **T** Told	One error
Intervention	**YTI** "You try it."	No error
Student uses initial sound to problem-solve	$\dfrac{\text{CHILD}}{\text{TEXT}}$ $\dfrac{\text{w ✓}}{\text{will}}$	No error

Guided Reading: Making It Work   Scholastic Professional Books

Scoring the Running Record

To calculate the **error rate**, **accuracy rate**, and **self-correction rate**, tally the number of each of the following:

RW = # of Running words

E = # of Errors

SC = # of Self-corrections

To find the **error rate (ER)**, the calculation is:

$$\frac{RW}{E} \quad \text{e.g.} \quad \frac{104}{8} = 13 \quad \textbf{The error rate is 1:13}$$

Convert the error rate to a percentage accuracy score by using the conversion table on page 252 for a shortcut, or use the calculations below.

Conversion Table for Error/Accuracy Rates for a Running Record

Error Rate	Accuracy Rate (%)	Reading Level
1:200	99.5	
1:100	99	
1:50	98	Easy/Independent Reading Level
1:35	97	
1:25	96	(95–100%)
1:20	95	
1:17	94	
1:14	93	Instructional Reading Level
1:12.5	92	
1:11.75	91	(90–94%)
1:10	90	
1:9	89	
1:8	87.5	Hard/Difficult Reading Level
1:7	85.5	
1:6	83	(89% or below)
1:5	80	
1:4	75	
1:3	66	
1:2	50	

To find the **accuracy rate (ACC)**, the calculation is:

$$\frac{(RW - E)}{RW} \times 100 = \text{ACC (as percent)}$$

$$\frac{(104 - 8)}{104} \times 100 = 92\%$$

The accuracy rate helps to determine if a text is EASY, INSTRUCTIONAL, or HARD.

EASY 95–100%   **INSTRUCTIONAL** 90–94%   **HARD** 89% or below

To find the **self-correction rate (SC)**, the calculation is:

$$\frac{E + SC}{SC} = \frac{8 + 4}{4} = \text{Ratio 1:3}$$

This means the child is self-correcting one out of every three errors.

A self-correction rate of 1:4 or less indicates that the student is self-monitoring.

Conversion Table for Error/Accuracy Rates for a Running Record

Error Rate	Accuracy Rate (%)	Reading Level
1:200	99.5	
1:100	99	
1:50	98	Easy/Independent Reading Level
1:35	97	
1:25	96	(95–100%)
1:20	95	
1:17	94	
1:14	93	Instructional Reading Level
1:12.5	92	
1:11.75	91	(90–94%)
1:10	90	
1:9	89	
1:8	87.5	Hard/Difficult Reading Level
1:7	85.5	
1:6	83	(89% or below)
1:5	80	
1:4	75	
1:3	66	
1:2	50	

Guided Reading: Making It Work   Scholastic Professional Books

Running Record

Adapted from *An Observation Survey* by Marie Clay · *Guided Reading: Making It Work* · Scholastic Professional Books

Child's Name: _____   **Date:** _____

Page	Title		Totals		Cues Used	
			E	SC	E	SC

SCORES: $\dfrac{\text{Running words}}{\text{Errors}}$ _____

Error Rate 1:	Accuracy %	SC Rate 1:

☐ **EASY** 95–100%   ☐ **INSTRUCTIONAL** 90–94%   ☐ **HARD** 89% or below

Observations/Analysis of Cues Strategies:

Running Record *(Back Page)*

Page	Title	E	SC	Cues Used E	SC

Adapted from *An Observation Survey* by Marie Clay

Guided Reading: Making It Work Scholastic Professional Books

Guided Reading Group Anecdotal Record Sheet

Students: _____

Date:

Title:

Level:

Instructional Focus:

Comments:

Date:

Title:

Level:

Instructional Focus:

Comments:

Anecdotal Record Sheet

Use with 3" x 3"
Sticky-Notes

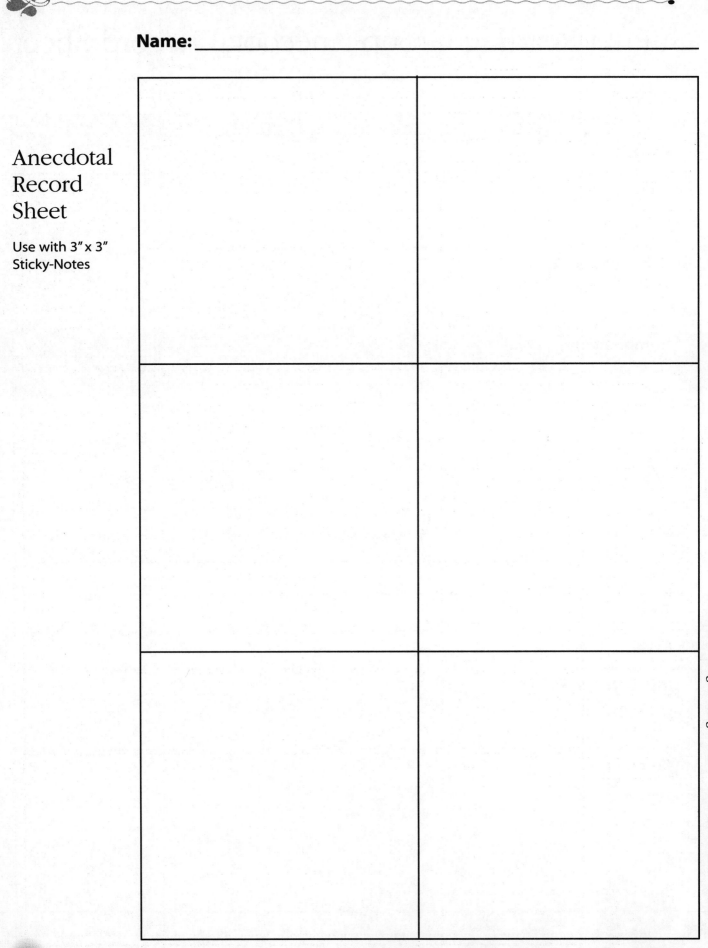

Anecdotal Record Sheet

Use with 2" x 1 1/2" Sticky-Notes

Name: _____

Status of the Class

Name	Monday	Tuesday	Wednesday	Thursday	Friday
1					
2					
3					
4					
5					
6					
7					
8					
9					
10					
11					
12					
13					
14					
15					
16					
17					
18					
19					
20					
21					
22					
23					
24					
25					
26					
27					
28					

Codes:

Independent Reading = **IR**	Writing Activity = **WTG**	Social Studies Activity = **SS**	Guided Reading with Teacher = **GRT**
Buddy Reading = **BR**	Word Study = **WS**	Math Activity = **MA**	Library = **LIB**
Computers = **CMP**	Poetry Journal = **PJ**	Science Activity = **SCI**	Art/Book Project = **ABP**

Status of the Class

Date: _____

Writing Sample Assessment Record
For Early Writing

Name: _____ Date(s): _____

To build a profile of the writer use a different colored highlighter pen to mark the learning behaviors observed each time a writing sample is reviewed. In the comments section make a note or two about future areas of focus.

Concepts/Conventions of Print

Knows where to begin writing
Knows writing moves left-to-right and top-to-bottom
Leaves spaces between words
Correct letter formation
Concept of letter
Concept of word
Uppercase and lowercase letters used conventionally
Approximate spelling
Conventional spelling of frequently used words
Uses punctuation: periods; question marks; exclamation marks; quotations;
    commas; apostrophes
Other:_____

_____

Understands That Writing Conveys a Message

Drawing/pictures
Scribble
Print-like symbols
Strings of letters
Writes own name: first name; last name
Letter/sound relationships: beginning; beginning/ending; beginning/medial/ending
Labels for pictures
Words
Phrases (groups of words)
Sentence
Several sentences
Beginning, middle, and end
Details or vocabulary specific to topic
Central idea organized and elaborated
Other: _____

_____

Comments:

Guided Reading: Making It Work   Scholastic Professional Books

Designed by Mary Browning Schulman and Carleen DaCruz Payne

Writer's Checklist

Name: _____ **Date:** _____

Guided Reading: Making It Work   Scholastic Professional Books

	Beginning	Developing	Skillful
Choice in writing topics			
Able to organize ideas prior to writing using web/list/notes/chart			
Willingness to write			
Content shows: ● logical sequence of ideas ● elaboration of ideas ● descriptive, creative, or unusual vocabulary			
Conventions of writing used: ● capitalization ● punctuation ● spelling ● paragraphing			
Revisions show: ● reorganizes ideas ● adds/deletes information ● varies word choices			
Writing conference participation			

Comments:

Guided Reading Group Lesson Plan Sheet

Literacy Level: _____

Students: _____

_____

Date:_____ **Title of Book:** _____

Instructional Focus:

Word Work:

Comments:

____'s Guided Reading Lesson Plan

Students:

_____

_____

_____

Date:

Title of Text:

Stage/Level:

Introduction:

Observations:

Word Work/Focus:

Date:

Title of Text:

Stage/Level:

Introduction:

Observations:

Word Work/Focus:

Guided Reading: Making It Work   Scholastic Professional Books

Guided Reading Lesson Plan

Students:

Book/Level:

Anecdotal Notes

Word Work

Next Running Record

Students:

Book/Level:

Anecdotal Notes

Word Work

Next Running Record

Terry Creamer '99

Guided Reading: Making It Work   Scholastic Professional Books

Literacy Center Icons

Cut out these icons and use them to label your literacy centers.

Guided Reading

Independent Reading

Literacy Center Icons

Cut out these icons and use them to label your literacy centers.

Buddy Reading

Book Basket

Literacy Center Icons

Cut out these icons and use them to label your literacy centers.

Read the Room

Reading Log

Literacy Center Icons

Cut out these icons and use them to label your literacy centers.

Writing

Letters and Words

cat   abc

mom

Aaa

Literacy Center Icons

Cut out these icons and use them to label your literacy centers.

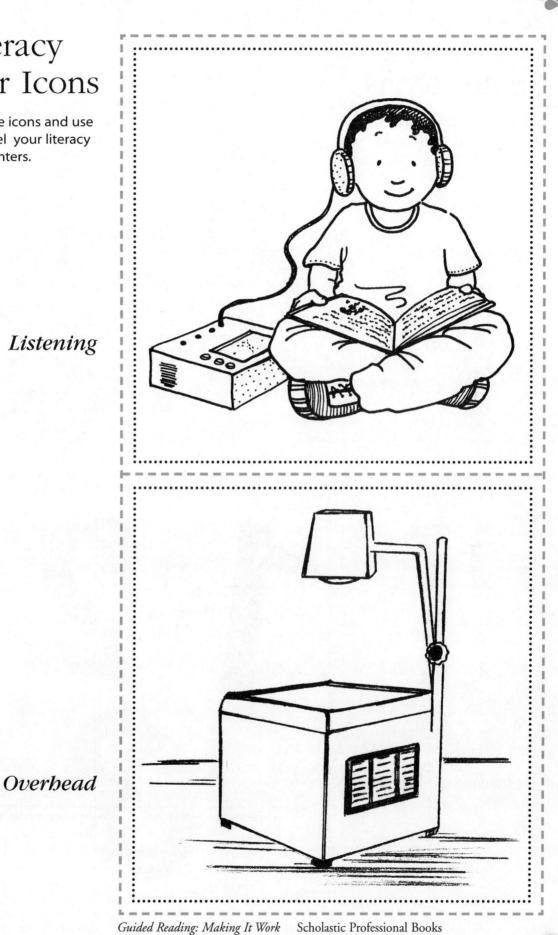

Listening

Overhead

Literacy Center Icons

Cut out these icons and use them to label your literacy centers.

Computer

Math

Literacy Center Icons

Cut out these icons and use them to label your literacy centers.

Art

Science

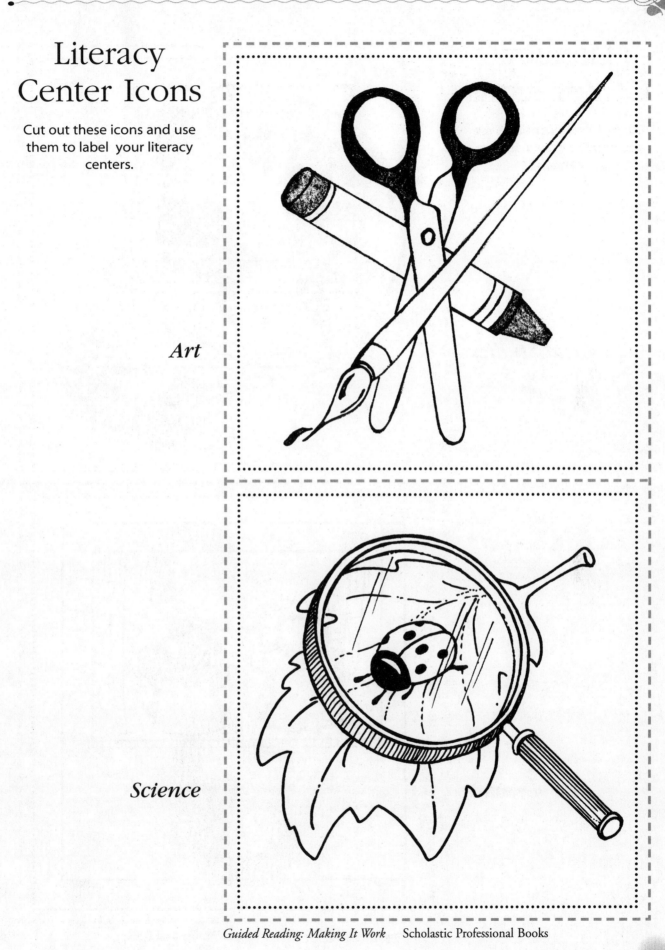

Literacy Center Icons

Cut out these icons and use them to label your literacy centers.

Social Studies

Drama